WHY LIBERAL CHURCHES ARE GROWING

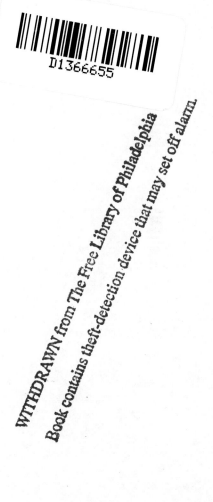

Why Liberal Churches are Growing

Edited by
Martyn Percy and Ian Markham

t&t clark

Published by T&T Clark International
A Continuum imprint

The Tower Building, 11 York Road, London SE1 7NX
80 Maiden Lane, Suite 704, New York, NY 10038

www.tandtclark.com

British Library Cataloguing-in-Publication Data
A catalogue record for this book is available from the British Library

Typeset by Free Range Book Design & Production
Printed on acid-free paper in Great Britain by Antony Rowe Ltd, Chippenham, Wiltshire

ISBN   056708163X (hardback)
         0567081737 (paperback)

CONTENTS

LIST OF FIGURES

FOREWORD

Is it the case, as so many Christians assume, that in order to grow in size and in vigour Christian congregations today, need to be theologically conservative and make more than average demands on their parishioners? Is it not possible that liberal congregations can faithfully live out liberal theologies in ministry and church life and still grow? This collection of essays insists that it is.

The reader will find a wide range of case studies, theological reflections and sociological research united by a common concern across two countries and many denominations about the health and vigour of Christian congregations in the twenty-first century.

In a multiplicity of ways, the authors take issue with Dean Kelley's thesis on the characteristics of growing churches. They consider not simply theology, but leadership, worship styles, the presence of youth, ecclesiologies, location, luck and the Holy Spirit as factors that affect the reality or absence of church growth.

Collectively, these essays, written by pastors, priests and scholars, give an interesting picture of thriving ministries and congregations informed by a liberal ethos.

Heidi Hadsell

INTRODUCTION

We want to set the record straight. So many commentators assume blithely that the only growing churches are the evangelical and fundamentalist ones. Yet those of us who are in the mainline, progressive churches know that this is not the case. There are plenty of mainline churches which are spiritually vibrant and growing. So this book wants to complicate the map: in it you will find leading specialists both in the USA and the UK reflecting on the mainline and progressive churches and illustrating that there are imaginative, innovative and spiritually vital congregations.

It is important to be clear as to what this book is not. It is not an uncritical celebration of liberal theology and liberal churches. There are good reasons why many mainline congregations struggle. In various chapters contributors reflect on certain key difficulties facing the mainline – some of which are entirely self-inflicted. Nor is this book a direct critique of Dean Kelley's well-known book, *Why Conservative Churches are Growing.*[1] Several contributors find themselves in conversation with Kelley's argument, but there is no sustained critique. In general most contributors find themselves critical of his link between 'strictness' and growth, although Scott Thumma takes a distinctive line when he points out that the 'strict' liberal churches (on the 'open and affirming' policy towards gay people) does not coincide precisely with Kelley's expectations.

So what is this book? First, it is a journey through different case studies, social science reflection and analysis. The contributors include sociologists, theologians and practical theologians. It is an interdisciplinary engagement with the issues around progressive and mainline churches. Second, the book is organized in four parts. Part 1 deals with the social justice witness (community organizing), church growth as conversational and the challenge of turning liberal churches around. Part 2 moves to three case studies – starting with congregations and moving to a denomination. In Part 3 we examine in more detail the underlying disposition of liberal churches and revisit such themes as social justice, homosexuality and alternative indicators of vitality. Part 4 concludes with three chapters on 'clergy and growth'. It is here we look at the relationship of the clergy-person with the congregation.

Turning now to individual chapters. In Chapter 1 Patrick Gray links the world of churches with the challenge of faith-based community organizing. He argues that we need to find ways that encourage churches to transcend the divisions over, say, sexuality and abortion, and recognize a shared obligation to those in need of community.

John Thomson takes the work of Stanley Hauerwas as a potential resource for those who want to challenge traditional church-growth models. With a strong emphasis on the 'Church being Church', Hauerwas provides an ecclesiology that can create a strong identity, which is committed to 'conversational church growth'.

Ian Jones argues that the progressive churches need to examine with more care the history behind the ascendancy of the evangelical churches in the UK. He shows that concentration on youth work, coupled with effective organization, is exactly what the progressive churches should strive for.

Part 2 opens with the first case study. The Nine o'Clock Service was a highly innovative example of a large congregation committed to a liberal theology. John Rogerson was closely involved with the service and the congregation. He brings together a description of the service with his own analysis of its sad demise.

Simon Taylor takes two parishes in the Church of England as a starting point to reflect on the context facing these congregations. He argues that these pressures require a rethink of the traditional ways in which organization and structuring of the Church takes place.

The third case study concentrates on a denomination. The Unitarian–Universalist denomination is the most progressive tradition in the USA. Terasa Cooley offers an analysis of why and how its congregations have managed to grow and avoid the dramatic decline of many progressive churches.

Part 3 begins with a chapter by Martyn and Emma Percy which recognizes the importance of congregational culture; and the fact that there are different aspects of growth.

Benjamin Watts explores the dynamic of African-American churches. He looks at the history of the Black Church, its concern with social justice and examines the reasons for its strength and growth.

Scott Thumma takes up the growing campaign in the USA for congregations to become 'open and affirming'. He looks at the process and notes the effects of it in creating an identity for a congregation.

Finally, in Part 3, David Roozen revisits the mainline churches (or in his phrase 'the oldline Protestants'). In a careful critique of the data, Roozen shows that we can too easily oversimplify the narrative. It is all much more complicated. And the interpretation of the data needs to be done with some care.

Part 4 looks at the significance of the clergy-person and growth. Adair Lummis shows it is important that there should be a match between the theology of the clergy-person and the congregation. She also illustrates the gender dimensions of these debates.

Ian Markham argues that liberal churches have encountered problems partly because of a commitment to a certain type of 'liberal theology' (twentieth-century sceptical theology) and partly because clergy-persons leading these churches have lost their sense of spirituality. He suggests if these two features are rectified then numerical growth might follow.

In the last chapter Martyn and Emma Percy start with Dean Kelley's famous thesis. After reflecting on the failure of many 'liberal churches' to challenge it, they offer four hallmarks of priesthood and a priestly church.

At the end of the book we hope that the reader will have a more nuanced picture of congregations and how some which would designate themselves as liberal are spiritually vital and growing. Now at this point, it might be objected that the term 'liberal' requires definition. We have deliberately resisted this temptation. Each contributor has been invited to define the liberal disposition in ways appropriate for his or her chapter. Suffice it to say, a liberal church is one that is not fundamentalist or even conservative evangelical. This deliberately minimalist and negative definition is shared, because one of the targets of this book is the opposite perception that the only growing churches are those that are evangelical and fundamentalist.

Finally, this book is offered in a spirit of hope and trust. It is an optimistic book. We do not share the perspective of those who think that in 50 years time the mainline in either the USA or Britain will have disappeared. We are confident that God will not allow the world to be left without a witness to a faith that is generous, open and hospitable. It is this confidence in the God we worship that keeps us involved in supporting churches that are 'liberal'.

Martyn Percy and Ian Markham

Note

1.   Dean M. Kelley, *Why Conservative Churches are Growing* (San Francisco, CA: Harper & Row, 1972).

Part 1

DEFINING THEMES

Chapter 1

COMMUNITY ORGANIZING AS LIVED FAITH

Patrick T. Gray

Since there are many definitions of 'postcolonialism' and 'postmodernity', I would like to suggest that within the ambit of both terms is the issue of power – who has it and (perhaps) shouldn't? who hasn't had it and should? what is it for? how to use it? Also inherent in both terms is the understanding that the 'old ways' haven't worked the way they claimed. And it is time for something new, something that will make power more available to the powerless. But how? If complete revolution is out, but so is maintaining the status quo, what mechanisms do people have to function publicly and power-fully? The recent American election quite clearly showed us that you have to be a multi-millionaire to run for President, and the captivity of political parties by special-interest moneys has almost become a truism. So what about us who fall a few million dollars short of being able to run for President? What about us whose lives are not defined by single issues, but by the multiplicity and complexity of life?

Besides these generalities concerning power, however, it is quite clear that there are four specific 'wounds' that need attention in our society today, at least from my white, middle-class American perspective – relations between religions, relations between 'liberal' and 'conservative', the race issue and the disparity between rich and poor. Professor Dan Hardy, in his inaugural lecture for the Society for Scriptural Reasoning, aptly spoke of the need for 'structures of repair'. And in his unpublished paper 'Society and Church after September 11th', Hardy, as the title implies, points to the events of September 11th as exacerbating the already strained relations between religions, thus making a 'structure of repair' between religions that much more necessary and urgent.[1] Within the Anglican Communion these days, we are acutely aware of the strain on relationships (if they exist) between conservatives and liberals. And we are not the only ones who have this problem. 'Red' and 'blue' are the current colours that seem to divide us in the USA, although the old divisions of 'black' and 'white' still apply, as well, despite the lack of attention race seems to garner these days, at least when put next to the issue of sexuality. And it is certainly a truism that the rich get richer and the poor get poorer, but never has that truism appeared truer, as the issues of the poor and working class now become middle-class issues (affordable housing is a recent example).

So what is there that could possibly speak to this myriad set of complex and apparently intractable problems? What addresses the issues of power, and at the same time acts as a structure of repair rather than division? Of course, there is no easy answer or quick fix, no simple formula that explains the problem. But I do think that the track record of what is known as faith-based (aka broad-based) community organizing (FBCO) goes far in addressing these issues.[2] But what is FBCO? How does it work? And how does it address the current issues of our day?

FBCO operates under the assumption that 'power' is the ability to act, the ability to accomplish something. Although power in our culture is commonly thought of as a noun, a thing, this method looks more 'verbally' at power, so that it is seen as a mode of acting. No power, no action. It's as simple as that. No doubt all of us have Lord Acton's maxim concerning power ringing in our ears, but as Rollo May reminds us, not only does power tend to corrupt, but so does powerlessness, and the absoluteness of both corrupts absolutely. There is no getting around the fact that if you act at all in the world, you are dealing with the dynamics of power.

But power is used in all sorts of ways, as we well know. In organizing terminology, there is either 'power over' or 'power with'. 'Power over' is more dominant and unilateral than 'power with', which is relational and based on compromise. There is of course a proper context for both uses of power, since using a relational approach with children can be disastrous, while a dominant approach with parishioners ('Father knows best') can breed resentment. So what approach to power works in our context as laid out previously? No doubt a unilateral approach would probably get action sooner, but at what cost? Hence, FBCO works much more from the 'power with' perspective, that lasting solutions start (and in fact end) with relationships.

But what kind of relationships? There is what I call the 'coffee hour' relationship, which, although important, is not the type of relationship used to build power. 'Coffee hour' relationships are more concerned with the question of 'how are you?' rather than 'who are you?' But it is only by asking the 'who' question that we start to get a sense of what is important to people, what is in their 'self-interest'. In other words, what they care about, and what they are doing about those things that are important to them. And here is where the role of the community organizer comes in.[3] An organizer's primary task is to initiate and develop intentional, public relationships that are based on respect, trust and mutual understanding, such that, after a conversation, the two dialogue partners have a sense of what the other cares about. And the organizer is to have numerous conversations like this, listening for what comes up again and again, because if not just two or three people care about something, but 200 or 300 people, then perhaps it is worth giving it attention; perhaps it is worth the effort to organize these people around the thing they care about. And the job of the organizer is to help them turn what is most likely in their mind an unactionable problem into an actionable issue that they are able to do something about.

Now to this point I have not laid out anything that might seem to require the label 'faith-based' community organizing. But what if you organize that which is already organized? In other words, what if you organize institutions? And what if those institutions that are organized are institutions where faith is the 'base'; that is, institutions that not only have some sense of the way the world is, but also some sense of the way the world should be? What if you organize institutions that not only recognize that people are multi-issue, but also acknowledge that they have a responsibility to participate in the issues that affect the lives of their members? What makes community organizing 'faith-based' is when institutions are organized together based on their vision of what 'should be'. For just as fear is a powerful motivator, so is faith.[4] Therefore, FBCO is motivating that which is already motivated, that which already cares about the world, that which is already thinking about 'lived faith', about how to act as agents of change, so that the 'world as it is' begins to look more like the 'world as it should be'.

Faith-based community organizations are then made up of dues-paying institutions,[5] institutions that care about the world and are acting in it. But here is one of the beautiful parts about FBCO. Because it organizes institutions which by definition are (or at least should be) multi-issue, diversity is truly a strength rather than a weakness. It brings together the 'arch-conservative' with the 'flaming liberal', the working-class Seventh-Day Adventist Haitian congregation with the upper-middle-class Jewish synagogue, the radical Unitarian–Universalist with the traditional and credally minded Episcopalian. What do they all share in common? A sense that the world, their cities, their communities do not need to be this way, *and* a recognition that they need to share their power with others if they actually want to see any substantial change. *That they have to work together if things are to be different.*

This is perhaps one of the most difficult aspects of FBCO, which is again where the leadership of congregations is so important. If the clergy are focused on, say, sexuality, to the extent that everything is coloured by this single issue, it becomes hard to imagine working with others who hold a contrary position. In other words, you cannot work with those on Monday that you just preached against on Sunday.[6] This does not mean, however, that you have to 'water-down' your positions in order to do FBCO. On the contrary, it is because of strongly held convictions that people come to the table *in the first place*. So the answer in our 'red' and 'blue' nation is not to be 'purple' (a combination of the two), but rather to find what 'red' and 'blue' have in common, and to help 'red' and 'blue' find the means to act powerfully together on what they care about. Distinctions and diversity matter, and may in fact be the driving force that brings substantial change.

So what are the issues that FBCO takes on? If we accept that the cultivation of relational power in an intentional fashion amongst diverse organizations is something to be desired, then what in fact should they (and can they) do together? As already mentioned, the first and most crucial step is the cultivation of intentional public relationships, both intra- and extra-institutional, in which people involved in the relationships know what the other cares about, and what they are doing concerning those things that are important to them.[7] But as often happens, people are not able to act in a powerful fashion around the problems they face, which are often the things that are important to them. But if hundreds of conversations like this occur in numerous institutions, and if certain problems come up again and again, that is a good sign that you have found something that cuts across ideology, race, religion and class.

For example, a few years ago when working at St Stephen's Episcopal Church in Lynn, Massachusetts, the leadership of the community organization for that area (the Essex County Community Organization [ECCO]) knew that there were myriad issues affecting the lives of people in their community, and initially thought that affordable housing would be on everyone's lips.[8] But once they started having intentional conversations with parishioners in the member institutions, and with others in the community, they discovered that housing, although an issue, was not what they worried about. For most of the people, their main concern was jobs. Not that they did not have one, but that they had too many. In other words, many of these people were stuck in dead-end 'McJobs', that did not offer a living wage, or benefits, or any hope of career advancement. Thus, they needed at least two 'McJobs' to pay the bills and provide for their families. So from the people's perspective, they needed training and access to jobs that provided them a living wage, with benefits, on a career path. This would free up more time for them to spend with their families and to be contributing members to their communities and to their churches.

Now the leadership of ECCO at this point could have said, 'Well, that's very nice, but we still think what you need is affordable housing', and gone ahead working on that issue. No doubt it would have made a difference, but it would have been yet another example of good-hearted people 'doing for' someone rather than 'doing with'. But in this type of organizing, *you always trust that the people in the situation know what needs to happen in order to change it.* So ECCO trusted the people, because they had (1) developed intentional relationships and (2) held numerous relational meetings that identified the problem to work on (jobs). Next, the third step – research.

Although jobs training programmes are well intentioned, many come with no guarantee that there will be a job waiting for the person once they finish the programme. So a community organization needs to spend a long time researching the problem so that it can be turned into an issue that can be acted upon. And through its research, ECCO discovered that there were approximately one hundred machine shops along the north shore of Massachusetts that were hiring people who needed to be completely retrained. So ECCO approached the machine shop owners, and negotiated with them, that if ECCO was able to find the money to develop a machinists' jobs training programme, they would allow the machine shop owners to develop the curriculum for the programme so that the graduates from the programme looked like the type of people they wanted to hire. But in return, the machine shop-owners had to 'set aside' a certain number of jobs, and actually hire those people who finished the programme (thus giving trainees the incentive to finish the rigorous year-long programme). The leadership of ECCO knew they had the people to fill the slots in the programme, who were desperate for a good job, and the machine shop owners agreed.

Which leads to the fourth step – action. Where was the money to come from for this apparently 'win–win' situation? It may come as no surprise that even when presented with something that benefits everyone, politicians are not quick to support such endeavours by making sure programmes like this one get funding. But when a thousand people from ECCO member institutions turned out at St Stephen's one evening to show their support for this programme, politicians who were invited to come to publicly state their support for this initiative had to think twice before turning it down. Here were a thousand people, many of whom were in need of these jobs: a thousand people who cared deeply about this issue and wanted to see some action. Thankfully, most of the politicians saw the benefit this programme could add to the community, and they came and publicly showed their support for it. What this community organization accomplished has now become a model for jobs training initiatives all over the country. And all because the leaders paid attention to the people, and empowered the people to take charge of their own situation.

Thankfully, faith-based community organizing is not rocket science. You do not need an upper-level degree to do it. But you have to love people. And you have to be patient and unafraid of power, for it is such, as St Paul reminds us (1 Cor. 4.20), that the kingdom of God depends on. So in conclusion, if I may paraphrase Samuel Taylor Coleridge: 'FBCO is not a Theory, or an Academic Endeavour; but ACTION – not a Philosophy of Action, but Action and a Living Process. TRY IT.'⁹

Notes

1. Hardy's example of a 'structure of repair' is the Society for Scriptural Reasoning.

2. The 'grandfather' of community organizing in the USA is Saul Alinsky, and his *Reveille for Radicals* (originally published 1946) and *Rules for Radicals: A Pragmatic Primer for Realistic Radicals* (originally published 1971) have become textbooks for organizers of all types. Edward Chambers, however, is most likely the 'father' of faith-based community organizing as it is known today. Chambers' recent book *Roots for Radicals: Organizing for Power, Action, and Justice* (New York: Continuum, 2003) completes the 'trilogy' begun by Alinsky in *Reveille* and continued in *Rules*, because Chambers was the one who took the 'Alinsky method' and gave it the sustaining quality that it lacked, as manifested in the Industrial Areas Foundation (IAF). For a biography of Alinsky, see Sanford D. Horwitt, *Let them Call me Rebel: Saul Alinsky, his Life and Legacy* (New York: Vintage Books, 1992). For recent books on faith-based community organizing, see Michael Gecan, *Going Public* (Boston, MA: Beacon Press, 2002) and Mark R. Warren, *Dry Bones Rattling: Community Building to Revitalize American Democracy* (Princeton, NJ: Princeton University Press, 2001).

3. I think that the role of the priest/pastor is not much different than the role of the community organizer. The one has been called a 'secular priest', perhaps a priest/pastor is nothing more (or nothing less) than a 'sacred organizer', whose vocation is to help and empower others to live into their vocation in the life of God, which would certainly include a 'public' life.

4. What I am assuming here of course is that churches, synagogues, mosques, civic organizations, etc. are already organized to the extent that the leaders (particularly the clergy) know who their people are and what they care about. I do not think, however, that most clergy are trained to view their vocation in this fashion. Although we clergy may be 'available' when

parishioners wish to meet with us, from my experience it is rare when clergy systematically and intentionally meet with their parishioners in order to discover not just what their 'problems' are but what their hopes and dreams might be, which goes far in revealing what people care about. In fact, I suggest that this may be a key means by which God raises up what a local parish should be concerned about; hence, the priest truly does become a 'sacred organizer'.

5.   Faith-based community organizations do not exist unless they are 'owned' by the institutions that constitute them, hence the need for dues. The bureaucracy of such organizations is therefore kept to a minimum (typically an organizer or two with perhaps an administrative assistant). One organizer commented that her job consisted largely of reminding the leaders of member institutions that it was *their* institution. The Iron Rule of Organizing is 'Don't do for others what they can do for themselves.' Bishops and clergy in the Anglican Communion would do well to heed such lessons.

6.   Besides sexuality, another issue in FBCO that is not organized around (or discussed much) is abortion. The difference between abortion and sexuality, however, is that, whether 'pro-life' or 'pro-choice', no one thinks abortion is a 'good thing', and some on both sides of this issue are able to recognize there are other factors at work that influence a woman's decision, thereby making it possible to work together on issues that get to the 'root', rather than simply whether abortion should be legal or not. The homosexuality debate, however, is more complex, in that one side truly does see it as a 'good thing', something that should be affirmed, blessed and celebrated. This makes it much more difficult to find common ground on this issue with those who hold a contrary opinion.

7.   The 'prequel' to this first step, however, is the establishment of a faith-based community organization, which usually comes about from the relationships that have developed already in a certain area (many times among clergy), and the realization that the community is facing issues that institutions are unable to overcome alone. In many respects, a faith-based community organizer is like a union organizer, in that they must be *invited* into the community, rather than forcing themselves upon a community, even if it is clear that the community could benefit from their presence.

8.   Affordable housing is *the* issue in Boston, and the community organization in that area (the Greater Boston Interfaith Organization [GBIO]) recently forced itself to find other issues to work on (civil rights for nursing-home workers and patients, and negotiations with a local bank for increased GBIO-member benefits), because GBIO was starting to develop the reputation as a housing organization. If a multi-issue organization becomes identified primarily with a single issue, the end of that organization is near.

9.   Coleridge, in *Aids to Reflection,* wrote, 'Christianity is not a Theory, or a Speculation; but a LIFE – not a Philosophy of Life, but a Life and a Living Process. TRY IT.'

Chapter 2

CONVERSATIONAL CHURCH GROWTH

John B. Thomson

Introduction

Reflecting on an incumbency now past inevitably offers possibilities of self-deception and simplification. Storytelling is always someone's particular narrative told within the horizon of the present. Memory is not the same as history.[1] In addition my perspective on this story is now informed by the research I undertook while incumbent of St Mary's, Doncaster, into the ecclesiology of Stanley Hauerwas.[2] Hauerwas confirmed, enriched and added to my own intuitions about ministry and Church. As a result, through living and retelling this story, I have become convinced that open, generous and conversational Christianity is both a creative expression of the gospel of God's grace in Jesus Christ and, in consequence, enables the Church to grow. It represents a properly broad and properly liberal Christianity without falling prey to the captivities of superficial contemporary relevance or uncritical biblicism. It is intrinsically open yet not formless, since while a conversation contrasts with a monologue in being unable to determine its conclusions in advance, a conversation can only happen from within the securities and stabilities of convictions. It is therefore a form of liberality rather than a form of cognitive control or irresponsible escapism. It is also broad and engaging in its attentiveness to alternative perspectives while offering a robust apology for its present convictions.[3]

In order to indicate the character of this open, generous and conversational Christianity and how it was embodied in the congregation at St Mary's, I will first delineate the contexts of the parish and myself. Secondly, I will provide a synopsis of Hauerwas's project and identify key features of this project, which I found to be illuminating. Thirdly, I will tell the story of my incumbency at St Mary's in a way that exposes the character and conditions of the congregation's growth. Fourthly, I will relate this story to the one often told in church growth literature. In conclusion I will distil key themes about conversational church growth which may help others in analogous journeys.

Context

The parish of St Mary's Wheatley in Doncaster is an inner-urban parish of about a square mile comprising some 6,000 residents. Geographically it falls into two halves: the terraced owner-occupiers to the north of the main arterial road (Beckett Road) and the mixed more substantial housing to the south. In the past the northern side of the road corresponded to traditional working-class culture, while the southern side represented the more affluent middle classes. The church and vicarage are situated just on the south side and initially were roughly at the centre of the original parish which had been developed in the late nineteenth century from St George's, the main parish church of Doncaster. However, with the interwar housing developments and then the postwar relocation of folk from the town centre to Wheatley Park, the parish church became geographically more distant from the majority of the parish population. Even when its 'daughter church', St Paul's, Wheatley Park, became an independent parish in 1992 (just before I became incumbent) the location of St Mary's was towards the town centre end of the parish. In addition, with the demise of domestic service, the rise of suburban living and the high cost of running large properties, quite a number have become bed and breakfast hotels, homes for the elderly or multiple-occupancy dwellings. I estimated, that within a generation the area had changed from being socially stable and respectable to being much more mixed, with a significant minority of dislocated and socially mobile temporary residents.

In the wake of these changes came the familiar problems of inner-urban areas, as wider tendencies to social anonymity combined with the particular pressures the social changes brought led to a sense that lower Wheatley was on the edge of 'respectability'. At one time the local primary school was reserving 20 per cent of its nursery and reception places for 'bed and breakfast' children. People often commented to me during my time as vicar that the area was not as it was. While aware that these voices represented contentious perspectives, there was a sense that longer-term residents were bearing the brunt of the social changes. Fecklessness was always at the frontiers in the form of drug-pushing, drug-abuse, theft, carelessness about the social fabric of the area and then, as a result of a change in police tactics, prostitution became a major issue in the streets around the church and vicarage.

In 1993 when I became vicar of St Mary's, the electoral roll stood at 120 adults of whom about 20 were actually associated with St Paul's, Wheatley Park (the daughter church, now a separate parish). Hence the congregational base of St Mary's was realistically about a hundred, of which about 60–70 were regular in attendance. My impression was that the parish, though low church, was not particularly 'card-carrying'. In addition it was clear that the relationship between congregation and parish had become detached and that the congregation was proportionately more middle-class than the surrounding communities. However, there was contact through occasional offices and by virtue of the integration of the parish with the predominantly artisan community. The latter represented a stable local population whose memory of the parish enabled the possibility of a conversation about God to take place. In short it was still possible to envisage a parish ministry.

Our arrival at St Mary's followed a three-year period in South Africa where I had been a tutor at St Paul's College, Grahamstown, one of the seminaries of the Church of the Province of Southern Africa. It had been a challenging three years, as the legislative framework of apartheid was dismantled and the leadership of Nelson Mandela emerged into public light. Before this I had served my curacy in the west Sheffield suburb of Ecclesall, an affluent area of Sheffield within a large congregation of open evangelical pedigree, and my formative years had been spent in Uganda, Scotland and England. Such a diffuse heritage left me with a sense of never being quite 'at home' with any particular constituency, whether it be East African revivalism, suburban and university evangelicalism, theological liberalism or radical liberationist catholicism, although each contributed significantly to my Christian journey. I was also ambivalent about the sufficiency of the Western tradition on its own to sustain a truthful way of life. Hence St Mary's offered me an opportunity both to put down roots and to explore, as a 'catholic evangelical' of 'liberal' tendencies, a number of conversations about Church, ministry and mission evoked by this pedigree.[4] Having lived and worked in a variety of contexts I was aware that incumbency could not be about imposing an abstract blueprint upon an existing congregation and parish as if nothing serious had been going on before my arrival. Rather incumbency was about partnership and conversation, since only together could the insights and wisdom, energies and gifts of God be employed in the ministry of this parish. Hence the importance of engaging in conversations.

The first conversation needed to be between my evangelical heritage and the robust liberationist and contextual Anglo-Catholicism of my experience in South Africa as I was serving in an English parish. Liberation theology and other contextual theologies present in the Church in South Africa challenged the individualism, pietism and relatively simplistic hermeneutics, which had informed my evangelical heritage.[5] Contextual theology, whether it was African theology, black theology or feminist theology helped me to recognize the situatedness of every theological enterprise. Hence the first conversation would need to grasp the story and stories of the area and those involving the relationship of incumbent to congregation. My disposition from the outset was to regard the congregation as the agent of ministry and mission with the incumbent acting in and through it.

The second major conversation was about the character and attention of ministry in the light of the challenges of liberation theology. In South Africa this had disposed me to identify Christ's missional focus as on the margins of life, and I had became aware that in the mission of the Church, the centre is the periphery. Hence the sense of vocation to a parish in a low churchgoing area such as the diocese of Sheffield and to a town such as Doncaster, which was often seen as marginal within the diocese itself. Given the recent history of the area a conversation would need to recommence between the congregation and the parish about what sort of congregational ministry was appropriate to serve this sort of community. Given that I was a stranger myself, this would involve careful listening on my part in partnership particularly with those who had depth awareness of the area, and an attempt on my part to learn the 'language' of the area. Church growth would therefore involve increasing the capacity of the congregation to engage with the social challenges of the parish as they became apparent. While numerical growth from immigrants to the area was always welcome, it appeared to me that the test of this congregation's vocation was whether it could engage those belonging to the area whose memory of churchgoing and vicars was quite ambivalent.

The third conversation was about the character and possibility of numerical congregational growth, given the superficially unpromising context of one of the lowest churchgoing areas of England and in the absence of the 'normal' supports for church growth, such as university students, articulate adults and a broadly middle-class parish. This element of the conversation was about whether this parish was the sort of context where ministry and church could flourish given God's commitment to those on the edge. In communities which had traditionally regarded the Church of England as a public utility for generations, this presented considerable challenge. It would require considering for whom the church existed, and being prepared to accept changes which would enable it to be more open and hospitable to those it served. Such a conversation would include attention to the culture of the church and how the congregation could welcome others to participate with them in the worship of God. Growth in imaginative congregational mission would therefore be necessary if numerical growth was to follow.

The fourth conversation was about the relationship between the international and historic Church and this parish. Could a parish situated in a predominantly monoethnic context discover an appreciation of belonging to the catholic Church and to the global, diverse human community? Such a conversation would need to explore what openness to the outsider might mean for a community relatively unfamiliar with difference. In addition my initial impressions suggested that there was considerable ambivalence about the financial relationship between parish and diocese, the latter being seen as a taxing agency draining the parish church of its resources. Growth therefore needed to include an enriched sense of ecclesial identity.

The fifth conversation was about how theology could reflect common worship, that is a common listening for God's voice by congregation and priest together rather than simply assuming that this was the vocation of the incumbent or activist core. The Anglo-Catholic tradition I had encountered in South Africa introduced me to the sociality of Christian discipleship in a way less evident in my evangelical pedigree. This suggested that, though personal commitment was important, 'person' should not be equated with 'individual'. In Xhosa the proverb '*mntu ngabuntu ngabantu*' (a person is a person because of other people) expressed an ancient African insight. To be a person implied relationality, whereas individual implied an atomistic isolated identity. Personal faith implied ecclesial faith represented in the gathering for worship of laity and clergy. Personal holiness and sanctified community life were not only witnesses to the grace of God, but also the premises for understanding the call of God. One could not grasp discipleship independently of ecclesial participation. Hence as incumbent my ministry needed to be conversational in the sense of participating with the congregation and any others who were so willing in a conversation with God about the character of congregational witness in this area of Doncaster. Congregational church growth, therefore, must include improved language skills as well as an expansion in the conversational community.

The sixth conversation was about what sort of congregation we needed to become better to embody the grace of God in Christ. In South Africa I already had a few uncertainties about aspects of liberation theology since they seemed to trade on unexamined notions of justice, power and rationality which had a particular pedigree in the post-Enlightenment Western tradition. This seemed to undermine the agenda of contextual theology since the sort of liberation spoken of was rooted in an alien liberalism. This suggested a continuing colonization by Western thought of African thinkers. It also raised questions about the adequacy of these concepts to offer Christians in the West a truthful freedom, since the premises of such liberal thought, as Alasdair MacIntyre has shown, are rooted in a particular anthropology which seeks independence from any theological moorings.[6] Given my ambivalences, a new English conversation would need to explore what sort of congregation we would need to become to be faithful to the gospel of Jesus Christ in this particular parish and yet free of the corrosive influences associated, ironically, with these elements of the liberal tradition.

Hauerwas's project

To those familiar with the diffuse writings of Stanley Hauerwas, it may seem strange to regard him as an ally of a broad and liberal expression of Christian discipleship and, in particular, to associate him with church growth. However, although Hauerwas spends much of his time attacking liberalism, his focus is upon that expression of liberalism, which emerged from the Western Enlightenment of the late seventeenth and early eighteenth centuries and is often equated with modernity.[7] This tradition of liberalism attempted to found human knowledge on the securities of a rationality rooted in the apparent stabilities of transcendental human consciousness and observation, free from the 'dogmas' of revealed religion.[8] It reflected a fatigue with the apparently insoluble and bloody theological controversies of the era of the Wars of Religion. However, for Hauerwas, this anthropocentricity not only divorced God from serious ethical enquiry but also denuded Christian discipleship and its correlative, the Church, of any significant contribution to the matter of truthful living. Christianity and the Church were rendered an unnecessary hypothesis and the apology for Christianity increasingly obscure. Furthermore, it encouraged space for human hubris and domination at the expense of the weak and vulnerable, such as the unborn, the child, the retarded and the elderly: in short any who did not equate with its notion of a universally normal human existence. While sympathetic to the deconstructive criticisms of modernity, expressed in the constellation of views called postmodernism, he still regards both as rooted in the same basic premise, with postmodernism simply taking modernity to its extreme and denuding the self of any sense of identity at all.[9]

In response Hauerwas developed a project, which sought to recover the true freedom of the Church and to demonstrate its pivotal place as the epistemological premise and agency for living the Christian 'ethos'. His intention was to restore an awareness of the significance of sanctification as the way by which God transforms Christian communities such that they can faithfully witness to his reign and be formed to see and act Christianly.[10] He called this church a community of character.[11] Characterized by distinctive virtues, in particular, peaceableness, this Church embodies the ongoing story of the risen Jesus whose core plot is narrated in the Scriptures, but whose story includes the contemporary, historic and eschatological Church. It is a Church whose presence is a prophetic sign of the present peaceable reign of Christ, a reign inclusive of the salvation of the cosmos. Its truthfulness is indicated by the character of its living and dying in ways which correlate with the living and dying of Christ. Hence people take precedence over texts, narratives or stories over ideas or ideology and embodiment matters more than rhetoric.[12] As such, the Church is a community of ordinary, often argumentative pilgrims, being trained, through the practices of worship and discipleship, to see, describe and inhabit the world as Christians rather than simply anybody.[13] Such formation disposes them to embody the practices of Jesus, namely to attend to the marginal, the stranger, the weak and the ordinary. It requires of them a political grasp of their diachronic and synchronic identity and from this communal attentiveness gives them the confidence and freedom to converse with the 'world' as Christians.[14] It is therefore properly broad and indicative of Christian liberty since it inducts Christians into a rich discursive theological community within which they discover that discipleship is the path to freedom rather than autonomy.[15] Furthermore it generates truthful church growth, since if the Church grows this is because it is Christian. For Hauerwas much church-growth thinking reflects unreconstructed post-Enlightenment liberalism, with its anxious survivalism, its equation of success with quantifiable effectiveness and its uncritical espousal of modern sociology.[16] Indeed, numerical congregational growth is not, for Hauerwas, a necessary indication of a truthful church.[17] Given his cruciform Christology, truthful witness may, under certain conditions, actually lead to numerical decline.[18] There may even be times when a catacomb existence is indicative of the truly catholic Church.

Hauerwas's project did not offer me a theory of church, which I needed to put into practice or to measure existing practice against. Such dualism, for Hauerwas, represented the timeless universalizing deceptions of the worst of the Enlightenment. Rather Hauerwas's role as a theologian, a servant of the Church, was to direct my attention to the significance of our ecclesial practices.

In short, he trained me to see what was going on more clearly. In so doing he helped me to answer the question 'why bother with Church?', when faced with popular ambivalence about churchgoing yet rhetorically high confessional claims.[19] His explorations of the significance of public worship enabled me to see how it is constitutive of discipleship.[20] His focus upon the Church as the key apostolic and apologetic agent of the gospel offered me an escape from the individualism of my evangelical heritage, a recovery of the vital missiological role of the gathered congregation and a way of integrating liberationist insights about the significance of the marginal into the currency of ordinary Christian discipleship.[21] The narrative shape of God's engagement with creation, illustrated in the form of the Scriptures, enabled me to see how the ongoing life of the Church formed part of the revelation of God's grace without diminishing the central place of the Scriptures, so important to one formed in the evangelical tradition. His emphasis upon self-conscious Christian identity supported a confident yet open conversation with the world without either withdrawal or capitulation. His concern with truthful witness and the active reign of Christ reduced, if it did not wholly remove, my anxiety about numerical growth. His attention to practices enabled me to see that Christianity is not a timeless ideology but a way of holy living before God which needs the contribution of all Christian people to be adequate to its calling. His focus upon peaceableness, while raising some difficult questions, suggested that the Christian community was constituted to befriend the stranger represented as the 'other'. In such a community living the peace of God, there is no need to destroy difference since the peace of the story integrates difference within the security of God's salvation. In addition, this peaceableness has space and time to let God web together the plurality of discipleship stories into the richness of his grand epic.[22] There is no need for someone to coerce all into a singular narrative. Essentially Hauerwas helped me to see that the Christian community is properly configured for a conversational if sometimes argumentative journey with God. Indeed, since for Hauerwas the term God is a name, and hence storied rather than a concept, God is actively involved in this conversation.[23]

The story I tell below, therefore, reflects a revisiting of my experiences as vicar of St Mary's, which I believe represents a symphonic relationship with Hauerwas's project. While this could be seen as simply the retrospective imposition of an alien architecture, it is my contention that this co-inherence is not one imagined but illustrative of the way things emerged. This is a form of *Nachdenken*. I am also aware that Hauerwas's project raised questions I continue to struggle with which may well have been screened out by me. I suspect that the elements of his project, which proved fertile and illuminating are the ones which I have been most drawn to. However, it may also be the case that what I was a part of gave embodied witness to those elements of Hauerwas's project which are most plausible.

Narrating conversational church growth 1993–2000

The challenge facing St Mary's in early 1993, as mentioned above, was how to recover confidence in the possibilities of being a faithful, growing Christian community situated as we were in the context of lower Wheatley, Doncaster, and engaged in the sort of conversations I outlined earlier. Our initial approach was to distil a core strategy reflected in three focal themes: worship, nurture and mission, and characterized by shared ministry. The congregation would be the agency of ministry and mission rather than simply the cleric and a few enthusiasts. In addition the relationship of congregation to parish was explored on the assumption that the gathered congregation did not equate with the parish church. This involved among other things consulting census records to see the profiles of those living in the parish and also a mapping of active links we had with people in the area. We had many associate baptized 'members' whose connection with church had to be respected. Looking for and listening to that community, an attentive conversation, would be imperative in developing a contextually appropriate way of being a church open to the 'strangers' on our doorstep. We were learning about the implications of Christian friendship, as Hauerwas would express it.

We therefore sought to find ways of becoming an open and porous community, hospitable to the baptized and to seekers from wherever they came. The church had to be a community whose first gospel 'word' to the stranger was 'welcome'; a 'yes' rather than a 'no' or 'not yet'. In order to enable this to happen, we agreed that more accessible acts of worship should be part of the menu of our devotional life. In the Lent of 1993 a 'prayer and gift' day took place to raise money for a new public address system and a large screen for the front of the church to cost £4,000. The money arrived, a member of the congregation built the screen, and by the summer we were able to have book-free acts of worship particularly at monthly all-age events during which baptisms took place. This did not mean that all acts of worship became screened. Instead we developed the existing patterns of worship to enable a variety of expressions of worship – some eucharistic, some not – to take place. Given the initial size of the base community, it was important that we learned to be together and to share different ways of worshipping. To have a consumerist approach to patterns of worship would have undermined the catholic character of the church and also prevented achieving the critical mass of people on a Sunday morning which acted as a magnet to newcomers.

To facilitate congregational formation we developed 'Root Groups' which met monthly on a Sunday afternoon for Evening Prayer, low-key Bible study and a tea-party. Root Groups nourished fellowship, gave other church leaders an area of responsibility and also offered a mission and service structure for the church when leaflet drops, coffee rotas, hospitality and celebration events, such as Harvest, Epiphany and Easter, etc., needed staffing. Furthermore they provided a structure, which configured the congregation towards growth, since they subdivided its pastoral and mission responsibilities. In addition, a music group began which embraced folk from across the church spectrum and acted not only as a creative enterprise but also as ecclesial cement, building trust which enabled difficult decisions to happen with relatively little conflict. In this way we were becoming more aware of our distinctive identity as an ecclesial community. This enabled us to converse with the wider community aware of who we were in God's story.

Consequently, teaching in church sought not to inculcate a timeless ideological view of Christianity, but instead to offer a conversational engagement with issues of the day, a conversation in which the Scriptures represented the core but not exhaustive wisdom of God. In addition the Scriptures were expounded in conversation with scholarly wisdom. This attention to the identity and character of being a Christian community was essential if we were to see the challenges of Christian mission and service in our neighbourhood. As Hauerwas indicated, the agenda for activity needed to be discerned by those formed to see what is at stake in a particular area rather than by attending to an abstract blueprint derived from somewhere else and masking its sociological address.

As the local theologian, my task was to make available the depth wisdom of the historic and contemporary Christian community to this particular church, both as congregation and parish. For example, the midweek eucharist was often the occasion for education about complex theological issues. For example, on one occasion, when discussing the controversy between Arius and Athanasius, the congregation was split into two halves, one responsible for chanting '*oti pote ouk en*' and the other '*ouk pote oti ouk en*', the Greek for 'there was a time when he did not exist' and 'there was not a time when he did not exist'. Such a dramatic pedagogy among folk of limited theological education enabled a richer conversation to take place about the issues underlying these slogans within a dramatic interactive learning environment. Similarly, the controversy between Augustine of Hippo and Pelagius could be construed as Africa sorting out the English, with all sorts of interesting implications for present perspectives on the two. This approach to adult learning was about ensuring communal ownership of theology rather than the imposition of a single agent's perspective. As incumbent my role was to introduce the community to the Christian tradition and with them listen for the word of the Lord in the conversation. As with all conversations, the outcome could not be guaranteed since growth in understanding was ongoing and inclusive of the participants. Even in larger contexts, I found it was still possible to engage in a dialogical sermon from the pulpit. Such congregational training was something which Hauerwas's stress on formation and agency reinforced.

To enable a conversation with the local community to recommence, the congregation as well as the priest needed to be outward-looking and engaged. Theologically, within the horizon of liberation theology, this was about a congregation following Jesus in his attention to the outsider. Hence visiting teams complemented the vicar, a generous approach to the occasional offices was agreed, links with the community were improved through the local schools, starting midweek clubs for youngsters, engaging the local jazz club, patronizing local shops, initiating a Christian Aid fair alongside the doorstep collections, etc. In addition we sought to be visible with ecumenical street processions and with me, as vicar, cycling and walking around the parish. However, as mentioned above, this went with a deepening sense of the character of a Christian community. An increasing sense of who we were and what this implied for mission enabled a confident engagement with the community. In addition it also enabled wisdom to be received from beyond the gathered community since this attention to our identity also enabled us to realize that Christ was ahead of us in mission rather than simply with us. We were discovering Christ before us in other people and situations rather than controlling the location of God's grace.

Alongside this we were surprised to find Christians from overseas, most of whom were working in the Doncaster Royal Infirmary, joining the congregation. This may partly have been due to the overseas experience of the vicarage family. However, more important was the warm welcome they received from the congregation. This hospitality was reciprocated when we began to hold international evenings. These enabled people from overseas to share their exotic cuisine with local folk. In addition, at one Remembrance Sunday we had testimonies from an Afrikaner Anglican woman priest, who had been a Black Sash activist in South Africa and a Nigerian Anglican visitor. Sadly our press release was not used by our local newspaper, but the occasion helped local people appreciate the way in which Christians in other areas of the world interpreted such memorials. Furthermore, local ecumenical relations were encouraged through colourful brass band-led street processions and common Lent groups. This enabled us to embody our sharing in a common story about God's grace, which Hauerwas regards as the most integrating form of ecumenism.[24] It is as we tell our stories of God that we find we cannot exclude fellow travellers in the tales. What this meant was that congregational growth happened as people of difference shared together vocally, in worship and also in participating in various activities. This was growth in understanding, numbers and also symbolic richness. It was also about becoming increasingly aware that this 'catholic' church was our primary if not exhaustive hermeneutical community. To grow in discipleship involved an awareness of our fellow travellers in the Christian community.

In all of this the initial strategy had to be contextually focused. Indeed, although at first I had joined one of the country's larger evangelical church's mailing networks I increasingly found that its agenda and suggestions seemed alien to our context. Similarly, as the Christian Basics course Alpha began to take off in the mid-1990s, I was cautious of taking it on board, partly due to some theological reservations, but also because it would have meant mothballing the locally generated Christian Beginners' Course which we had developed using local church leaders.[25] Growth in confidence was better encouraged by joining with local people to develop a Christian Basics course rather than buying one in from elsewhere. In addition this enabled us to engage in a more conversational style of learning since we were not beholden to a fixed syllabus or timescale.

The first three years of any incumbency engender a sense of realism about a church and although St Mary's was not particularly conflictual, there were challenges in our various conversations and not all initiatives flourished. I remained perplexed at the ongoing view of church as a public utility rather than a community of faith held by much of the surrounding community. However, congregations grew and commitment deepened. By 1995 the electoral roll stood at 170 and financial giving had been rising significantly. Average Sunday attendances were now about 90 adults and 20 children/youth; the monthly all-age baptism services filled the large 300-seater building on a regular basis, and our midweek children's clubs had begun to take root. Links with the local community were growing, although I had to wait two years before local primary school ministry was invited. There was a sense of partnership in ministry as various teams of people shared ministry with me. However, it was still slower progress than I had expected.

The second half of my incumbency involved giving early initiatives time to mature and, as mentioned above, undertaking doctoral research in Hauerwas's ecclesiology. Participating in a congregation growing in a variety of ways and reflecting upon the character of church in contemporary Western society seemed a fertile use of time. It also clarified the role of the parish priest as organic theologian, attentive to the distinctive role of the contextual theologian parasitic upon both the local context and the tradition of Scripture, Christian discipleship and wisdom. Nevertheless, it was also a time of struggle. The curate who had joined us in 1995 retired in 1997 on the grounds of ill-health. While this was not directly to do with St Mary's, it left me disappointed that the opportunity had not succeeded. Similarly, although we could attract large congregations to baptisms, major festivals and memorial services, and were visiting assiduously, this did not translate into swift numerical growth. It would also be true to say that we only approximated to the sort of disciplined Christian community Hauerwas pointed me to. Nevertheless, the congregation continued to grow gradually, until by 2000 the roll was over 200 adults and we had about 60-plus youngsters linked to our midweek clubs all led by members of the congregation. However, the visiting and other local initiatives were inculcating a greater sense of active responsibility for mission to the parish among a wide range of congregational members. This was deepened by a renovation project we embarked on in 1995, which aimed to raise the quality of the church premises as a contribution to this mission. The £100,000 needed for the renovation project was raised predominantly through regular 'prayer and gift' days, fundraising events, two major legacies and a grant from the diocese. The second of the two legacies came just as we reached the £75,000 mark and covered all the congregational giving to that point. Hence what individuals had prayerfully and sacrificially given was given back to the Christian community as a whole. I detected in this a profound insight about faith, church and the character of being a giving community.

Through these experiences we were discovering that an open, generous yet challenging conversation about the gospel was proving fruitful. Illustrative of this was the climax of my time at St Mary's when we took part in a community performance of Roger Foster's *Hopes and Dreams* musical as our major Millennium celebration. This involved folk from a local dance school, the Jenny Riley School of Dance, three local primary schools, the South Yorkshire Crusade Choir and pupils from Danum Comprehensive School, all coordinated by our ecumenical forum, Wheatley Churches Together. Over 1,200 people came to watch the performances and it was a remarkable sound to hear them – many were not churchgoers – singing the Millennium Prayer. Here was an experience of popular piety given focus and space. It reflected churches as singing societies welcoming the participation of other voices in the celebration of God's grace for all.

Conversational church growth and Church Growth Movement

For those conversant with the Church Growth Movement rooted in the Fuller Theological Seminary and particularly associated with Donald McGavran, much of what we were about had affinities with their suggestions and conclusions.[26] Indeed, given my evangelical background, this is not surprising. Where I found myself raising questions about the movement related to my concerns about the legacy of post-Enlightenment thought and the particular sort of liberalism which it represents. Although McGarvan, for example, is highly critical of 'liberalism' as a contributor to church decline, it is clear that by 'liberal' he means those whose view of Scripture does not concur with a conservative evangelical view. However, his own approach is very liberal in the sense that its assumptions, method and view of human identity uncritically reflect the Enlightenment thinking which I was already questioning when I began my incumbency and which Hauerwas's project illuminated more radically.

In terms of church growth methodology there is a presumption that contextual differences, important as they are, remain secondary to the possibility that a universal theory of church growth can be distilled independent of time, identity, tradition and context. Involved in this is the assumption that underneath the distinctions of culture, language, gender, race etc. is a transcendental subject. Yet, as Gadamer (following Heidegger) has convincingly demonstrated, this is impossible to achieve.[27] There is no transcendental stable subject. Persons are relational creatures situated in particular contexts, which webbed as they are with one another, nevertheless prevent universal theories from representing an adequate understanding of what is at stake.

In contrast, a conversational approach engages with the particulars of each context, in a way superficially like McGavran's, though not with the intention of generating a universal missiological theory but rather in order to narrate the story of this particular community and to relate this community with the story of the gospel, which the missioner brings. The capacity to converse in this way is rooted in the common linguistic environment of which both are a part and in which God as part of the social order is also a speaker.[28] A properly liberal approach involves liberating Christians to see the contexts they are a part of through the formative experience of worship so that other wisdoms, such as sociology, anthropology and psychology, which McGarvan believes can offer him secure knowledge of the human condition, are positioned and discriminatingly evaluated in terms of where the Christian tradition has got to. Such a task is incumbent upon each ecclesial community as it engages in mission and involves conversation rather than simply analysis, since only a situated wisdom can offer light.[29] Hence the challenge is not to generate a theory about church growth but to attend to the stories of particular Christian communities located as they are within the horizon of Christian tradition. The latter offers formative resources for generating Christian communities faithful to their apostolic vocation but in ways appropriate to their particular contexts. In this way congregations discover a new liberty in mission and are spared the colonizing of abstract theories or methods. Discipleship rather than technique is the resource for churches to grow. Coherence is achieved not by controlling people's intellectual grasp of faith through theories of discipleship, but by nourishing the bonds of love and respect as people discover that the faith story they are a part of is connected with that of the Christian community they are part of.

Reflections on conversational church growth

The possibility of the sort of liberal and conversational ecclesial evangelicalism I am advocating may seem a contradiction in terms both to those sceptical about the resources of the evangelical tradition to sustain such an approach and also to those seeking a more categorical and delineated expression of this tradition. However, this would be to caricature the evangelical tradition. While it is true that there are significant elements within this company who fit this caricature, I have never been convinced that to be evangelical implies that one must be conservative or rigid. Indeed, given the story shape and character of Scripture itself, a more open, peaceable and liberal expression of the tradition seems quite consonant with a high doctrine of Scripture.[30] Bishop Kenneth Cragg is exemplary in this regard, as he has engaged in this form of conversational evangelical outreach to the Islamic tradition for decades. In addition it is noticeable that many evangelical clergy who find themselves called to inhabit the strange lands beyond the 'evangelical heartlands' often find that their ministry becomes more conversational and less proclamatory as time goes on. For myself this conversational approach, as mentioned above, proved fertile in all sorts of ways and seemed to enable a congregation to grow in character, giving and also numbers. I learned a number of insights, which were ones concurrent with what I found myself exploring in conversation with Hauerwas's ecclesiology.

(1) Conversational church growth is rooted in a church exploring its worship. A conversational church is a singing society inviting others to be nourished in the free grace of God.[31] Only by a primary attention and response to God could the congregation of St Mary's be theocentric and thereby formed to 'see' and serve the parish in company with God. God's imparted right-

eousness mediated through the openness of worship was about being transformed into a Christian community rather than simply a religious club. Such
worship was common in the sense that it involved all of us, not simply the cleric
leading and instructing the passive congregation. However, it was not about
our attempt to understand God, but rather our openness to let God illuminate
us. We were not controllers of the divine identity. Worship, furthermore,
required that we took the liturgy seriously so that the contemporary,
Doncaster-based congregation was not prey to the limitations and deceptions of its own perspectives, but nourished and challenged by the wisdom of
the wider church, past and present.[32]

(2) Conversational church growth involves prayerful formation or training.
My prayer was that St Mary's would grow numerically and in terms of its
income. However, the key was the character of this growth and, in particular,
the character of the community, which was growing. Sanctification took
precedence over statistics. Genuine growth would not necessarily be numerically evident, but would be relative to a faithful prophetic calling to display
Christ to the world in worship, nurture and mission. Thus being trained to
attend to Scripture and also to the Christian tradition was important, since the
story of God is ongoing. This was about growing in catholic awareness.
Similarly, listening for God with others on the journey – particularly those least
interesting or engaging – was vital if the community was to be properly
formed. Furthermore, this involved giving space and permission for questions
to be raised and engaged with without dismissal or rejection and a recognition
that common discipleship did not require consensus on all issues.

(3) Conversational church growth embraces rather than excludes and hence
seeks to retain people as they explore. At St Mary's, growth was as much about
keeping people within the ecclesial conversation as attracting newcomers.
Certainly it was important to see new faces, but the key was to pray that they
would be engaged by the worship and hospitality of the congregation, its
embodied apologetic. A confrontational approach to evangelism is unhelpful
in a context when most are already struggling to engage with church at all.
Believing was present in the local community, but it needed care in order to
encourage belonging so that believing could intensify and, through belonging,
grow.[33] This was particularly so given those whose background disposed
them to be suspicious of church, or who were fragile people. Befriending rather
than berating folk not only attracted them to church, but as Hauerwas argues,
displays the Christian disposition to love the stranger and is itself an invitation
to conversation.

(4) Conversational church growth required risk-taking or faith. It was
important that the congregation took risks, in terms of outreach, giving,
renovations, liturgies, delegation, shared ministry, etc. The church had to
learn to live its life as Jesus did, orientated and open to those on the fringe,
rather than following the Pharisaic defence of secure sacred space. It was
important that the plant as well as the people conveyed the story that God
cared about this place. Hence the importance of care of the buildings and
gardens and the importance of the vicar's involvement, along with others, in

local neighbourhood issues, such as the struggles surrounding prostitution, drugs and theft, was vital to the credibility of the church. Similarly active support of Christian Aid and the Jubilee Debt Relief campaign were all part of this engagement with the vulnerable and marginal.

(5) Conversational church growth involves patience and faithfulness evident in ongoing visiting, involvement with local schools and other local agencies, without immediate dividends. The congregation of St Mary's, therefore, began to have affinities with a quasi-religious mission order as when 50–60 people took part in the Millennium visitation on Advent Sunday in 1999. Christian Aid street collecting and general visitations also developed this identity. These community practices established the congregation as the primary apostolic and apologetic agency of the church rather than the vicar alone.

(6) Conversational church growth entails shared ministry and teamwork. As priest I may have had a distinctive role but it was always one within and with the body, which itself was a loose but distinctive congregational polity acting as a prophetic sign to the neighbourhood. The vicar's role was to challenge and encourage that community to live up to its proper identity. Hence inviting others to develop their gifts and take areas of responsibility was a major part of my role. It was important not to regard oneself (or be regarded) as a soloist, instead of being part of a choir.

Conclusion

Four words summarize this conversational church growth: hearing, hallowing, hosting and hospitality. They also speak of the heart of Hauerwas's project in a way often missed by his critics. I was privileged to explore this embodied apologetics as part of St Mary's, Doncaster, a church which though attracting little public attention sought to hear God's call, to witness God's hospitable grace, to hallow a local community and thereby to host that community in the eucharist of God's life.[34] In this way its growth displayed the broad embrace and generous liberality of God.

Notes

1. Miroslav Volf, *Exclusion and Embrace: A Theological Exploration of Identity, Otherness and Reconciliation* (Nashville, TN: Abingdon Press, 1996), pp. 233–40.

2. John B. Thomson, *The Ecclesiology of Stanley Hauerwas: A Distinctively Christian Theology of Liberation* (Aldershot: Ashgate, 2003). A bibliography of Hauerwas's works is included in this book.

3. For a discussion on the character of understanding as conversational dialogue see Hans-Georg Gadamer, *Truth and Method*, 3rd edn (London: Sheed & Ward, 1993), pp. 359–79, 462–3 and Lewis Edwin Hahn (ed.), *The Philosophy of Hans-Georg Gadamer* (Chicago and La Salle, IL: Open Court, 1997), pp. 33–4. The commitment of Anglicans to common worship has many affinities with this conversational discernment of the ways of God in life.

4. For a fuller exploration of this identity see John B. Thomson, *Church on Edge: Practising Ministry Today* (London: Darton, Longman & Todd, 2004).

5. I am not implying that this is characteristic of the whole evangelical tradition, with which I am associated. However, it was certainly true of me and I suspect is a tendency within most of the tradition.

6. Alasdair MacIntyre, *After Virtue* (London: Duckworth, 1985) and *Whose Justice, Whose Rationality?* (London: Duckworth, 1988).

7. For Hauerwas's understanding of liberalism, philosophically, ethically, and in socioeconomic terms see Stanley Hauerwas, *Vision and Virtue: Essays in Christian Ethical Reflection* (Notre Dame, IN: University of Notre Dame Press, 1981) p. 229; Stanley Hauerwas with Richard Bondi and David B. Burrell, *Truthfulness and Tragedy: Further Investigations into Christian Ethics*, 2nd edn (Notre Dame, IN: University of Notre Dame Press, 1985), pp. 10, 16–37; *A Community of Character: Toward a Constructive Christian Social Ethic*, 4th edn (Notre Dame, IN: University of Notre Dame Press, 1986), pp. 11, 78, 107; *The Peaceable Kingdom: A Primer in Christian Ethics*, 3rd edn (Notre Dame, IN and London: University of Notre Dame Press, 1986) pp. 7–8; *Against the Nations: War and Survival in a Liberal Society* (Notre Dame, IN: University of Notre Dame Press, 1992), p. 18; 'Will the Real Sectarian Stand Up!', *Theology Today* 44.1 (April 1987): 93; *Unleashing the Scripture: Freeing the Bible from Captivity to America* (Nashville, TN: Abingdon Press, 1993), p. 35; *Dispatches from the Front: Theological Engagements with the Secular* (Durham, NC: Duke University Press, 1994), pp. 6–13.

8. Hauerwas uses modern medicine as a case study in the pathology of liberalism with its loss of the particular, its confusion of caring with curing, its inability to deal with the tragic and vulnerable in the quest for normality, efficiency and technical prowess. See *Suffering Presence: Theological Reflections on Medicine, the Mentally Handicapped and the Church* (Edinburgh: T&T Clark, 1988) and *Naming the Silences: God, Medicine and the Problem of Suffering*, 2nd edn (Edinburgh: T&T Clark, 1993).

9. Stanley Hauerwas, 'The Christian difference: surviving postmodernism', *Cultural Values* 3.2 (April 1999): 164–80.

10. Stanley Hauerwas, *Sanctify them in the Truth: Holiness Exemplified* (Edinburgh: T&T Clark, 1998), pp. 215–16.

11. See Hauerwas, *A Community of Character*.

12. *A Community of Character*, p. 9; *In Good Company: The Church as Polis* (Notre Dame, IN: University of Notre Dame Press, 1995), p. 58; *Sanctify Them*, p. 5. See also 'The Church as God's new language', in Garrett Green (ed.), *Scripture, Authority and Narrative Interpretation* (Philadelphia, PA: Fortress Press, 1987), pp. 179–98.

13. *Vision and Virtue*, p. 117.

14. See *A Community of Character*, pp. 105–6 and *Against the Nations*, pp. 112–13.

15. Stanley Hauerwas, *After Christendom* (Nashville, TN: Abingdon Press, 1991), p. 89.

16. See 'What would Pope Stanley say' in *Christianity Today* (November/December 1998): 2 and 7.

17. *Truthfulness and Tragedy*, p. 6.

18. *Vision and Virtue*, p. 102.

19. In the 2001 census, south Yorkshire recorded a 75 per cent Christian population, despite having one of the lowest churchgoing rates in the country.

20. See 'The liturgical shape of the Christian Life: teaching Christian ethics as worship', in David F. Ford and Dennis L. Stamps (eds), *Essentials of Christian Community: Essays for Daniel W. Hardy* (Edinburgh: T&T Clark, 1996), pp. 35–48. Interestingly, Robin Gill's work in *Churchgoing and Christian Ethics* gives cautious empirical support to the thrust of Hauerwas's contention that being actively part of a Christian community shapes people into disciples with particular character. Gill feels Hauerwas is too idealistic. I would argue that Hauerwas's emphasis upon practices evoking distinctive living suggests that what emerges should indicate the sort of distinctiveness is realistic. Otherwise expectations are once again

anthropocentric rather than relative to the grace of God among his people. For Gill's discussion, see Robin Gill, *Churchgoing and Christian Ethics* (Cambridge: Cambridge University Press, 1999) pp. 1–23.

21. See Stanley Hauerwas, 'The gesture of a truthful story', *Theology Today* 42 (July 1985): 181–9 and *Wilderness Wanderings: Probing Twentieth-Century Theology and Philosophy* (Boulder, CO: Westview Press, 1997), pp. 165–6.

22. Hauerwas, *A Community of Character*, p. 40.

23. William H. Willimon and Stanley Hauerwas, with Scott C. Sage, *Lord Teach Us: The Lord's Prayer and the Christian Life* (Nashville, TN: Abingdon Press, 1996), p. 31.

24. Hauerwas, *In Good Company*.

25. Alpha is a ten-week introduction to Christianity developed by the the the Anglican Church of Holy Trinity, Brompton, London. It works within the more charismatic-evangelical tradition and is based around meals, hospitality and conversation.

26. For McGavran's thinking, see Donald Anderson McGavran, *How Churches Grow* (New York: Friendship Press, 1973); *Understanding Church Growth* (Grand Rapids, MI: Eerdmans, 1978); *How to Grow a Church* (Glendale, AZ: Regal Books, 1974).

27. See Thomson, *The Ecclesiology of Stanley Hauerwas*, pp. 44–6.

28. Brad J. Kallenberg, 'Unstuck from Yale: theological method after Lindbeck', *Scottish Journal of Theology* 50 (1997): 201, 209–11.

29. For a discussion on Heidegger, Gadamer and MacIntyre see Thomson, *The Ecclesiology of Stanley Hauerwas*, pp. 42–6, 55–7.

30. For a discussion on this issue see John B. Thomson, 'Time for church? Evangelicals, scripture and conversational hermeneutics', in *Anvil* 21/4 (2004): 245–57.

31. For an exploration of the theme of the singing self see, David F. Ford, *Self and Salvation: Being Transformed* (Cambridge: Cambridge University Press, 1999).

32. 'The Liturgical Shape of the Christian Life: Teaching Christian Ethics as Worship', in David F. Ford and Dennis L. Stamps, (eds), *Essentials of Christian Community: Essays for Daniel W. Hardy* (Edinburgh: T&T Clark, 1996), pp. 35–48. Also in Stanley Hauerwas, *In Good Company: The Church as Polis* (Notre Dame, IN: University of Notre Dame Press, 1995), pp. 153–64.

33. For an outworking of the relationship between believing and belonging in English Christianity see Grace Davie, *Religion in Britain since 1945* (Oxford: Oxford University Press, 1994).

34. For the description of Hauerwas's ecclesiology as 'embodied apologetics' see Brad J. Kallenberg, *Ethics as Grammar: Changing the Postmodern Subject* (Notre Dame, IN: University of Notre Dame Press, 2001), p. 156.

Chapter 3

REORGANIZING THE CHAIRS ON THE *TITANIC*: A CASE OF A CHANGE IN PRIORITIES

Pete Ward

In the summer of 2004 around 18,000 young people gathered in central London. The event organized by the charismatic youth organization Soul Survivor centred around worship and local community projects. The previous Easter over 80,000 people were reported to have attended the long-running evangelical conference Spring Harvest. At around the same time EMI were surprised at the chart success of their compilation album of charismatic worship songs *The Best Worship Songs Ever*. Every day on my way to work I seem to be cycling behind a bus which has an advert on the back inviting me to explore the 'meaning of life', evidence of the extent to which the Alpha course has achieved a Christian presence in the popular consciousness which was reserved only for Cliff Richard, the Pope and the Archbishop of Canterbury. Clearly the evangelical/charismatic sections of the Church are thriving. More than that they are entrepreneurial, ambitious, well funded and on something of a wave.

This has not always been the case. In the 1930s evangelicalism was a small and somewhat ineffectual group within the Church of England. David Bebbington illustrates the weakness of the movement by pointing out that in this decade there was not a single episcopal appointment from among evangelical ranks (Bebbington 1994, p. 367). In 1944 Max Warren, general secretary of the Church Missionary Society could lament that 'all too commonly today an Evangelical in the Church of England is a person labouring under a sense of frustration and discouragement often so deep as to engender … an inferiority complex' (quoted in Bebbington 1994, p. 367). In a period when other sections of the Church have experienced a loss of confidence and decline, how have evangelicals managed to buck the trend? I would like to suggest that the answer is very simple: youth ministry.

In this chapter I will explore the way that the charismatic/evangelical movement has transformed itself through a long-term investment in work with young people. While I would not wish to underplay the importance that theology has played in shaping the fortunes of the various groupings in the Church, I think there are some key social and cultural insights arising from developments in youth ministry which may be of use to those outside the evangelical/charismatic world. I should perhaps preface these observations by sharing something of my own biography.

I came to faith through an evangelical youth group at my local church in Cheltenham, and in the 1970s I, like many others, was affected by charismatic renewal. Through 20 years involvement in various forms of youth ministry I have remained committed to an evangelical and charismatic expression of the faith. At the same time I have with my family worshipped in a wide range of Anglican churches, including over ten years in a catholic parish. Working for Archbishop George Carey, I was often involved in dialogue with catholics and liberals on how we could develop youth work within the broad spread of the Church of England. Through these and other encounters I have become convinced that the only hope for these wider traditions of the Church lies in a reordering of priorities towards a genuine long-term engagement in work with young people. Not only those young people currently in the Church but perhaps more importantly those who never darken our doors. This is not simply about adding to the numbers in the pews. The lesson of evangelical/charismatic youth ministry suggests that such engagement changes the culture and theology of the Church. Youth ministry keeps the Church young and energetic. What I mean by this is that a commitment to sharing faith and growing faith among young people has led evangelicals/charismatics to a distinctive contextualization in contemporary culture. It is out of this contextualization that new forms of Church life, worship and leadership have emerged. It may seem unlikely, but the spread of Alpha and other large-scale initiatives owe their origins to the hard work of many volunteers and young clergy over a 60-year period.

Turning evangelicalism around: the early years

Even before the Second World War evangelicals were clear that the future lay in ministry among young people (Bebbington 1989, p. 225). Working largely outside of parish or formal church life a series of youth ministries had begun to emerge. The most important of these came from the unlikely and rarefied context of the leading English public schools. In 1932 a young Anglican clergyman named Eric Nash was appointed by CSSM (the Children's Special Service Mission) to lead a section of their work know as the Varsities and Public School Camps (or VPS). Bash, as he was known, followed a very single-minded policy. He was called, he said, to minister to the small group of privileged upper-middle-class young people found in the elite public schools of the day. His reason for this was strategic. If he could win significant numbers of these young people for Christ they would in turn have a disproportionate impact on the life of the nation, because overwhelmingly the leaders of the academy, the military and indeed the Church of England, were drawn from this group (Eddison 1982, p. 19). At the heart of this ministry lay a number of very important commitments and values. First, Bash stressed the importance of building long-term relationships with young people. Secondly, he formed patterns of ministry which encouraged young people to develop as Christian leaders. He trained these leaders 'on the job' as evangelists, preachers and pastoral workers. Thirdly, while maintaining an unswerving commitment to a particular expression of the faith he was quite prepared for this to be located in a style and cultural form which connected to the social norms of the young people with whom he was working.

The result of this ministry was quite extraordinary. Bash effectively trained a whole generation of evangelical Anglican clergy. The future leaders of the postwar evangelical/charismatic movements were to a large extent shaped by their long days spent at the VPS camps at Iwerne Minster. These included: John Stott, Dick Lucas, Michael Green, David Watson and many others. It was these leaders who were to begin to shape church life during the 1960s and on to the present day. Chief among these was John Stott.

In 1950 Stott became Rector of All Souls, Langham Place. His decision to accept this appointment is significant. He was widely regarded as the brightest star within evangelicalism at the time, and his decision to focus on parish ministry was to have an energizing effect on evangelicals not only in the UK but around the world. What made this move so important was that Stott decided to take the lessons he had learned in youth ministry and apply them to the local church. (Dudley-Smith 1999, p. 251) There were two main influences on Stott's life as he set out on this task. The first was the Varsity and Public School camps, the second was his experience in the Christian Union at Cambridge (Dudley-Smith 1999, p. 251).

Born out of theological controversy within student groups, the Cambridge Intercollegiate Christian Union (or CICCU) developed a pattern of ministry which was to spread throughout the universities and colleges of Britain. The history of this movement and the eventual forming of the Intervarsity Fellowship (IVF) lies outside this present study (see Johnson 1979). The significance of the spread of evangelical Christian Unions around the country is that they served to initiate young people into a particular cultural expression of the faith. The student-led nature of the groups meant that many young people took their first steps in Christian leadership and ministry while they were active members of the Christian Union (Johnson 1979, p. 301). In a very short time this resulted in evangelical parishes being continually reinforced by keen young Christians out of the universities. At the same time, following the example of John Stott, these churches were now led by clergy whose sensitivities and expectations had grown from ministry among students and young people. In evangelical churches around the country youth fellowships were established. Through the Church's Youth Fellowship Association (CYFA) these groups were not only supported and networked, teaching resources were also produced, but most significantly these clergy set up a number of camps and house parties along the lines of those pioneered by Bash. The intention was that young people in local parish would benefit from the style of ministry pioneered by VPS. Staffed by volunteers, many of them young clergy, these camps were to generate thousands of well-taught and highly motivated young Christians. In the 1970s and 1980s there can have been few evangelical Anglican clergy who had not cut their teeth on CYFA Ventures or the Pathfinder Camps which catered for the younger age groups.

A *culture of production*

Evangelicalism grew through youth ministry, but this was not the whole story. Youth ministry actually shaped evangelicalism, and as it did so it changed the culture of the Church. The postwar culture of religious production within evangelicalism grew initially from a public school and university context. The new breed of evangelical clergy had learnt how to preach, how to do evangelism, how to run groups and how to express theology as they had become involved in student and youth ministry. Student leaders soon became clergy and when they entered into parish life they ran the church in much the same way as they had the Christian Union.

In other words, as evangelical leaders move from youth ministry into the ordained ministry they tend to take the style and innovation from one context to another. This is true not only of evangelicals in the UK, it is true of most evangelical groups. Billy Graham learnt how to run his evangelistic crusades during his time in Youth for Christ in Chicago. The present-day mega-church movement in the USA has grown out of youth ministry. Two examples would be Bill Hybels from Willow Creek Community Church and Ed Dobson from Calvary Chapel in Grand Rapids, Michigan, both of whom are explicit about the way their present-day ministry has been shaped by involvement in youth ministry (Creasey-Dean 2004, p. 14 note)

Creativity in youth ministry is generated out of the desire to reach out to young people. In the UK, during the early years early of CICCU and VPS, the culture of young people was primarily shaped by formal institutional structures. The result was a culture of production which reflected this educational setting: the student association or membership group. When Stott and others came to local parish ministry they reproduced the cultural style and theological expression they had seen to be effective in the universities. As the 1950s gave way to the 1960s it was clear to many evangelical clergy that reaching young people would mean some kind of engagement with the developing youth culture. One of the first attempts in this direction came when in 1966 Falcon Books launched a new songbook: *Youth Praise*. The list of acknowledgements makes it clear that the book came out of the combined effort of a number of evangelical Anglican clergy. These included Richard Bewes, John Stott, Michael Baughen, David Watson, Michael Botting and Kenneth Habershon (*Youth Praise*, p. vi). Over the next decade these individuals, and others involved in the spread of *Youth Praise*, were to be the movers and shakers in the evangelical movement. This is highly significant because it shows how creativity in youth work was a priority and focus for some of the most talented within the evangelical movement. Moreover, *Youth Praise* also shows these 'conservative evangelicals' being quite prepared to contextualize worship in contemporary youth culture.

Born out of public school life and Oxbridge, evangelicalism was clearly willing to change its style and culture. It was the desire to share faith with young people which led to a growing interaction between evangelicalism and youth culture. Soon evangelicals were to be swept up by two movements: the

Jesus movement and the Charismatic movement. In both of these young people and those reaching out to young people were to be at the forefront of shaping the life of the Church. In the 1960s a number of key evangelicals in the Anglican Church began to be influenced by the theology and experiences associated with Pentecostalism. In 1965 Michael Harper, then one of Stott's curates at All Souls, set up the networking organization the Fountain Trust (Hocken 1997, p. 115ff.). The Fountain Trust promoted the charismatic renewal for those within existing denominations. By the early 1970s, however, it is arguable that the momentum behind the movement may have begun to slow. All of this changed when news of a new youth-orientated Christian style was brought from the USA. Starting on the West Coast, the Jesus Movement (or Jesus Revolution) had emerged from young people who had become disorientated and disillusioned with the drug-soaked hippie scene (Enroth, Ericson and Peters 1972). Soon key figures from the Jesus Movement in the USA were visiting the UK. These included Arthur Blessit, the minister from California who carried a huge wooden cross around with him, and perhaps most significantly the long-haired hippie musician Larry Norman (Leech 1976, p. 117). Blessit and other 'Jesus freaks' openly advocated a pentecostal spirituality, but this was articulated with the hippie style of dress and expression. For young evangelicals this mix was irresistible. Now it was possible to be Christian and dress like a hippie, now there were albums and bands and a new way to worship with hands raised in the air and a sense that all of this was 'cool'. Inevitably, within a few years the creative heart of evangelical culture had shifted once again: Oxbridge and the public schoolboy had been replaced by the Jesus festival and the Christian musician.

The significance of the Jesus movement was that it offered the young evangelical Christian a new youth-orientated version of the faith. Key evangelical leaders such as Billy Graham and Michael Green were quick to endorse the Jesus People (Graham 1971). Indeed, Green saw in the movement the possibility of the renewal of the wider Church. (See Green in Palms 1972.) The energy associated with the Jesus movement spawned a new generation of Christian musicians, including Graham Kendrick, Ishmael and Andy and Judy MacKenzie. A number of record and music publishing companies came to prominence, including the fledging Thank You Music. Alongside all of this activity a number of Jesus festivals were to start, including Greenbelt and later Spring Harvest.

By the end of the 1970s evangelicals had engaged in local relational youth work, and through this activity had developed a number of very able leaders. With the Jesus movement a new youth style was added to the mix, and evangelicals became familiar with and skilled in the use of popular music and media. What gave this cocktail its final burst of energy was the link made between a media-based religious culture and charismatic worship. Through worship musicals such as *Come Together* and on to the publication of the house church-inspired worship material of *Songs of Fellowship*, the youth style and musical expression of the movement was taken into the daily life of the Church. What people heard at Spring Harvest or later at New Wine and Soul

Survivor festivals appeared in the local church the next week. With worship music promoted on CDs through the local bookstore, at specialized tours and events, and made available through the Internet, evangelicalism had transformed itself into a consumer culture (Ward 2005).

Spring Harvest, Alpha, the March for Jesus and the whole web of evangelical initiatives exist within this media-related environment. At the same time they have a history. They have grown from a sustained commitment to working with young people and students. If we want to learn the lessons from evangelical rejuvenation then they are most evident in the long-term picture, rather than in the more spectacular evidence of this movement in the present. I am sure that many look at the financial clout of evangelical churches or the media presence of Alpha or the numbers of young people at Soul Survivor, and they see no way in which their section of the Church can compete. In my view this is to misunderstand what has taken place over the last 50 or so years. The lessons are actually more basic and probably much more challenging.

Lessons for the wider Church

Long-term investment

For over 80 years evangelicals have prioritized work with young people. What this means is that in every evangelical church, even in a relatively small congregation, there will have been a group of volunteers spending time with teenagers either in youth fellowships or in some kind of organized outreach and these groups will have been running for decades. As congregations have grown most evangelical churches have made it a focus to raise money from the congregation to employ a part-time or full-time youth worker. The growth in the numbers of youth ministers in the Church of England has been one of the quiet revolutions in the life of the Church. When I first came to Oxford in 1983 there were probably four of us working as youth ministers in the churches. None of us had received a formal training for our role. We had to form a pressure group to persuade the local diocesan youth officer to recognize us in any formal way. Today there are more than 30 full-time paid youth ministers in Oxford city alone. There is also a degree-level training course linked to Oxford Brookes University.

In the early days young clergy would focus a good deal of their time on working with the parish youth club. Senior evangelical bishops such as Michael Baughen, David Shepherd, Graham Cray and many others spent a significant proportion of their early ministry concentrating on work with young people. Alongside ministry in parishes and on CYFA camps from the early 1980s there have also been groups of evangelicals working closely with local schools. Many of these are linked or networked together by Scripture Union. This work has been fragile, tough and often struggles for financial support, but it is for many a vocation. The activities of a group such as Message to Schools in Manchester, with their band The Worldwide Message Tribe, may be seen as successful and high-profile, but it should be stressed that their work has developed over a 20-year period. It is hard to imagine what this means in terms of commitment and investment in local schools and churches, but what is clear is that the work has grown from 20 years of visiting local high schools taking lessons on faith, appearing at assemblies and running evangelistic meetings in local churches.

There is an urban myth from where I live in Oxford, which I find appropriate to the question of investment. The myth has it that an American tourist is admiring one of the college lawns. On seeing the gardener the American says how much she likes the lawn. 'How do you make it so green and beautiful?' she asks. 'Well', says the gardener, 'We feed it in the autumn and early summer, rake out the old growth and then mow it twice a week.' 'We could do that at home', says the enthusiastic American. 'And you do it for six hundred years', adds the gardener. This is the point: evangelicals, as far as I can see, are alone in making young people a central priority in their church life. The vibrant scene we see today is the result of this investment. The numbers of young people involved in charismatic/evangelical churches come directly from this long history. There is no quick fix in youth work: the festivals and bands and so on may seem to be the answer, but in reality they are just the icing on the cake. Youth ministry is about the willingness to spend time with young people, listen to them and share your life with them. Evangelicals have been doing this for years, and this is why their churches are full of young people and young adults.

Organize

The Church of England has generally been poor at organizing on a regional and national level when it comes to youth work. Yet evangelicals have failed to let this get in the way of their efforts to work with young people. The result has been the growth of organizations such as CYFA or Scripture Union (SU) or the Universities and Colleges Christian Fellowship, or organizations such as Spring Harvest or Soul Survivor. Most youth work is grassroots, based in a local parish and staffed by volunteers, but from the earliest times evangelicals have realized that there is a need for a range of regional and national gatherings to support the local work. The most important of these networks were linked to the various camps and house parties run by groups such as SU and CYFA. These camps offered support, fellowship and encouragement throughout the year with newsletters and other meetings as well as two or three weeks together engaged in running the event. For the leaders these camps were not only culture carriers they were also a vital means of support. Parish youth work can be a lonely and at times tough job, especially if you are a volunteer or an inexperienced curate. The camps gave a vision of something bigger. The energizing effect that this had not only on the leaders of youth groups but also on the many thousands of young people who have attended them is enormous. These camps continue to run, and every year thousands of young people attend them. The camps remain largely uncelebrated but they are the vital organs or cell structure that lie beneath the evangelical world. They make all the other stuff work.

The lesson here for the wider Church is that while youth ministry must be relationship-based and located in the parish, school or local community, if that is all that it is it will very soon wither on the vine. Isolated youth workers, be they volunteer or paid, need to feel part of a larger, deeper and faster-flowing stream. In my view it is a mistake to look to a diocese or the national structures of the Church of England to deliver this kind of network. Even if the will is there to do this (which in my experience it is generally not) diocesan youth officers are poorly resourced and their energies are often focused on issues such as child protection, relationships with the local authorities, and so on. This means that the non-evangelical traditions in the Church of England need to learn to organize around youth ministry. There need to be dynamic regional and national structures developed where individuals and parishes can organize together and focus their activities in joint action which supports and builds local youth initiatives. This need not be an enormous undertaking. What I have in mind is something like a CYFA house party where four or five parishes or younger clergy might agree to run an annual youth gathering for a week and use this to generate a more energized and dynamic work in the parish. Of course the real value of such an activity is only seen after ten years of working together and that I am afraid brings us back to the college-lawn dilemma.

Contextualization

Charismatic/evangelical religious culture has evolved dramatically over the last 30 or 40 years. It has done this by generating the next wave of innovation among young people. At the same time this innovation has been guided by a clear commitment to a theological position. A glance at the advertising associated with Alpha or the marketing indulged in by Christian record companies may lead to a view that charismatic/evangelicals have in some way sold out to culture. In my view this judgement fails to take account of the extent to which evangelicals and charismatics have remained consistent in many of their core theological commitments. This gives a continuity and identity to the movement, while at the same time it has also sustained a considerable movement towards cultural innovation.

There doesn't seem to be any reason why those from a more catholic or liberal tradition in the Church might not embark on a similar journey. The thousands of young people who flock to Taizé would indicate that it is not just charismatics who can connect to young people. What is interesting about Taizé is that it has maintained an authenticity in its community life, theology and worship, and yet it has responded to young people. It has done this by becoming more than a monastic community. Indeed, the process of engaging with young people has helped the authentic culture of the community to develop around the particular commitments of Brother Roger and in response to a much wider global and ecclesial scene. It is worth comparing Taizé to Alpha or to the New Wine Network. Alpha and New Wine have both grown out of a local parish church: Alpha from Holy Trinity Brompton and New Wine from St Andrew Chorleywood. What these parish churches have achieved is that they have become more than a local church. Like Taizé they have developed culturally and innovated structurally. They have done this largely in response to a desire to connect with young people. Their priorities have led them along this path. Contextualization has grown out of the desire to do youth ministry.

Contextualization is a chicken-and-egg question. If the Church attempts to do something for young people by imitating a particular cultural expression it will invariably fail. If, however, out of relationship with young people new forms of worship and church life can grow organically then there is much more chance of success. Making contact with young people outside of a church context is still very difficult and demands a measure of sensitivity to context. This means that in the first place leaders are required to embody a relevant and relational Christian presence. (This is what I mean by chicken-and-egg.) There is a new generation of young people in a local church every four or five years. What this means is that youth ministry is a constant flow of relationships and cultural responses. In my view it is only the evangelical/charismatic section of the Church which has given significant time and energy to sharing faith in this fast-moving world, and because they are focused, the chicken-and-egg problem is transformed into the learning and adaption which characterize ministry in these kind of contexts. To mix metaphors: to solve the problem you have to get into the water and start to swim. Evangelicals have been willing to do this; I fear this has not been the case with other sections of the church.

Culture and the Church

Richard Holloway once remarked that evangelicals were characterized by a willingness to embrace bad taste for the sake of the gospel (France and McGrath 1993). It is an amusing and telling observation, not simply for what it says about evangelicals but also for what it may imply about Holloway and others in the Church. It was youth ministry and a commitment to young people that has led evangelicals to express faith in terms of popular culture. Holloway and others may feel that a commitment to taste goes hand in hand with their version of faith. The challenge really lies in the extent to which such a commitment is dysfunctional for the long-term health of the Church. My sense is that for Holloway and others involved in the Church a link has been made between particular forms of Anglican spirituality and worship and notions of 'high culture'. The problem is that good taste can be less than helpful for youth ministers and the young people they seek to involve in Christian worship and Church life. It is my sense that the location of certain forms of Church life in an aesthetic formed by a particular view of culture has held sections of the Church back from a real engagement with young people. The willingness of charismatic/evangelical Christians to utilize methods of communication from popular culture and then to incorporate these into the worshipping life of the Church has in turn been one of the reasons for their success. The challenge then for the wider Church is how do we with integrity and authenticity to our tradition connect with and communicate within a media-constructed consumer culture? I am convinced that it is only when creative energy and resources are given over to finding solutions to this question that we will see vibrant and renewed churches outside of the charismatic/evangelical scene. Interestingly the success of the cathedrals is firmly located in good taste, but it utilizes consumer culture through the increasingly commercial and sophisticated world of classical music. This should suggest that there are ways for a creative and innovative parishes to connect with young people in their neighborhood without the vicar resorting to an ill-advised baseball cap and attempting to rap the sermon.

A word to those who may object

I am aware of the objections that might have arisen in readers' minds as they read this piece. In the first instance I know that many will feel that the kind of creativity and energy which is demanded in a commitment to engage with young people may not be easily forthcoming in their particular parish or Church tradition. Some may argue that evangelicals have a culture of entrepreneurial activity which is quite simply absent in the catholic and liberal traditions. I honestly do not think this holds water.

   In the area of Oxford where I live the parish church has a strong catholic tradition. Walking the streets around my house I am struck by the number of institutions and buildings which owe their origins to the energy and dynamism of the local Anglican church. These include two foundations for religious orders, three schools, a working men's club, a youth club and a community theatre. Many of these date back to the nineteenth century. Clearly at some point there was enough energy and activity in this small area of the city to rival any contemporary evangelical church. Again with regard to those in the liberal tradition there also seems to have been enormous energy for the creation of institutions and creativity in developing new initiatives for work in the local community and for social justice. Those from the centre of the Church have been behind a number of hugely successful and significant charitable organizations including the Samaritans, Help the Aged and Oxfam. Through these and other creative initiatives Christians have transformed social care in our society. Yet this leads me to a key point. These activities, although not an exhaustive list, indicate that the creative efforts of many Christian people have lain outside of formal church life. Not only that they have tended to be the kind of activities which do not, and should not necessarily, result in a numerical growth in the Church. Essential as it has been to witness to the life of the gospel in founding schools and setting up major charities it is perhaps worthwhile asking why similar energy has not been devoted to developing the life of the Church and in particular why we have not seen the emphasis upon working with young people replicated in the whole of the Church. My sense is that this relates to priorities and a choice to work outside of specifically Church life. Now maybe is the time to reassess these priorities.

   Perhaps in response to this some may argue that their particular theology either of the Church or indeed of the nature of mission means that they simply do not believe it is right or proper to pursue what I have suggested. In support of this it could be said that the conversionist theology of the evangelical lends itself to dynamic youth work and the focus on building a vibrant church life, while the catholic and the liberal identity is set against adopting such an approach. My second point then in response to this is to say that I recognize that there are theological issues at stake here, as well as the question of institutional survival. I would want to suggest two ways forward. For the liberal tradition it seems clear that a concern for social justice and a commitment to the environment and ecological issues are echoed strongly in many aspects of youth culture. Young people in the main would sympathize with the agenda of many within the Church. Indeed there are organizations, such as Amnesty International and CND, who have generated their own culture and creativity from engaging with young people. Surely the Christian Church can follow this lead and develop spiritualities and Church life which link these worlds together? For those in the catholic tradition I am sympathetic that identity and liturgical practice are linked together. This makes innovations in worship such as those associated with the charismatic movement particularly problematic. At the same time there is considerable evidence that there is a groundswell in the wider youth culture and among a large number of young Christians towards a more ritual-based, sacramental form of worship. On the whole, catholics in the Church of England have been outside of these developments, leaving charismatics and post-evangelicals to access the tradition for themselves. The fact that this is taking place seems to indicate that there is at least a window of opportunity for the catholic tradition.

Conclusion

In the summer of 2004 over 19,000 young people attended Greenbelt Festival at Cheltenham racecourse. While Greenbelt is rooted in an evangelical history it has long since drifted and become 'post-evangelical', or at least it has embraced the wider Church. Archbishop Rowan Williams preached at the Sunday eucharist, and it was announced that he is to be the patron of the festival. In the last five years Greenbelt has pursued a policy of developing relationships with mainstream Christian organizations. As a result Christian Aid has been joined as the main sponsor of the event by the *Church Times* and the Church Missionary Society. The event featured a seminar by Jeffrey John and a talk by the founder of the Body Shop, Anita Roddick. This is a far cry from the regular fare at an evangelical/charismatic festival! Greenbelt seems to me to hold out some hope that a youth- or young-adult-orientated expression of the faith is possible outside of the charismatic/evangelical paradigm. With Greenbelt as something of a rallying-point it might be possible to imagine that some of the grassroots initiatives I have argued for might come into being. The bottom line, I suspect, is that this will depend upon a willingness to turn the tide.

My fear is that the present disputes over sexuality and the episcopacy will absorb the energies of too many people. This is not an argument about the rights and wrongs of these causes, simply my own belief that in the absence of a clear change in priorities towards young people we may simply be reorganizing the deckchairs on the *Titanic*.

References

Bebbington, D., 1989 *Evangelicalism in Modern Britain: A History from 1730s to the 1980s* (London: Unwin).

———, 'Evangelicalism in its settings: the British and American movements since 1940', in M. Noll, D. Bebbington and Rawlyk (1994) *Evangelicalism: Comparative Studies in Popular Protestantism. The British Isles and beyond 1700–1990*.

Creasey-Dean, K., 2004 *Practicing Passion: Youth and the Quest for a Passionate Church* (Grand Rapids, MI: Eerdmans).

Dudley-Smith, T., 1999 *John Stott: The Making of a Leader* (Leicester: Intervarsity Press).

Eddison, J. (ed.), 1982 *Bash: A Study in Spiritual Power* (Basingstoke: Marshalls).

Enroth, R., Ericson, E. and Peters C., 1972 *The Story of the Jesus People: A Factual Survey* (Carlisle: Paternoster Press).

Graham, B., 1971 *The Jesus Generation* (London: Hodder & Stoughton).

Hocken, P., 1997 *Streams of Renewal: The Origins of the Charismatic Movement in Great Britain*, 2nd edn (Carlisle: Paternoster Press).

Johnson, D., 1979 *Contending for the Faith: A History of the Evangelical Movement in the Universities and Colleges* (Leicester: Intervarsity Press).

Leech, K., 1976 *Youthquake: Spirituality and the Growth of the Counter-culture* (London: Abacus).

Palms, R.C., 1972, *The Jesus Kids* (London: SCM Press).

Plowman, E., 1972 *The Jesus Movement* (London: Hodder & Stoughton).

Ward, P., 1996 *Growing up Evangelical: Youthwork and the Making of a Subculture* (London: SPCK).

———, 2005 *Selling Worship: How what we Sing has Changed the Church* (Milton Keynes: Paternoster Press).

Youth Praise, 1966 (London: Falcon Books).

Part 2

CASE STUDIES

Chapter 4

'The Lord is here': The Nine o'Clock Service

J.W. Rogerson

It may come as a surprise to readers that a book on how liberal churches grow contains a chapter on the Nine o'clock Service. In the first place, the Nine o'clock Service ceased formally to exist in the August of 1995, and although attempts were made to continue it in the form of a Nine o'clock Community Church, most of its original members had left and ceased to be active, or had joined other churches, and to the best of my knowledge the Nine o'clock Community, if it still exists, has never succeeded in recreating anything remotely resembling the Nine o'clock Service. In the second place, at the time of its closure, the Nine o'clock Service was widely represented as a sect in which women members were being abused. This hardly sounds like a liberal church! Yet, as I shall argue, the Nine o'clock Service was liberal in many ways, and the popular ideas that were put about concerning it were gross misrepresentations.

In what follows in this chapter, the reminiscences and ideas expressed are entirely personal ones, and are not based on any research which I have undertaken in order to write the chapter. The few former members that I know have understandably moved on in their lives and are not especially keen to go over old ground. At the same time, I have a clear memory of such history of the Nine o'clock Service as was told me by one of its founding members, and for several years before its demise, I was as regular a member of the Nine o'clock Service as my duties as head of a university department allowed me to be.

Origins and early history of the Nine o'clock Service

The Nine o'clock Service originated in St Thomas's Church, Crookes, a well-known and thriving charismatic Anglican church in an area of Sheffield close to the university and popular with students. Its founder, Chris Brain, was the bass guitarist in a rock group which, apparently, was on the verge of breaking through into the 'big time'. However, the group turned its back on the possibility of success in the world of rock groups, with all that that meant for a lifestyle that was perceived by many to be bound up with drugs and sexual licence, and decided instead to use its talents in the service of the Kingdom of God. Although St Thomas's was a very well-attended and successful church by modern-day standards, Chris Brain and his friends felt that it was completely failing to establish any contact with those young people for whom the rock scene and clubbing were important parts of their life, and this would eventually lead to Brain and his friends being allowed to provide experimental worship directed towards this particular group of young people. It was because this could only happen on Sunday evenings at 9 p.m., after the other services at St Thomas's had finished, that the idea of the Nine o'clock Service came to be born. However, prior to that, Brain's circle had formed a community based in Nairn Street in Crookes, in which some members worked in order to support others who would undertake full-time ministry.

In one of its earlier phases, the Nine o'clock Service was influenced by the teachings of John Wimber, and at this stage (I was not yet a member) most likely resembled a 'signs and wonders' charismatic church, distinguished by its use of rock music and an attempt to identify with the culture of those the service sought to reach. By the time that I came to be associated with it, which was in the early part of 1992, its influence had shifted from that of John Wimber to that of the German theologian Jürgen Moltmann. In its public worship, at any rate, there were no indications that it was, or had been, a 'signs and wonders' church, although it was made clear that if people wished individually for private counselling, prayer and other ministries, these would always be available. The association with Moltmann gave the service a strong political dimension, and a concern for justice at local and international level. Its members were challenged to think radically about their lifestyles, and whether these reflected the values of an acquisitive and materialist society or whether they were such as would lead to greater social justice. It was a small step from this Moltmann phase to its view of cosmic justice which would be articulated through the theology of Matthew Fox. I shall come to this phase later. For the moment, I shall describe the Nine o'clock Service as I encountered it in the early part of 1992.

From 1992

There were several reasons why I was drawn into the Nine o'clock Service. On the one hand, there was a desire on the part of the leadership to recruit me. As an external examiner of the Northern Ordination Course (at which Chris Brain was studying for ordination in the Church of England), I was invited at the beginning of each academic year to give a talk about the meaning and use of scripture. It appears that on the occasion when I gave this talk in the presence of Chris Brain it enabled him to see beyond the fundamentalism which he had previously embraced, to the creative use of the Bible through the insights and questionings of liberal biblical criticism. From that point on he became to keen to meet me and to get my views on certain matters, and members of the leadership team began to enrol in the Sheffield Department of Biblical Studies to do either a postgraduate diploma or an undergraduate degree. A day consultation was held with me, one of the topics being relationships between members of the same sex. In the course of this Brain was very sympathetic to my view that the gospel meets us where we are, and that if we are attracted to members of the same sex, this is something that has to be worked out by the congregation as a whole. If God has accepted us for Christ's sake as we are, then fellow Christians must do the same.

My contact with Brain was made easier by the fact that some of my best graduate students from the Sheffield Department of Biblical Studies were active members of the Nine o'clock Service, and one or two were in his closest circle. For my part, knowing these particular students as I did, it was clear to me that they would not be involved in anything that was mindless and extremist, and in any case, having a lively interest in types of liberation theology and the need for evangelism among young people, I was sympathetic to the whole Nine o'clock Service project, for all that I was a total stranger to the rock scene. Had I not studied theology I would have studied music, and classical music had played an extremely important part in my own progress into faith from a largely non-church background. My ignorance of rock music was such that I became aware of Queen and Freddie Mercury only several years ago because of the very lively interest taken in this group by one of my nieces, then aged 12. (She, needless to say, could not understand how anyone who was alive when Queen and Mercury were at their zenith could have remained ignorant of their existence!)

The pattern of worship in the Nine o'clock Service in 1992, when it was at St Thomas's, Crookes, was that of a one communion service and two teaching services per month, with one Sunday evening being retained for a more general church meeting. The teaching service was very simple. It began with worship, which consisted largely of songs composed by members of the service, accompanied by both live and pre-recorded rock music, to which members of the congregation danced. This was then followed by 30 minutes or more of teaching, usually based on the exposition of a biblical passage, in which rapt attention was paid to what was being said. The service concluded with another session of worship. The communion service was quite different. It included worship, as described above, and culminated in one of the clergy at St Thomas's saying the words of institution of Holy Communion before this was received by the communicants. It also included elements of confession and absolution, the background for the latter being an intoned voice reciting prayers in Latin. Latin (with suitable translations) was also used in other parts of the service, some aspects of which were outwardly 'catholic' with the use of genuflexion and the sign of the cross. Many candles were placed on window ledges about the church, as were small bowls containing incense. The point of all this was to emphasize that although the service was trying to identify with the culture of those whom it sought to reach (members of the inner circle of the service deliberately wore black and other clothes similar to those of the rock and clubbing youth), it was trying to do this in conjunction with ancient traditions of the Church in order to add a new dimension to the experience of those who belonged and were attracted. The clergy and those taking part in the service (this was always a team effort) wore black cassocks. Chris

Brain was ordained to the priesthood at Petertide in 1992, and celebrated his first communion on 16 August. I was invited to preach on this occasion, the first of a number of times that I did so at the Nine o'clock Service.

From St Thomas's to Ponds Forge

Brain's ordination to the priesthood gave an independence to the Nine o'clock Service that meant that it could move from its situation at St Thomas's to an independent venue. This was necessary because St Thomas's was a comparatively small building and the numbers of people attending the Nine o'clock Service made it uncomfortably crowded, quite apart from the fact that it was not possible to begin to rearrange the seating and décor for the service until the normal Sunday evening service had concluded. (It was quite often the case that it was not possible to begin the service until well after 9 p.m.) In 1993, therefore, the Nine o'clock Service moved to Pond's Forge, a building housing a swimming pool built for the World Student Games and a number of gymnasia and other recreational facilities. A circular gymnasium was hired for use on Sundays. The circular design was favoured because it resembled a Byzantine basilica. A good deal of research was done into devising an appropriate liturgy, and a circular altar was designed in such a way as to imitate the sun and the moon. The circular gymnasium also made possible the deployment of large video screens on which the words of the liturgy and the songs could be projected, and which also enabled people to see the leaders, preachers and celebrant from wherever they were. Also on the surrounding walls of the gymnasium it was possible to project images which created an atmosphere associated with whatever theme was chosen for the occasion. The lighting was dim and anyone familiar with discos and clubs would have felt immediately at home. Every kind of posture was catered for, from those who wanted to sit on chairs to those who wanted to sit on the floor on foam mats, to those who wanted to stand. The pattern of worship altered so that a Planetary Mass was held twice a month, with the other services being teaching services. The form of the Planetary Mass differed fundamentally from the previous communion service.

It began with the statement that there was no right way to take part in the service and everyone should feel free to do what was felt to be comfortable and natural. The only 'compulsory' part was that those present were asked to hold hands at the very beginning of the service for the preparation and opening prayer, culminating in the words 'The Lord is here; his Spirit is with us', after which there were songs and worship. This was followed by a period of meditation in which the congregation was invited to do body prayers led by a member of the team. These were accompanied by primal sounds from the highly efficient amplification system, sounds which were very moving and helpful in sustaining meditation. This usually lasted around ten minutes and was then followed by the readings, the gospel being introduced with the words 'Wisdom: let us attend'. After the address which followed the reading of the gospel there was the offertory. This did not mean the collection of money (the Nine o'clock Service had an extremely efficient and well-supported method of committed giving) but a remarkable sequence of events in which not only bread and wine were presented on the altar, accompanied by appropriate prayers, but the elements of earth, air and water, representing those things that sustained life on the planet. With the offering of the earth, the celebrant rubbed his hands in the earth and with the earth made the sign of the cross on his white alb, reciting the words 'I wash my hands in this earth your body makes perfect.' The purpose of this action was to emphasize the humanity and mortality of the celebrant as representative of those present.

The 'canon of the Mass' began with a rehearsal by the celebrant of the words of institution at the Last Supper. This was followed by a form of epiclesis at which those who were assisting with the distribution and who had presented the elements on the altar stood around the celebrant, and one of the assistants prayed freely for the descent of the Holy Spirit upon the elements of bread and wine. This was followed by the elevation of the host and its fraction, the latter being accompanied on the video screens by the release of enormous bursts of energy and sometimes by a recording of the crying of a newborn baby. The words said at this point by the celebrant were 'The broken bread: the rebirth of the universe'. The celebrant then added the words 'Christ said: "Take this it is my body. Drink this: it is my blood."' Administration was by intincted wafer directly into the mouths of the communicants, with the words: 'The body and blood of Christ'. During the administration of the communion the intercessions were led by a member of the congregation. There then followed a brief period of praise and worship, and the service ended with the blessing and words: 'The Mass is ended. Go in peace.'

This description of the service has necessarily failed to do justice to its richness and complexity, and has not explained that there would sometimes be extracts from films such as *Jesus of Montreal*, and that praise would be accompanied by dynamic and ever-changing images on the video screens. Needless to say, the preparation of such a service entailed an enormous amount of work on the part of artists, musicians and designers, and indeed the whole service, including the address, was rehearsed in the afternoon before it took place in the evening. It is the only time in my life that I have had to preach a 'trial sermon' before a service and have it subjected to criticism in order for improvements to be made when given at the proper time! As one who dislikes muddled and ill-prepared services, I could not help admiring the care and preparation that characterized the Planetary Mass.

Evaluation

In what sense was the Nine o'clock Service a liberal church? In the first place, it was not fundamentalist in its view of the Bible. Whereas I have never been invited to preach in a conservative church in Sheffield during the 26 years that I have lived there, the Nine o'clock Service welcomed my presence and preaching, and sent students to study in the Department of Biblical Studies. It was highly sensitive to liberation and feminist issues, and I vividly remember an occasion at which the gospel was the Parable of the Talents from Matthew 25.14–30. The version read was deliberately altered so that the first two (good) servants were women, and the third (bad) servant was a male! I have often wondered whether there was a church anywhere else where this could have been both contemplated and performed.

Another respect in which the Nine o'clock Service was liberal was in its readiness to embrace new ideas and new ways of trying to understand Christianity. Indeed, this aspect of its work was certainly quite bewildering to a number of its members. This was particularly the case when the service began to be interested in the work of Matthew Fox and the 'creation spirituality' that he advocated. I never made any secret of the fact that I was extremely unhappy with many aspects of Fox's theology, and especially his treatment of the opening chapters of Genesis in his book *Original Blessing*.[1] I was particularly concerned that Fox's theology involved a minimalizing of the fact and power of evil, and I insisted that from a Christian perspective, as I understood it, one should be concerned with the re-creation and redemption of the natural order and not with the attempt to affirm what is, paradoxically, a compromise creation.[2] On the positive side, Fox's theology was part of a wider phenomenon in the Nine o'clock Service which sought to be open to spiritualities from faiths other than Christianity, and which sought to give a cosmic and planetary dimension to its own Christian worship and witness.

An important aspect of the Nine o'clock Service, and one reason why its closure was so catastrophic for many of its members, was the fact that it provided ministries for many people. The planning and execution of a Planetary Mass involved something in the region of a hundred people, if one counted the artists, designers, musicians, technicians, singers and dancers – not to mention the leadership team. What the Nine o'clock Service offered to its members was not merely the possibility of attending a church or a church service: it offered the possibility of exercising a ministry in a church that was trying to articulate an alternative way of living in a materialist and acquisitive world. This alternative way of living was profoundly linked to Christian values. In this sense, the Nine o'clock Service came closer than any other Christian body which I have known to putting into practice the idea of the priesthood of all believers. This is why its closure was so catastrophic.

Why did people attend the Nine o'clock Service? They probably did so for many reasons. In some cases, it offered a type of church which both resonated with, but presented strong alternatives to, the rock and club culture of its teenagers and 20-year-olds. Secondly, it provided forms of worship that enabled creativity and spontaneity to be expressed. When I first attended a teaching service in 1992 while the service was still at St Thomas's, I was confronted with something that I had never experienced before in the context of church worship. This was not a happy-clappy middle-class congregation sitting on chairs or in pews in ordered ranks. It was an open space in which people were able to express or not express themselves in movement and dance as they felt best. It had a stunning exuberance and joy. It was not surprising that these things would appeal to young people for whom even charismatic church worship was an alien experience in class and cultural terms. From the point of view of the beliefs of those who attended the Nine o'clock Service, I had little opportunity to discover why people belonged to it doctrinally. My guess is that people were attracted to it in the first instance for aesthetic and cultural reasons. On the other hand, I have never been associated with a church that laid so much stress on the importance of study and education, as indicated by the fact that members were encouraged to take A-level Religious Education or courses in the Sheffield Department of Biblical Studies if they were qualified to do so. There was also the outreach side of the service, with work among young people who were addicted to drugs – a side of the work that I had no opportunity to become involved with.

I have deliberately said nothing about the bad things that came to light when allegations were made against Chris Brain. It became apparent that whether or not there had been sexual improprieties, there was certainly a culture of psychological control and manipulation at the heart of the Nine o'clock Service, possibly a hangover from the time when St Thomas's itself had passed through a phase of 'heavy shepherding'. There was a blatant contradiction between this attempt to control the lives of some members and the repeated official line at services that each member should be responsible for his or her own Christian life and for his or her own decisions in connection with it. I had been gladdened by this stress upon the responsibility of individuals, and was saddened to hear the stories about psychological control and manipulation.

The question I have often asked myself is whether the Nine o'clock Service could have been saved substantially in its existing form in August 1995. It is not generally appreciated that Chris Brain had left the service in March 1994 in order to plant Nine o'clock Service churches elsewhere, including in San Francisco. From March 1994 to its closure in August 1995, the service was run by a leadership team of around six men and women. There was no permanent priest, which is why I was often called upon to celebrate at the Planetary Mass. It has never been clear to me why it was necessary to close a church because of allegations made against a founder and leader who had, however, not been at any of its services for the previous sixteen months. Perhaps this will be investigated in future years when the passage of time will have healed the wounds of all those involved. For my own part, I greatly miss what I saw of the Nine o'clock Service which, admittedly, was the bright side and not the dark side of the whole picture. It was a bold and imaginative attempt at contextual theology, not just in theory but in practice. Whether in its present parlous state the Church of England can afford *not* to learn or benefit from such bold experiments, only time will tell.

Notes

1. Matthew Fox, *Original Blessing* (Sante Fé, NM: Bear & Co., 1983).

2.   See J. Rogerson, *Genesis 1–11* (Sheffield: Sheffield Academic Press, Old Testament Guides, 1991) pp. 21–4 where the implications of the contrast between the 'vegetarian' creation of Genesis 1.30 and the 'meat-eating' creation of Genesis 9.3–4 after the flood are discussed.

Chapter 5

THE SHAPE OF THINGS TO COME?
TWO CHURCH OF ENGLAND PARISHES IN A TIME OF TRANSITION

Simon J. Taylor

Let me begin with a story. At 7 a.m. on Easter morning a group of about 80 people gathered outside a former Congregationalist chapel now used as an Anglican parish church.[1] They came from three groups: the congregation of Cotham Parish Church, where they were all gathered; the congregation of St Paul's, Clifton, the neighbouring parish that has been together in a united benefice[2] with Cotham Parish Church since 1999; and members of Resonance, an alternative worship community[3] which has strong links to the vicar of the benefice and which has used Cotham Parish Church as a base since his appointment there. So this is the story – three communities coming together to worship.

But there is another way to tell the story. The service began with quite traditional catholic ritual – the lighting of the paschal candle from a new flame, its procession into church and the singing of the *Exultet*. But then, while passages from the Old Testament were read, the congregation were invited to explore some installations relating to them. The story of creation was explored by making figures out of clay; reflecting on the delights and frustrations of being created; and magnetic poetry. Calvin and Hobbes cartoons lent it a humorous flavour. In the installation reflecting on the Exodus, one was greeted by Charlton Heston's Moses (on a video loop) parting the Red Sea. Two shower curtains, covered in advertisements and symbols of addictions and imprisonments led to an icon, where candles could be lit and liberations prayed for. In all there were four stations. After some time to explore these, the congregation was called back together by the singing of 'Alleluia' for the gospel reading. Then they entered the sanctuary, which had been screened off from the body of the church. Inside was a paddling pool full of water, draped in white cloth with lilies around it. Here baptismal vows were renewed, then people splashed themselves with the water, took a piece of white cloth and were anointed with oil. Finally, the eucharist was celebrated, using an authorized Anglican liturgy with ambient music playing in the background and projections of the cosmos on screens overhead. This is story 2: an imaginative attempt to marry two very different styles of worship, the gifts of each being offered to enrich the other.

But, you will forgive me, I am a curate and for me the story begins the day before. It takes a great deal of preparation for such an event, and most of

Holy Saturday was spent moving furniture, setting up installations and the like. It also saw a dreadful row between one man setting up part of the service and the lady who arranged the flowers. This led, ultimately, to her leaving the church, at least temporarily. Story 3, therefore, is 'how we lost our flower-arranger'.

There are other ways of telling the story of our Easter vigil, most of which are for others to relate. None of these stories begin or end with the Easter vigil, each are part of a longer history which began before the vigil and continue in the life of the churches today. But the vigil provides a focus for these stories in which they can be identified. I want to suggest that the three stories reflect three different pressures that are felt by these two parishes at the present time. These pressures come from the church, wider society and also from within the parishes themselves.

Pressure from the Church

The reason why the Easter vigil service marks the coming together of three communities, two of them parish churches, is that since 1999 the two parishes concerned have been a united benefice. This was a decision made by the diocese of Bristol at the time of the appointment of the current vicar of the parishes. The effect of this has been that each parish runs separately, while sharing ministerial resources in the form of a vicar and, latterly, a curate.[4] From the vigil, the vicar went on to preside at an all-age eucharist at Cotham, and the curate to do the same at St Paul's. Ministerial time is not allocated in a fixed way between the parishes, as it might be in the case of a parish job being shared with a diocesan job. Instead a more flexible approach is taken.

Nevertheless, the sharing of resources and the legal status of the parishes as a joint benefice sometimes require decisions to be made as a benefice. This creates problems in that very few people see the operation of the benefice *as a benefice* (rather than as a parish within the benefice). Three or four benefice eucharists a year is the extent of the impact most feel, but even these must be agreed as deviations from the normal pattern of services. The weekly staff-meeting is the only decision-making forum that has a benefice-wide view, and it has no status to make some of the necessary decisions.[5] Earlier this year, each parish within the deanery was asked to provide an outline of themselves as part of the consideration of future provision of ministry. The clergy of the benefice felt strongly that the two parishes could only do this adequately as a benefice. This required both Parochial Church Councils (PCCs) to assent to a document drafted by the clergy – a rushed process, with complex negotiations required, which did not happen without some resentment.

Recently, the PCCs of both parishes met together for a study day. At the end of the day there was an exercise asking people to say in single words and short phrases how they saw the benefice. Most of the responses described features that the two parishes had in common ('liberal', 'intellectual', 'predominantly old-ish'). Some looked at what might be the case ('waiting to fly'; 'open sky';

'potential-filled'), and others reflected the experience of being in the benefice. In this latter category, some responses reflected the separateness of the churches and the sharing of ministers: 'two churches', 'two parishes', 'vicar-share' and 'Paul [the vicar]'. Others spoke of the experience as 'theoretical'; 'unreal'; 'frustrating'; 'a marriage of convenience' and 'a push-me-pull-you'.

This experience of sharing clergy among otherwise separate parishes is set to continue. The diocese of Bristol is committed, largely on financial grounds, to a strategy which requires a 20 per cent-plus reduction of the number of stipendiary parochial clergy in the diocese by 2010. No church closures have been envisaged. As yet there have been no decisions taken formally, but it seems likely that in the near future a neighbouring parish will be included with the benefice in the allocation of ministerial resources, and that in the medium term the benefice will form two of around seven parishes sharing ministerial resources.

Pressure from society

Without wanting to enter the debates about the role of secularization in the UK,[6] it is true to say that church attendance is a minority sport. In a city such as Bristol, parish boundaries have little influence on where people attend church. In both parishes the majority of the Sunday congregation live outside the parish boundaries, and this is unremarkable. These churches are chosen by the congregation for a number of reasons. For some it is an issue of churchmanship – both churches fall in between the extremes of evangelical and Anglo-Catholic practices which are seen in neighbouring parishes. For others it is because they have found the community to be welcoming to them. Both churches have a policy of welcoming gay and lesbian people. Historic links of churchgoing are also important. St Paul's has many members who are former students of the university and have continued to worship at St Paul's after graduation. Many people travel to church at Cotham long after they have left the parish.

Other more widespread changes in society have an effect on the parishes. The increase in house prices, a particularly acute issue in the areas of Bristol served by the two parishes, has led to an increase in multi-occupancy houses in the area. People in such accommodation are rarely long-term residents. The increase in mobility and in the dispersion of families across the country, combined with the rise in leisure activities, makes Sunday morning churchgoing part of a competitive 'market'. What constitutes 'regular attendance' at church is more likely to be once a month than once a week.

The role of the occasional offices (baptisms, marriages and funerals) as a point of contact with the wider community is negligible. In 2003 there were five baptisms, five weddings and five funerals in the benefice.[7] Demographic trends, linked with the increasing value of property in the parishes explain some of this. However, particularly in terms of the low number of funerals in either church (or at the crematorium), it is clear that for many, perhaps most, of the local population the parish church is no longer a feature of their lives. People resident in the parishes no longer look to the parish church as an integral part of their rites of passage. This is not a pattern that is repeated throughout Bristol, and a combination of economic prosperity and fluid patterns of employment in Cotham and the lack of residential accommodation in St Paul's parish is significant in explaining the peculiarities of this relationship with the communities in which they are set. Indeed, to speak of 'community' at all in these areas starts to beg some difficult questions.

The pressure brought to bear on the parishes of the benefice from the society in which they are set is that the churches will become increasingly irrelevant to that society. One particularly good example of this is the way the two churches minister to residential homes for the elderly. There are five such institutions in the parishes and four are regularly visited by clergy or laity. In each, a notable decline is being detected in the numbers wanting traditional patterns of ministry and those wanting to receive the sacrament of Holy Communion. Here we can see that even people in their sixties and seventies are part of a wider social trend that has little or no abiding connection with the Church. Such experiences can only increase.

Other forms of engagement with the community go on at both churches. Cotham runs an open drop-in group for carers and children. St Paul's has a long-established link with the university chaplaincy, which used to be run from the church. Both also let their halls to community groups.

Alternative worship such as the Easter vigil, focused particularly at Cotham, seeks to serve a constituency that comes from across the city and even beyond it. A service in November 2004 brought about 80 people from all over Bristol to worship. Some were habitual churchgoers elsewhere in the city. Many were 'dechurched' people, who had stopped going to church but who continue to call themselves Christian.[8] This brings an engagement with society outside the church in a wider sense to more parochially focused work, attempting to engage culturally with 'postmodern' and consumerist trends.

These are important ways in which the churches seek to serve and engage with their surrounding communities. Both churches continue to rethink the ways in which their mission and ministry can deepen this engagement. Both continue to be shaped by their encounters and by the way in which they struggle to make these encounters possible.

Pressure from within

Pressure for change from within is of a different nature than the external pressures I have already identified. It comes from various sources, is often contradictory in nature and there are various timescales attached to it. Some are reactive to changes forced upon or foreseen as coming. Others are more concerned with the type of church people would like to belong to. But there are ideas and initiatives that arise from individuals and groups. The PCCs of the parishes are places where some of these ideas are discussed and decided upon. Cotham PCC has spent a good deal of time dealing with issues of how it welcomes people into the community. For a time this found a focus in proposals for changes to the church building, but now it is more concerned with building relationships within the church community and with those in the wider community. Recently, therefore, with the support of the PCC, a series of small groups known as Transforming Communities[9] have been set up. These have two aims. The first is 'to build people of Christian faith by strengthening relationships, deepening prayer and worship, growing in the knowledge of the Bible and the Christian tradition, and by enabling and supporting participation in mission and evangelism'. The second is 'to help us to meet the challenges and opportunities of changes within the church and in the wider society that we seek to serve'.[10]

St Paul's, similarly, has found a focus on building relationships to be crucial. In 2003 St Paul's celebrated its 150th anniversary, and a forward-looking focus was achieved through a series of '150+ groups' which considered where the church should go in the future. High on this list was the setting up of small groups in order to deepen relationships and explore matters of faith together. In October 2004 a series of Emmaus groups was launched.

But, as my story of how we lost our flower-arranger shows, the effects of external pressure is often to reveal internal tension. The effect of pressures from the diocese has been to change the relationship between the clergy and the congregations of the benefice. Clergy are no longer experienced as constant features of a church, but instead are seen usually fortnightly. A greater division between clergy and congregation is introduced as a result, deepened by the sense that the loyalties of the clergy are at least partly divided between the parishes. Pastoral work is increasingly performed by lay people, while the (primarily eucharistic) worship of the churches continues to depend on clergy, but as a class rather than as individuals.

Worship too is an area that both churches are re-examining. Current patterns of eucharistic worship do not appear to be sustainable in the light of declining numbers of clergy. Yet these patterns are carefully constructed compromises between different interests and different preferences within the churches. To take the example of music: St Paul's has an auditioning choir, largely made up of university students, but this choral tradition does not sit well with children and young people in the congregation, or their parents. Some members of Cotham have a strong aversion to choirs in any form, while at the same time demands can be heard that we learn new music. The compromises of each church are being opened up for scrutiny.

What shapes the Church?

Pressures are a constant feature of the lives of churches. At a time of transition, such as the present one, the pressures are felt more acutely. Old accommodations are no longer possible; new ways of operating must be found. Pressure from the Church is felt most from the diocesan rather than the national or international level. This, in part, reflects the tension within the ecclesiology of the Church of England between episcopal and congregational models. Martyn Percy speaks of a 'creeping congregationalism' coming into the Church of England,[11] created not least by changing financial arrangements. The diocesan movement towards multi-parish arrangements (whether formalized as benefices or not) reinforces the shift towards congregationalism by treating congregations as sacrosanct. Yet at the same time, it is the *diocese* that is calling the tune. Wherever the balance of power will lie in the future, it is certainly being renegotiated.

Pressure from society is felt by the strengthening of the distinction between the Church and the wider society. Again in relation to funding, Percy speaks of the change wrought by the way 'a comprehensive national ministry is now funded by *congregations* rather than its parishes'.[12] It is clear the parish system, understood as the clear identification of a parish church with a bounded geographical area, is simply irrelevant to many both within the congregation and within wider society. Yet at the same time, the clearly established legal and organizational basis provided by the parish system continues to have a huge impact on where the churches choose to engage in mission and ministry. It is still largely to those within the parishes that service is offered.

All of this has the effect of bringing to light internal pressures. Much of this is due to the changing relationship between clergy and congregation. Due to competing pressures for time and attention, the clergy are no longer able to occupy the same role within the congregation. Yet they remain an important part of the church community. How roles and expectations are negotiated between stipendiary clergy, non-stipendiary clergy, congregations and lay ministers will be of vital importance as change progresses.

Of course, all of this has been simply some reflections by one of the participants in the transition about which I have been speaking. The various stories that can be seen in our Easter vigil service have one thing in common – they are all focused on the worship of God. This is not worship despite the various pressures that I have identified in this chapter, but rather worship which takes place as all these pressures become the stories of the people of God in two parish churches, seeking in faith to follow their Lord.

Notes

1. At the formation of the United Reformed Church in 1972, the Congregationalist congregation moved into another church building in the area. Two Anglican parishes were being merged and rather than close one church building, both were merged into the former chapel. It was dedicated for Anglican worship in 1975.

2. Technically, the two benefices of the parishes of Cotham and St Paul's, Clifton, are held in plurality by the incumbent of both. See Mark Hill, *Ecclesiastical Law*, 2nd edn (Oxford: Oxford University Press, 2001), p. 110.

3. On alternative worship see Paul Roberts, *Alternative Worship in the Church of England* (Cambridge: Grove, Grove Worship 155, 1999).

4. All licensed ministers, lay and ordained, are licensed to the benefice rather than to either

of the individual parishes. Other than the vicar and curate, most minister almost exclusively in one or other parish.

5.   The staff-meeting is open to all licensed ministers within the benefice and in practice attended regularly by the vicar, curate, two licensed readers and a youth worker. Others attend as their commitments permit. Notes of the meeting are sent to all members of the ministry team, the churchwardens of the two parishes and the benefice administrator. The administrator is the only non-ministerial person who has any day-to-day experience of the benefice.

6.   For an assessment of different theories of secularization see Timothy Jenkins, *Religion in Everyday English Life: An Ethnographic Approach* (New York and Oxford: Berghahn, 1999), pp. 23–39.

7.   These break down in the following way: St Paul's: one baptism, four weddings, no funerals. Cotham: four baptisms, one wedding, five funerals. Of these five funerals, three were taken by clergy from outside the benefice ministry team and one other was a memorial service held at the same time as a funeral took place in Denmark.

8.   On 'dechurched' people, see Philip Richter and Leslie Francis, *Gone but not Forgotten* (London: Darton, Longman & Todd, 1998). Richter and Francis suggest that the dechurched make up 40 per cent of the population of England. They divide them into the 'open' and the 'closed' dechurched, depending on their continuing attitudes to the Church. This analysis has been very influential in current thinking within the Church of England. See, for example, the General Synod report *Mission-Shaped Church: Church Planting and Fresh Expressions of Church in a Changing Context* (London: Church House, 2004), pp. 36–40.

9.   These are consciously modelled on Steven Croft, *Transforming Communities: Re-imagining the Church for the 21st Century* (London: Darton, Longman & Todd, 2002).

10. Paper to Cotham PCC, March 2004.

11. Martyn Percy, *The Salt of the Earth: Religious Resilience in a Secular Age* (London and New York: Continuum, 2002), p. 340.

12. Martyn Percy, 'The priest-like task: funding the ministry of the Church of England', in Martyn Percy and Stephen Lowe (eds), *The Character of Wisdom: Essays in Honour of Wesley Carr* (Aldershot: Ashgate, 2004), pp. 3–21 (quotation from p. 3).

Chapter 6

IT'S NOT ALL ABOUT UUS:
GROWTH IN UNITARIAN–UNIVERSALIST CONGREGATIONS

Terasa Cooley

'Why aren't there more Unitarian–Universalists? It sounds like such a reasonable thing for people to be.' The college student who made this remark to me was responding to a talk about Unitarian Universalism I had just given to her college 'Religion and Philosophy' class. I had given a broad sketch of its history over the last two centuries in America, and explained its basic premise: Unitarian–Universalists (UUs) unite around a behavioural covenant in which we agree to certain principles rather than particular beliefs; human reason, experience and conscience are the tests for what is 'believable' rather than a strict interpretation of a particular tradition. Having been properly schooled in the philosophical development of our culture, the student proclaimed: 'It's so post-Enlightenment!'

Indeed, Unitarian–Universalism in its precepts and approach corresponds neatly to a postmodern, pluralistic, democratic philosophy. So why hasn't our tradition lived up to Thomas Jefferson's expectation that most Americans would become Unitarians?[1] While UUs often include a disproportionate number of public figures and are prominent figures in American history, they represent only a small fraction of contemporary churchgoers (roughly 218,000). Yet, in the context of current theories about the decline of liberal churches in America, one might easily ask why UUism continues at all, given that it certainly occupies the most liberal end of the religious spectrum.

There is considerable debate about whether UUism is growing as a movement (which will be explored more fully below), but it is clearly not experiencing the precipitous decline that has befallen most mainline, more liberal churches. There are some large, growing, highly sustainable UU congregations that have garnered attention and study of what creates these seeming anomalies. While there is no comprehensive study of these growing congregations which can give us definitive data on a 'recipe for success', there is at least some general evidence that can help us understand and perhaps replicate their accomplishment. Beneath this data I find some theological and ecclesiastical directions as well that can help build our movement as a vital force within American culture.

The 'numbers'

Is Unitarian–Universalism a growing liberal faith? As with almost any issue in UUism, this is difficult to clearly define. On the one hand, we can say that with the exception of the year 2003, the UUA (Unitarian–Universalist Association) has posted growth of roughly 1 per cent per year over the last two decades, and that the lack of demonstrable growth in the year 2003 was due to the secession of the Canadian Unitarian Council congregations that took place that year. Of UU congregations as a whole, 42 per cent grew by 10 per cent or more between the years of 1995–2000. And the numbers reported to the UUA may only represent a small percentage of UUs, for national surveys regularly report that the number of people who identity themselves as UUs is somewhere around 630,000 in 2001, compared to only 502,000 in 1990.[2] This growth-rate, while very small, stands in considerable favourable contrast to the decline-rates of other mainline denominations.

On the other hand, say some, trumpeting this tiny rate of growth is ridiculous when one looks at how we compare to the total population. The total number of UUs today (roughly 218,000 reported members) doesn't even match the past peak in UU membership of approximately 282,000 in 1968. This would represent an aggregate decline of 7 per cent, while the total population of the USA has increased by 37 per cent. If we look closely at particular congregations we find that only 1.5 per cent of the congregations account for 24 per cent of all UU growth in the last 8 years, while 30 per cent of our congregations have shrunk by 10 per cent or more. Less than 10 per cent of those participating in congregations are lifelong UUs, and one must ask what has happened to those who grew up in the UU tradition over its 200-year history. In other words, these numbers make us only a tiny drop in the vast American population, and only a small percentage of UU congregations are significantly growing. People of this perspective warn of a slow but steady death of UUism, not just a decline, given the trends in the growing conservatism of American religious people.

Of course, one of the sources of this dispute is the difficulty of tabulating membership and participation in UU congregations. Congregations are notoriously poor reporters of numbers in some cases they deliberately underreport their membership in order to avoid paying the per-member dues to the UUA, while in others they overreport their numbers due to poor record-keeping or a desire to look good in the eyes of the denomination. Even when a congregation is quite vigilant, however, it is quite difficult to track the comings and goings of a very transitory population, and considerable difference of opinion about what makes one a 'member' of a UU congregation. Does a person have to go through all the rituals of membership, or can we count as UUs those who attend or participate in programmes but who haven't 'signed the book'?

This is not just an issue of tabulation, however. Nor is it just a matter of rosy optimism versus doom-and-gloom apocalypticism. Those who care about the future of liberal religion must look closely at this most liberal of liberal denominations and ask what potential for growth there might be. It is abundantly clear in the research that success begets success in UUism (i.e. congregations that are already sizeable and well staffed are the most likely to grow and prosper). Rather than ask whether UUism as an entire denomination is growing or not, one might more profitably look at the characteristics of those UU congregations that are growing and what might be replicable in them not only for other UU congregations but within liberal religion as a whole.

General characteristics of growing congregations

There are two excellent sources for information about large or growing UU congregations: one is a detailed study of the data collected by the 'Faith Communities Today' (or FACT survey) related to UU congregations compiled by the Revd Charlotte Cowtan of Triad Consulting.[3] Another is a survey of nine large and growing congregations conducted by a group of lay people from the Unitarian Universalist Church of Berkeley, California.[4]

From the FACT survey we learn that rapidly growing congregations see themselves as:

- spiritually and vitally alive (62 per cent of rapidly growing as compared to 43 per cent of rapidly declining congregations)
- being a moral beacon in the community (42 per cent compared to 27 per cent)
- having well-organized programming (57 per cent compared to 45 per cent)
- having a clear sense of mission and purpose (47 per cent compared to 35 per cent)
- work for social justice (42 per cent compared to 31 per cent)
- dealing openly with disagreements and conflicts (50 per cent compared to 39 per cent), and
- welcoming new ways of ministry and worship (49 per cent compared to 38 per cent).

Rapidly declining congregations were much more likely (47 per cent) to see themselves as a 'close-knit family' than rapid growth congregations (34 per cent).[5]

The Berkeley survey indicates that growth in the largest and most rapidly growing congregations did not necessarily come about because of intentionality. Indeed some of them had no growth plans or activities whatsoever. Growth was more a result of 'excellence in two major driving factors: Leadership and Programs/Activities'.[6] They acknowledge 'excellence' as hard to define, and describe excellence in leadership in these terms: 'Growth often seems to be driven by a Senior Minister committed to and galvanizing a team for delivering exceptional programs ... An active footprint in the outside community ... excellence in preaching ... a willingness to champion change and see some growth opponents leave ...'[7] are some of the attributes described. In terms of programming they note: 'Growing churches have a dynamic energy. These people are passionate about excellent offerings on Sunday mornings and well beyond.'[8] This report also notes that attractive, well-maintained buildings, proximity and visibility have some effect on growth, but interestingly they could find no correlation between outside demographic factors and growth in terms of dramatic shifts of population or significant cultural events.[9]

The analysis of the FACT survey brings forward some interesting statistics that are worthy of some brief attention.

- Of large congregations surveyed, 85 per cent were in older suburbs of large metropolitan areas (defined as a population over 50,000).[10]
- Large congregations offered the greatest range of programming, from community service, to theological study, to music or fitness programmes;[11] 95 per cent of large congregations offer some kind of small group ministry programme;[12] and 100 per cent of large congregations have an organized programme to serve the needs of their members (such as caring committees, etc.).[13]
- Large congregations offer the greatest variety of social service programmes from food donation (100 per cent) to organized social issue advocacy (95 per cent) to support groups (86 per cent).[14]
- Large congregations' growth efforts were more likely to be focused on planned outreach programmes, stressing the importance of sharing one's faith, special public worship services and purchasing radio or television ads, rather than direct contact (visiting individuals), whether through lay members or ministers.[15]
- In terms of internal demographics, large congregations are more likely to have more highly educated, wealthier, married or partnered, and younger members; they are less likely to have lifelong UUs, and larger proportions of their membership have been involved for five years or less.[16]
- Of rapidly declining congregations, 73 per cent were established before 1965; whereas 27 per cent of rapid-growth congregations were established after 1985.[17]
- The largest gains in membership came from congregations in the midwest, mid-Atlantic, west and southwest regions of America; the greatest losses in membership came in the northeast districts.[18]

All this is a measurable and objective view of UU congregations. What follows is an analysis of less easily defined issues that are nevertheless of central importance to growth. I will include some more statistics, but also my own anecdotal observations and opinions as well.

Can liberals be disciplined?

As we read in other chapters of this book, the criticism often levelled at liberal congregations is that they do not have a sufficiently disciplined approach to religion, and that their very lack of definition and central focus are what lead people to prefer conservative churches. So one could ask whether the larger liberal congregations indeed offer a greater sense of discipline than their declining fellow liberal congregations.

There is some evidence to show that the larger congregations have clearer expectations than those that are declining. The FACT survey demonstrated that more people from growing congregations felt their congregations made expectations fairly clear of members, even if they were unevenly enforced (51 per cent of growing congregations as opposed to 41 per cent of declining ones);[19] as well as the opposite: more declining congregations said their expectations were implicit and seldom, if ever, enforced (46 per cent compared to 39 per cent).[20] One might also look at giving levels as an indication of evidence of discipline, but clear statistics were unavailable in this regard.

It has been my observation that newer Unitarian–Universalists are more willing both to articulate expectations and to give more unquestioningly and generously. Longer-term UUs often bristle even at the use of the word 'expectation' and consider such a concept incompatible with the principle of freedom of choice. In this view, the desires of the individual 'trump' the needs of the community. Larger congregations seem to have learned that it is not possible to revolve the institution around the individual and still be able to grow and function effectively, and that articulating expectations of financial and volunteer support early and often ultimately means that the institution may serve a greater number of needs.

Larger congregations also tend to have far more centralized structures of decision-making and authority, as would be demanded by a larger number of people. It would be unwieldy and impractical to call a congregational meeting for every decision needed, and yet inevitably such structures limit the ability for individuals to have input into and 'ownership' of their ecclesiastical processes. A certain kind of 'discipline' is then required that is unfamiliar to UUs who revere the democratic process as a central principle: they have to allow their leaders to make some decisions without them. It is interesting to note, however, that in larger congregations with more authoritarian structures, more choices in programming are available to meet more diverse needs simply because there are staff and building space to provide them. UUs in these congregations seem to have learned the beneficial trade-off: discipline in one area allows greater freedom in another.

There is another way in which this issue of 'discipline' is much more complex than it might seem. One must ask what the source of the discipline is. If discipline is about giving authority over to religious leaders or a particular tradition or interpretation of scripture, then UUs would seem the least likely to qualify, even in larger congregations. In every survey taken recently, the great majority of UUs still hold that personal experience is the primary source of authority for them. They are unwilling to give over to an externally imposed discipline of thought that emphasizes exclusive truth claims.

Yet I would argue that in another sense being a religious liberal in the extremely pluralistic sense that UUs uphold requires tremendous inner discipline. It takes a kind of strength of purpose and moral courage to open our beliefs to a wider perspective and acknowledge that true certainty may not be had in today's world. Discipline may also be a deeper inward orientation which continually calls us to the hard work of facing the challenge that different beliefs and perspectives pose to our faith – particularly so when those challenges come in the form of members of your own congregation who have differing beliefs from you. It can require great discipline to construct your own faith perspective in the midst of so many competing choices and easy materialistic substitutions.

The challenge for UU congregations is how to support this kind of inner discipline, without falling into dogmatism. In recent years it has become a trend to place more and more emphasis upon the UU Purposes and Principles as a method of providing this sense of structure and definition. These Purposes and Principles are not intended to be a creed, but rather a detailing of the covenant which members agree to and the principles upon which we attempt to build community.[21] The UUA in its resources makes regular use of these statements to try to unify our programming, and most congregations list them on their orders of service and use them liturgically and in religious education.

A number of prominent ministers have strenuously objected to this usage as 'creeping credalism' and find them so vague as to not serve a definitional purpose. It is interesting to note that the larger congregations seem to make much less use of the Purposes and Principles than other congregations,[22] and are willing to rely on the stories of personal and spiritual experiences of their minister to explicate or explore religious concepts. Does this mean that members of larger congregations give over some of their discipline to their ministers? Perhaps so, but the wide variety of programming, particularly the universal usage among large congregations of small-group ministry programmes, would also seem to suggest that members desire support for their own explorations as well.

To grow a liberal congregation, therefore, does not seem to imply that congregations need to impose greater discipline upon their members in the conservative theological sense, but it does seem to ask for a shift in understanding the relationship of the individual to ecclesiastical authority, which represents a significant cultural change for UUs.

Conservative or liberal?

The kind of nuanced discussion above about discipline reveals some tensions within liberal communities about what makes them liberal. This understanding has shifted in recent times in subtle yet discernible ways. For some UUs the kind of ecclesiastical change in which decision-making authority may be more centralized in the hands of a few lay leaders and the senior minister represents a move away from the liberal value of democracy. Yet such a move would seem to be required to grow a congregation.

There are other shifts that are threatening to those who would uphold a particular image of liberal integrity. For many UUs of the past, the involvement of UUs in movements for social change and social justice has been definitional. Despite the rifts that have been created over time and in many congregations about taking stands on public issues, the demand for liberal congregations to provide prophetic witness continues, and indeed dominates the denominational landscape.

There is a growing divide between generations of UUs in this regard, as well as a growing divide between growing and smaller congregations. For the older generations, as well as for many in smaller congregations, the focus of the congregation ought to be first and foremost on social justice issues. But for many newer UUs, and quite clearly in the larger congregations, spiritual growth is proving to be of greater importance. The statistics dramatically emphasize this: for example in large congregations the focus of the sermon is likely to be upon spiritual growth 90 per cent of the time, and upon social justice 38 per cent of the time; whereas smaller congregations feature social justice 51 per cent of the time, as compared to spiritual growth at 71 per cent.[23]

Recent critics of the political emphasis of UU communities and discourse have been growing in number and prominence. Congregational consultant Michael Durall, in a book newly published by one of the largest UU congregations, *The Almost Church*, not only points to the ways in which embracing secular causes distracts congregations from their spiritual purpose but also notes how unsuccessful these efforts have been:

> ... the Association has embraced many causes over the past forty-three years ... An impressive list, but does anyone remember what the issues were at last year's General Assembly? ... General Assembly has devolved into a traveling Chautauqua, selecting multiple causes and issues that receive little attention after everyone has gone home. Were any of these issues acted upon to any significant degree in UU congregations across the nation?[24]

From the look of the data, many smaller congregations spend a great deal of time and energy discussing these issues, but perhaps at the cost of their growth.

But perhaps this is once again presented as a false dichotomy. Perhaps there is not such a stark distinction between efforts for social justice and desires for spiritual growth. Another interesting statistic from the FACT survey is that large congregations were more likely to describe themselves as working for social justice than any other size (52 per cent of large, 41 per cent of medium and 37 per cent of small).[25] What are we to make of this seeming contradiction? I believe the issue is not one of either/or, but of which is primary. In large and growing congregations the primary understanding of their purpose is clearly that of spiritual growth. Just as clearly they understand an attention to the justice issues of the world and a willingness to partner with the surrounding community as a key component of spiritual growth. Understanding oneself as a part of the larger world and responsible to the community are attributes that require spiritual centredness and perspective, and growing congregations understand that and offer to support members in their reflection as well as their action.

The above description of understanding social justice as a part of spiritual growth does not necessarily allay the concerns of some of those UUs who fear encroaching 'conservatism'. For their central understanding of the liberal nature of the UU endeavour was that it stood in opposition to conservative religion. Again we see a generational and church size divide between those who understand liberal religion as intellectually centred and those who desire it to be spiritually centred. Debates about the use of God-language and other traditional religious terminology continue in all UU congregations to some degree, but it seems apparent that in larger, growing congregations there is a considerable shift toward a willingness to understand themselves as in relationship to God and the mysterious Holy.[26] Interestingly enough, there is also less interest in larger congregations in experimenting with worship styles or elements, and greater desire to have a more formal and consistent liturgy.[27] All this makes those who understood themselves as UUs to be *not* traditionally religious as a point of pride very uncomfortable.

For some UUs it will simply always be the case that the use of traditional religious language will evoke traditional religious concepts, no matter how much they might be redefined. For a growing number of UUs, however, and for growing UU congregations, a willingness to see themselves as a part of a larger reality and to accept that experience does not always lend itself to rational, objectifiable description in no way makes them less liberal. They are intent upon seeking meaning that is both experiential and reasonable, celebrating the unique gifts of the self as well as acknowledging that we are not self-sufficient. It is to this complex understanding of the self in relation that I now turn.

A healthy self-image

Throughout all the studies quoted a consistent theme emerges: large and growing congregations have a 'dynamic energy',[28] their worship is 'joyful', 'exciting', 'reverent', and there is a 'sense of expectancy' as well as a 'sense of God's presence'.[29] These are congregations in which people actually enjoy themselves! At the same time this almost visceral sense of pleasure does not seem to be about self-satisfaction or selfishness. As I have noted above, there is a great degree of attention given to the larger community and the experience of a larger reality. How is this balance achieved?

Despite our insistence upon being a contemporary religion, UUism continues to carry a great deal of baggage from our Puritan past. Congregations often seem much more intent upon reminding their members how inadequate they are politically – how racist, homophobic, sexist, imperialistic, etc. – than reminding them of their potential for good. At the same time, we have such dislike of the punitive side of traditional religion which emphasizes how sinful and inadequate we are inherently, that we have a difficult time acknowledging our personal limitations and little language for forgiveness.

We are a tradition steeped in the culture of individualism, which understands personal experience to be the primary authoritative source, and which endeavours to protect individual rights and expressions. At the same time, we often find it difficult to plumb the depths of our souls and truly understand and affirm our own individual needs, desires and callings. Unitarian–Universalists are not alone in struggling with these dichotomies and contradictions: they are endemic to contemporary life. But I believe that we have the potential to offer a unique – and yes, very liberal – way to reconcile these difficulties.

The dilemma is in understanding these different influences as dualistic dichotomies: self vs community; self vs God, good vs evil, etc. Instead of understanding these things as opposed to one another, it is possible for us to point a way toward understanding them as relational continuums, and to structure a religious experience that supports us in our multiple facets, rather than assuming a static identity.

Let me illustrate. Religious experience ought to be about helping us understand the deepest parts of ourselves – our loves and longings, our callings and our gifts, our limitations and our potential. *And* religious experience ought to be about helping us live in community – reminding us that we are who we are because of the influences upon us, that we are not self-sufficient nor in complete control, that other people both known and unknown help complete our true selves by affirming and challenging us. *And* religious experience ought to be about helping us see ourselves as a part of a larger whole that both embraces and bewilders us, that points to the great gift of creation and acknowledges our subservience to powers beyond our control, that affirms that good and love exist where reason would dictate them not, and recognizes that all of us are capable of evil and destruction.

There is a precarious balance here that I believe only liberalism helps provide: a mosaical quality of understanding that resists totalitarian impulses and perspectives. At our best, UU congregations can provide a joyful embrace of this understanding, for we can provide sustenance for living in a confusing, unstable and pluralistic world. If UU congregations found this balance I believe we would grow beyond our wildest dreams and expectations.

In other words, our purpose as liberal religious communities is to help people understand what it is about them, what it is about others, what it is about God, that is meaningful and worth pursuing in their lives – and seeing all these things as a complex whole, not a series of either/ors. It's not about 'UUs' in the sense of promoting how wonderful and right and unique we are, but about what we provide to the world that helps bring meaning and balance to people's lives.

A perspectival shift

I have deliberately chosen in these latter sections not to talk in typical categories of conversation about church growth: worship, programming, leadership, etc.

What became clear to me in looking at the research about growing congregations was that there was no universal 'technique' or 'tool', no particular style of minister, no prescription for a special programme that could be applied across the board and replicated in any congregation. Rather it seemed to me that what is required is a shift in perspective whereby we understand ourselves as serving a larger purpose, attending to a greater power in the world than just our own programmatic efforts. If we are trying to grow our churches just so that we can continue to fulfil our own desires we will not succeed. If we are trying to grow our churches so that we may offer a place for weary and seeking souls that embraces the complexity of our spiritual existence we may just stand a chance.

Notes

1. During Jefferson's time, the Unitarians and Universalists were different denominations; they merged in 1961.
2. ARIS survey:
3. Charlotte Cowtan, *Faith Communities Today: Large UU Congregations*, unpublished report Unitarian Universalist Association, June 2002.
4. Earl Koteen (ed.) *Large UU Church Growth Best Practices Study*, unpublished report from UU Church of Berkeley, CA, May/June 2004.
5. Cowtan, *Faith Communities Today*, p. 5.
6. Koteen, *Large UU Church Growth Best Practices Study*, p. 2.
7. Ibid., p. 3.
8. Ibid.
9. Ibid.
10. Cowtan, *Faith Communities Today*, p. 3.
11. Ibid., p. 9.
12. Ibid., p. 11.
13. Ibid.
14. Ibid., p. 10.
15. Ibid., p. 12.
16. Ibid., Appendix, pp. 10–11.
17. Ibid., p. 5.
18. Ibid., p. 8.
19. Ibid., p. 20.
20. Ibid.
21. *We, the member congregations of the Unitarian Universalist Association, covenant to affirm and promote*
   • The inherent worth and dignity of every person;
   • Justice, equity and compassion in human relations;
   • Acceptance of one another and encouragement to spiritual growth in our congregations;
   • A free and responsible search for truth and meaning;
   • The right of conscience and the use of the democratic process within our congregations and in society at large;
   • The goal of world community with peace, liberty, and justice for all;
   • Respect for the interdependent web of all existence of which we are a part.
The living tradition which we share draws from many sources:
   • Direct experience of that transcending mystery and wonder, affirmed in all cultures,

which moves us to a renewal of the spirit and an openness to the forces which create and uphold life;

- Words and deeds of prophetic women and men which challenge us to confront powers and structures of evil with justice, compassion, and the transforming power of love;
- Wisdom from the world's religions which inspires us in our ethical and spiritual life;
- Jewish and Christian teachings which call us to respond to God's love by loving our neighbors as ourselves;
- Humanist teachings which counsel us to heed the guidance of reason and the results of science, and warn us against idolatries of the mind and spirit;
- Spiritual teachings of earth-centered traditions which celebrate the sacred circle of life and instruct us to live in harmony with the rhythms of nature.

Grateful for the religious pluralism which enriches and ennobles our faith, we are inspired to deepen our understanding and expand our vision. As free congregations we enter into this covenant, promising to one another our mutual trust and support.

22. Cowtan, *Faith Communities Today*, Appendix, p. 5.

23. Cowtan, *Faith Communities Today*, p. 6.

24. Michael Durall, *The Almost Church: Redefining Unitarian Univeralism for a New Era* (Tulsa, OK: Jenkin Lloyd Jones Press, 2004), p. 24.

25. Cowtan, *Faith Communities Today*, Appendix, p. 2.

26. Cowtan, *Faith Communities Today*, Appendix, p. 2.

27. Ibid., p. 5.

28. Koteen, *Large UU Church Growth Best Practices Study*, p. 3.

29. Cowtan, *Faith Communities Today*, p. 5.

Part 3

Macro-issues

Chapter 7

PARADOX AND PERSUASION:
ALTERNATIVE PERSPECTIVES ON LIBERAL
AND CONSERVATIVE CHURCH GROWTH

Martyn Percy

Conservatism works, apparently. As I sit down to write this essay, British teenagers are being treated to an intensive PR onslaught from a North American organization called 'Silver Ring Thing'. It has the backing of President George W. Bush, and aspires to persuade teenagers to abstain from sex until marriage. Britain, it is said, has the highest rate of teenage pregnancy in Europe, and therefore current sex education models must be failing. The only solution, it is argued, is abstention. This partly accounts for why the 'Silver Ring Thing' has received over $700,000 of aid from President Bush, as part of a $270 million programme in 'virginity training' to combat teenage pregnancy and sexual diseases among the young.

The Conservative argument appears to be playing a winning hand here. The USA and Great Britain have high levels of teenage pregnancy, despite a great deal of investment in sex education. Ergo, the solution is to cut back on ('liberal') tried and tested forms of sex education, and invest public money in programmes that advocate abstention. Right? Wrong, actually. The logic of the argument is deeply flawed, even on its own terms. If one accepted the diagnosis and prognosis asserted by the Conservative viewpoint, one would naturally expect that countries where access to 'liberal' sex education and contraceptives were more widely available, would lead to greater levels of teenage pregnancy and sexually transmitted diseases among the young.

But the truth is, at least in Europe, quite the opposite. America and Britain are two countries where puritanical and Conservative sexual attitudes flourish, and where sex education among the young is comparatively weak. The figures tell an alternative story that rather undermines the Conservative narrative. In the USA, there are 53 teenage pregnancies per 1,000 of the population – a record that is marginally worse than in India, Rwanda or the Philippines. In the UK, the figure is 20 per 1,000, in contrast to Germany and Norway (11 per 1,000), Finland (8 per 1,000), Sweden and Denmark (7 per 1,000) and Holland (5 per 1,000).

In contrast to the message of the 'Silver Ring Thing', these figures suggest that explicit sex education is more effective than the advocacy of ('Victorian'?) restraint and implicit moral values focused on abstinence. The latter only leads to secrecy and guilt; it keeps important social, moral and personal issues locked away. But it fails to stifle desires and urges, the consequences of which are all too plain to see. To put it bluntly, abstinence programmes probably do more harm than good. Or perhaps to press the point more forcefully, 'Conservative' agendas tend to breed the very 'liberal' cultures that they seek to check. 'Liberal' cultures, in contrast, can lead to the establishment of more conservative cultural values, where, in this case, teenage pregnancy becomes less socially normative.

These points may seem tangential to a discussion of church growth, but my purpose in beginning this way is to highlight just how unhelpful the labels 'conservative' and 'liberal' can be in describing not only ethos, but also outcomes. To be sure, there are plenty of complex cultural and demographic reasons why explicit and widely available sex education in one country leads to enhanced moral and social responsibility, and in another, leads to embarrassment and prurience. We are all, I suppose, studies in contradictions. Take Japan: is it a conservative or liberal society? Many cultural commentators would be quick to assess it as conservative and progressive. But then what does one make of that same country that has one the lowest ages of consent (13) in the G8 economies, and thinks nothing of selling rather 'childish' sex toys in almost any corner store?

Labels such as 'conservative' and 'liberal' are notoriously unreliable as guides to church growth. Too many exceptions suggest that Dean Kelley's rules for success have been broken long ago. There are theologically conservative churches, which are at the same time organizationally progressive and liberal, at least in so far as they sit light to their parent denominational structures. There are theologically liberal churches (the rise of 'mega' gay and lesbian metropolitan churches comes to mind) that unashamedly borrow growth strategies from evangelicalism. There are burgeoning numbers of post-evangelical churches, cell churches and new church movements, which are neither conservative or liberal, theologically or otherwise. There are substantial Christian Unions at universities and colleges, but much evidence to suggest that the conservative religion that is espoused by such groups fails to captivate and equip most individuals beyond the thrall of years as students. Quite simply, the map of 'growing' churches does not show an easy delineation between the profits brought about by conservatism and the deficits allegedly created by liberalism. The economy is much more complex than this.

In this chapter, therefore, I want to look at two specific areas that go deeper than the superficial analysis that all too readily identifies conservative growth and liberal decline. I want to suggest first that, stories of growth and decline are often stubbornly rooted in particular cultures (that make space for both 'liberal' and 'conservative' worldviews), which unless understood and deconstructed can paint a rather distorted interpretation of the ecclesial landscape. Second, I consider some of the recent theorists and strategists in 'mainline' or 'liberal' church growth, and how their contributions might alter prevailing ecclesial horizons. A brief conclusion looks at the possibility of empowering mainline churches for growth and mission in a way that is spiritually consonant with their tradition.

Conservative culture and the narrative of decline

To tackle the first of these sections, we will turn to James Hopewell's fine book *Congregation: Stories and Structures*,[1] and use his insights to 'read' a fictional Anglican diocese. The diocese of Northfield is a northern Church of England diocese that comprises about 200 or so stipendiary clergy and parishes, in an area that is largely post-industrial. In Hopewell's narrative analysis of local congregations or churches, he identifies four genres of story that characterize ecclesial life and worldviews. These genres closely correspond to Northrop Frye's[2] analytical categorization of literature: irony, comedy, romance and tragedy. Hopewell holds that irony relates to 'empiric', comedy to 'gnostic', romance to 'charismatic' and tragedy to 'canonic'. Now there is not enough time here to discuss these genres in detail, and, suffice to say, they can all be found in virtually every congregation and diocese, irrespective of its theological commitments. But my purpose in introducing the notion of genre at this point is to identify the diocese of Northfield and its churches as primarily (but not exclusively) 'tragic' or 'canonic' in their storytelling. In turn, this identifies the diocese, in Hopewellian terms, as 'conservative'. But it is a form of cultural conservatism that is in fact wedded to a traditional understanding of socialism, rather than being a particular form of theological conservatism. (There is a paradox here, about which more later.) The 'tragic' genre 'fits' with the prevailing 'low church', post-industrial and working-class culture that dominates the diocese. But there are also deeper reasons why Northfield's narrativity is primarily 'tragic' in outlook.

For example, in listening to congregational stories around the diocese, one is immediately struck by how deprivation and struggle are identified as 'true' and 'authentic'. Correspondingly, stories of 'success' or 'growth' are often seen as deviant, 'unreal' or 'inauthentic'. The clergy, particularly those who are native to the region, seem to share and cultivate these perceptions with the laity. The self-perception of the diocese is that it has the lowest church-going population in Europe – a mantra often repeated by senior clergy of the diocese. But the claim (ironically several other dioceses in the region also believe it of themselves) is used as a way to *validate* the story of struggle. In other words, it is a kind of trope; it *sounds* like a complaint, but actually it is more of a boast.

Further attention to congregational and clerical narrativity also reveals some interesting binary paradoxes. Sacrifice is valued, but positive trans-formation is seen as illusory, and perhaps false. Suffering solidarity is a dominant and valued motif, but stories of 'slow resurrection' are essentially mistrusted by clergy and laity alike. It is not unfair to say that numerically growing churches are almost uniformly resented by the wider church culture within the diocese. It is almost as though 'growth' were somehow a betrayal of the gospel; the pathology of the diocese is that it anticipates a tragic worldview, in which its destiny is already settled, and the future ('faithful struggle in the midst of decline') already predetermined.

Thus the 'mission statement' of the diocese places a stress on empathy with 'the pain of the world', but is reticent when it comes to articulating the role of the Church as an agent of change or transformation, except in the most general of terms. At a clergy conference (based on the theme of resurrection), senior staff chose the theological input for the residential gathering. It was not a lecture or a seminar led by a theologian (this was deemed to be potentially 'too contentious'), but the film *Regeneration*, from the novel of the same name by Pat Barker. In the story – a good fit for the tragic genre – shell-shocked officers during the First World War are rehabilitated at a special centre in the Scottish Highlands, but only to be sent out to the front line once again to face further injury or death. Of course, *Regeneration* is not a story of resurrection or transformation at all, but one of ultimately hopeless and wasteful recycling. But as a story, it would speak (subconsciously) to many in the diocese, especially clergy, and would frame their sense of calling and destiny.

Arguably, the choice of such a film to convey a theological message could be seen as odd, even ironic. But in actual fact, its emergence at the conference (and the absence of any challenge to the storyline) shows that the 'tragic' worldview is part of the established semi-conscious life (or identity) of the diocese. So it is not the case that any one person or group *consciously* artic-ulates the necessity of tragic actors and plots. Rather, the tragic worldview emerges out of a long, multilayered oral history in which expectations are already shaped. Semi-consciously, in the very act of local ministerial engagement, ministers find themselves quite unwittingly colluding with the tragic worldview and ethos. So for many congregations and dioceses, there is a close match between *ethos* (the way things actually are) and *worldview* (the way things could or should be), since the Church seeks to embody kingdom values.

In the case of Northfield diocese, the 'sacrificed hero' (either a minister or congregation) often emerges (in individual and congregational narratives) as the ikon of suffering in the midst of adversity; triumph lies in the ability of ministers or congregations to *indwell* tragedy, not in overcoming it. And, rather as in *Regeneration*, the task for younger ministers is to simply follow in the footsteps of their fallen or wounded comrades, who can only prove their worth to their peers by further acts of sacrifice. In other words, demonstrative suffering (but not necessarily acute failure) is actually *valued*. Correspondingly, those clergy that need rehabilitation are often regarded as those that have been *truly* engaged in the struggle (and are therefore heroic). Those who have no need of such help can therefore find themselves being characterized as less engaged in the sacrificial struggle – not really working on the 'front line'. But the 'war' is never won or lost by such ministerial tactics and tropes. It is only lives that are sacrificed (which is, strangely, what counts). In the world of the tragic genre, Christ and his ministers are perpetually called to crucifixion.

Thus, and typically, many of the illustrative stories that are told by senior staff in sermons or at large diocesan occasions are ones where consolation, affirmation and 'making do' emerge as major motifs. Theologically, their sermons often place a stress on 'sacrifice' – either that of the laity or the priest

– and then resource this from a catholic perspective or through evangelical doctrine. Consistently, oblation is offered alongside consolation. (Where this does not happen, the tragic outlook quickly shifts into a romantic worldview, but reifying the visions and dreams as inevitably 'just out of reach'. The most frequently prescribed opiate to take away the pain of tragedy is a dose of romance – of what could be, if only…) Stories or strategies of transformation or radical revision are rare. Sacrificial self-expenditure frequently emerges as the key value that shapes the horizon of possibility.

Furthermore, the culture of clerical obeisance in a primarily working-class diocese ensures that there is little self-critical awareness at any level that might lead to revision or transformation. This, coupled to an abundance of pride and paternalism that regards malfunction as confirmation of the authentic nature of the 'gritty' ministerial struggle, ensures that the diocese lives under a pervasive cloud of 'low-grade' depression, which is then, oddly, celebrated. The narrative of pride in suffering becomes sanctimonious. One is reminded of Monty Python's famous 'Four Yorkshiremen' sketch, which satirizes glorying in poverty and the lack of resources, in one of many famous tropes: 'We were happy in those days, though we were poor … ay, *because* we were poor!' In effect, then, it is the Christ *of* or *under* culture that constantly emerges in diocesan narrativity. Pain is shared, and spread around as much as possible, but it is seldom challenged. The Christ who is against culture – who would resist struggle, pain and sacrifice – is conspicuously absent in the canonical litany of socioecclesial stories that shape the life Northfield.

In a diocese where a tragic worldview dominates, outcomes are accepted as they are predictable: 'Christ lays aside his prior glory and accepts the tragedy of his life'.[3] Or, as Northtrop Frye puts it, 'tragedy seems to lead up to an epiphany of law, of that which is and must be'.[4] So the diocese consoles, comforts and affirms its clergy and parishes as they fulfil their destiny in the arena of tragic sacrifice. But little changes in a diocese that has a primary tragic or canonic worldview, because obedience to the plot is ultimately the path to fulfilment: 'the pattern for life in the present land is that of Christ, who was willing to take the cross and, in the words of the famous evangelistic hymn, willing to suffer all of life's misery'.[5]

To be sure, I am conscious that such remarks can only be generalizations. Any diocese will be bigger than the theory applied to it; churches will invariably exceed any analytical interpretation. And in sketching the narrativity of one diocese and its congregations, it is important to remember that other dioceses will have different emphases in their narrative structures and outlooks (or worldviews), and that these will frame quite different attitudes to organization and expectation. Certainly, historic patterns of church attendance will have a bearing on congregational expectations and the shaping of local narratives of growth and decline. However, the paradox of this particular conservative working class is that it seems fundamentally to mistrust concepts of growth, whether 'organic' or 'engineered'. Interestingly, this means that virtually all initiatives that foster growth, whether or not they hail from radical–liberal or theologically conservative quarters, are more often than not placed at the periphery of the life of the diocese. Put another way, one can identify a form of conservatism, alive in churches, that is suspicious of growth. This, in turn, undermines at least part of the thrust of Kelley's thesis. As we shall now see, there are further complications when considering patterns of growth and decline in mainline church situations.

Mead and Mann on mainline church growth

Among those who have reflected theologically and sociologically on the subject of growth in mainline denominations, Loren B. Mead is, by any standards, a name to be reckoned with. His ground-breaking *The Once and the Future Church*[6] was first published in 1991, and has gained a steady following amongst the mainline denominations within the USA, and indeed beyond. Mead is very conscious that the paradigms of being Church and local congregations in any given community were rapidly eroded during the latter part of the twentieth century. He makes a remark that has an eerie resonance with some of Callum Brown's[7] thinking (i.e. secularization began suddenly, in 1963, with the advent of popular culture). Mead notes:

> When and how did we change? Although it may sound trivial, one of us is tempted to take the shift sometime on a Sunday evening in 1963. Then, in Greenville, South Carolina, in defiance of the State's time-honored blue laws, the Fox Theatre opened on Sunday. Seven of us – regular attendees of the Methodist Youth Fellowship at a Buncombe Street Church – made a pact to enter the front door of the church, be seen, then quietly slip out of the back door and join John Wayne at The Fox.[8]

That said, Mead identifies three core ecclesial paradigms. The first, the Apostolic, can be understood as the initial Church, which followed in the wake of the death and resurrection of Jesus. These were the churches that sent people out, and their period of expansiveness fundamentally altered a variant of Jewish spirituality into a full-blown faith that embodied a myriad of cultures, creating pluralities of churches and congregations. This in turn, second, led to the second paradigm, that of Christendom, in which sacred and secular combined to legitimize Christianity across the Mediterranean world, and in time beyond Europe to other continents. The third paradigm is Mead's identification of the gap between the first two paradigms, namely the Church between the Apostolic and the Christendom models. Mead sees this as a set of conditions that have already been present in Christian history, but are arguably returning again in late modernity, albeit with some important cultural differences. He argues that

> The third way of being Church has begun to be born, but its birth is not complete. Once again the Church and the individual person of faith are beginning to discover a sense of a new mission frontier. That frontier has not yet become clear or compelling enough; we see the horizon, but the path that we must follow remains obscure.[9]

Mead then goes on to explore the tension between these paradigms that typically find their expression in churches today. For example, there is a tension between being a church of the parish as against being the church of the congregation.[10] Similarly, there is a tension between an emphasis on servanthood, and conversion.[11] The stress on servanthood might well lead to the notion of the Church being actively engaged in a form of social service and cultural renewal, which may, in order to achieve its ends, downplay the differences it has between itself and its community, and in so doing place little emphasis on conversion. On the other hand, churches that are actively engaged in 'saving souls' may be inclined to emphasize conversion, even if that risks the alienation of the very community in which the Church finds itself situated. Mead contends that all churches have a tension between being exclusive and inclusive, which can also have a profound impact on their sense of mission and identity.

Although one may dispute the sweeping diagnostic tendencies in Mead's work, the freshness with which he addresses the situation of churches in late modernity is nonetheless appealing and challenging. Specifically, Mead is interested in challenging those impediments to change that prevent numerical growth in mainline churches, especially those where atrophy and indolence has set in. For example, he identifies different kinds of resistances that are built into the systems of success that were developed by the Christian paradigm.[12] These include strong, conservative institutional frameworks, leadership patterns, dependency-affirming relationships and financial systems. Mead also shows that inadequate leadership can be an obstacle to growth, partly because many leaders have a poor theology of institutions, which in turn allows personal resistances to change to flourish. In an intriguing turn, Mead uses the work of the behaviourist Elizabeth Kubler-Ross[13] and her work on bereavement. Kubler-Ross, you may recall, identifies several key stages in the bereavement process: beginning with denial, working through to depression, coming through to bargaining, arriving at anger and finally resting in acceptance. Mead suggests that the anatomy of change (including change directed at growth) within many congregations and denominations is essentially a form of bereavement process, albeit masquerading (in the bargaining and anger phases) as passion and innovation. To be sure, this is challenging material, but what does Mead have to say about the future Church and the particular ways in which mainline denominations might extricate themselves from their gradual disintegration?

Mead, wisely perhaps, offers general principles that can be applied to specific congregations and denominations. Mead begins his prescription by identifying the four dimensions of congregational life that are normally accepted by those within the discipline of congregational studies. These are

1. Programme – the sum total of the things a congregation does, including what is on its calendar.
2. Process – the way in which the congregation does what it does: how its leadership works, and how its people and groups make choices and relate to one another.

3. Context – the setting of the community and the denomination, the external forces that constrain or influence what the congregation and its members are and do.
4. Identity – that rich mix of memory and meaning that grounds the congregation defining who it really is in its heart.

Mead obviously argues that the field of applied congregational studies needs to address each of these areas, and their interrelationship. He suggests that working experimentally with congregations is a key to finding a way forward, which in turn means that congregations have to be willing to be patient with new initiatives. Tellingly, he also suggests that congregations need to pay attention to boundaries. These include: the boundary one crosses in choosing to go to church; the boundary a pastor crosses in moving from one congregation to another; the boundary a person crosses in moving from one town to another; life boundaries, and the like. In all of this, Mead says that paying attention to margins, congregations can begin to understand how easy and how difficult it is for the churches to become open and closed, welcoming and unwelcoming and open or resistant to change. Steadiness and accountability also play their part, as congregations learn to trust those processes that begin to develop spiritual needs, not only in the congregation but also in those beyond them.

In a later book, *More than Numbers*,[14] Mead develops his earlier thinking, exploring the different kinds of growth that occur within congregations. He begins by acknowledging that many congregations will never grow in numbers – but, and this is crucial – this does not render those churches pointless. On the contrary, the varieties of growth that occur in congregations are to be identified and encouraged if the church is to have a future. Mead understands that some communities will benefit by churches deepening their spiritual growth, but that this in itself may not lead to numerical growth in the congregation. Similarly, the growth in the congregation that occurs because of a charismatic new leader might well be extensive, but it is not necessarily intensive and rooted, and may leave the congregation in a worse position (ultimately) than a position where there was less obvious growth before.

Mead illustrates the polarities in perceptions of growth by examining a case study. A small bequest is left to a congregation, but the question is, what to do with it? There are several ideas, which include repairing the church, increasing the amount of time that the pastor can be available, setting up a feeding programme for the hungry and revamping the education programme. But as Mead describes the debate, he points out that one fact seems to capture people's imaginations more than anything else: there were simply no resources in the area to help people to figure out how to get a job. So the bequest is used to rent some space in a shopping centre in order to broker services from public agencies, and also solicit help of a nearby university, to enable local people to analyse their skills, locate training opportunities and get some help seeking work. As Mead points out:

The congregation's decision was not primarily shaped by jobs and money, but by a concern that people discover their gifts and learn how to use these gifts in service to the community. So while the community sees a Job Centre, the congregation sees it as a place for people to discover their ministries in the world. So far there has been no impact on membership of the congregation, although a number of neighborhood groups and agencies now relate to the congregation.[15]

With a vignette like this, Mead suggests that there are four different categories of church growth:

1. *Numerical growth* – that is growth in the ways we ordinarily describe it. Sunday attendance, size of budget, number of activities and growth in numbers of active members.
2. *Maturational growth* – this is growth in the stature and maturity of each member and congregation, spiritual development, etc.
3. *Organic growth* – this is the growth of the congregation as a functioning community, able to maintain itself as a living organism and one which engages with other institutions within its context.
4. *Incarnational growth* – this is growth in the ability to take on the meanings and values of the faith story and make them real in the world outside *the congregation.* The congregation grows in its ability to enflesh in the community, which is what the faith is all about.

The kind of growth that very often applies to mainline denominations is organic and incarnational. Mead states that

organic growth is about the task of building the community, fashioning the organizational structures, developing the practices and processes that result in a dependable, stable network of human relationships in which we can grow and from which we can make a difference. Organic growth is about interaction; between frustration and hope in all congregations. Many people find the structures of their congregation are an obstacle to their ministries, draining energy away rather than generating it to spark mission. Organic growth is the call to shape congregations themselves to become communities that generate life and energy. Organic growth helps the organizational structures of the congregation, becoming a launching pad for the ministry rather than an institutional albatross around the collective neck of its members.[16]

Here I can offer two local examples of incarnational growth where the signs of the kingdom are present but not immediately obvious. In one case, a businessman takes on a disused factory in a run-down part of town, where the economy is depressed. Through the development of an innovative product, the company grows from a tiny outfit into a sizeable organization. However, each of the workers is given a share in the management of the company, its future development and a share of its profits. Jobs bring hope; workers are empowered; the area in which the factory is begins to experience regeneration.

In a similar but slightly different vein, another company structures its business so that all the workers subscribe to a core ethos and affirm a common set of workplace values. The company is placed in 'common ownership' by its founders, so that all those engaged in its employ can share in its profitability. The directors agree to be paid no more than ten times the amount that the lowest-paid worker receives. The company creates a climate of opportunity, empowerment and responsibility.

Intriguingly, the founding directors of both companies attend the same church, and while they know each other slightly, have quite independently developed patterns of incarnational growth that marry their Christian commitment to their everyday commercial life. As Barth notes, tellingly:

> The true growth which is the secret of the upbuilding of the community is not extensive but intensive; its vertical growth in height and depth ... It is not the case, that is intensive increase necessarily involves an extensive. We cannot, therefore, strive for vertical renewal merely to produce greater horizontal extension and a wider audience. If it (the Church and its mission) is used only as a means of extensive renewal, the internal will at once lose its meaning and power. It can only be fulfilled for its own sake, and then – unplanned and unarranged – it will bear its own fruits.[17]

The strength of Mead's work lies in the precision and angularity of his questions. He suggests, for example, that one problem liberal churches face is their failure to identify the bad (spiritual) news that is the antithesis of the good news of the gospel. More conservative churches have less problem with this: Hell, a life forever without God, damnation and judgement might all feature as 'penalties' for failing to accept the gospel. But what do mainline churches suggest might be the consequence of ignoring the gospel? Can liberalism preach the Good News without saying what the Bad News is?

Another writer in the field of applied congregational studies worthy of attention is Alice Mann. In her ground-breaking fieldwork, she has been concerned with explorations of size transition that puzzle many clergy and lay leaders of congregations. Mann provides analytical tools, stories from real situations, research and practical hints when looking at expansion and decline in congregational contexts. In her book *The In-between Church*,[18] she suggests that there are optimum sizes of Christian gatherings, which to some extent dictate both the style and process of leadership. In each of the four 'models' she identifies, the numbers refer to average worship attendance on any given Sunday.

First, there is the *family-sized church* (1–50 members). Mann points out that this is a kind of single-cell organism, a social system resembling an extended biological family in which everyone knows each other. Second, the *pastoral-sized church* (50–150 members), is a multi-cell organism with a coalition of several overlapping family friendship networks, which are unified around the person and the pastor. When a congregation is portrayed in literature, films or in television, it is often made in this pastoral image: a church on the green with a single resident parson. Third, the *programme-size church* (150–350 members) is known, as the name suggests, for the quality and the variety of its programmes. Its larger and more diverse membership will contain a critical mass of people from several different interest and age groups. Typically, the church will have part- and full-time staff, and lay leadership that is concerned with pastoral care, new-member incorporation, community outreach and education. Fourth, the *corporate-size church* (350–500+ members) is usually a significant institutional presence in the community. It may even have a cathedral-like building in a prominent location, plus associated institutions like a day-school or a community centre, and a sizeable staff of highly skilled professionals.

Mann places no particular value judgement on each of these four models, but the distinction between single-cell bodies, multi-cellular bodies, coalitions and conglomerates is intriguing. She understands that the negotiation between sizes, while not exactly a science, is nonetheless part of a complex nexus of social interactions, which includes the evaluation of the church by the community and its own sense of belonging. Critically, Mann's analysis raises a question about the suitability of the size of the congregation in relation to its environment. Should the congregation be growing? Should the congregation be attempting to try something different that engages the community? What is the relationship between spiritual and numerical growth? What is the relationship between resourcing and staffing and outreach? To be sure, it does not follow that the more congregations do try and spend, the more likely they are to succeed. What Mann's research shows is that congregations need to centre on themselves, their core spiritual values, and what kind of community they belong to, in order to identify new prospects for growth and mission.

Building on this work, Mann suggests that there are real factors that may inhibit growth that need addressing. In *Can our Church Live?*[19] she suggests that certain demographic realities are factors. People can move away, and new incomers may have different tastes that do not relate to what is already available within a given community. She also suggests that a more powerful factor in church decline is 'the loss of our first love'. She suggests that many churches have forgotten that God is primarily in the business of *redemption* rather than being engaged in the (undoubtedly wholesome) enterprise of *maintenance* – an immaculately tidy building, tidy records, ordered worship and regular fellowship.

To be sure, she acknowledges that these are all fine, but she argues that unless the Church can re-enter the redemption business, it will soon be out of business. Mann also understands that a factor in church decline is the difference between form and content. By this, she simply means that many churches implicitly assume that they must first convert individuals and groups to a style of life, values and preferences, and it is only then and through those things that they can be introduced to the gospel. Finally, Mann suggests a further factor in church decline: brittleness, the lack of flexibility and intransigence that bedevils many mainline denominations can make individual congregations unappealing and inhospitable.

So, what of redevelopment? Interestingly, Mann champions 'organic church growth'. Granted, social organisms are different from biological ones, but nevertheless they often manifest similar patterns of emergence and decline. Thus it is necessary to identify key stages in the life-cycle of the congregation if the church is to engage in or maintain its growth. This includes an understanding of the birth of the church, its formation, its stability and maturity, as well as what leads to its decline and death. The temptation in this organic life-cycle of the congregation is to attempt to pivot the church on an axis between stability and formation. But the danger of this, in attempting to stave off death, is that it prevents new birth. Correspondingly, the congregation becomes fixed in its sights, on efficiency and maintenance. Mann suggests that regaining flexibility, renewing identity of purpose and being willing to entertain dramatic transformation are key principles for mainline denominations as they seek to grow.

Again, Mann develops these ideas in *Raising the Roof*[20] by suggesting that congregations that seek to actively grow must move from implicit and indirect assumptions about mission and spirituality to explicit and direct activism in relationality. This is important, because it allows the congregation as a whole to own afresh the spiritual charismas and core values that make up its life. Instead of the congregation being allowed to become comfortable by investing time and energy in institutional maintenance, Mann suggests that congregations need actively to own the spiritual and religious reasons they have for being there together. Typically, this will involve them engaging in steep learning processes that centre on Christian education. they will explore the ways in which power flows in and out of the church, and will seek to understand individual and corporate faith-formation frameworks that determine how and why people belong to local congregations. It is only at this point that congregations can begin to truly explore the barriers to growth (which may well be within them). By placing the emphasis on spiritual growth, Mann understands that it is from that perspective that numerical and organic growth can be truly addressed. Here, her work complements the early work of Loren Mead, by calling congregations to pay attention to the barriers and boundaries within them that may inhibit growth, and those barriers and boundaries that both identify and constrain the local congregation.

Conclusion

Concurring with these insights, Roozen and Hadaway[21] suggest that there are now four types of growing liberal church. First, there are those that are market-driven, and barely differ from those evangelical churches, except in their content and style. Second, there are growing mainstream churches in many denominational settings where the demographics make organic church growth relatively easy. These might include particular kinds of rural or suburban areas, or occasionally certain kinds of inner-city areas that are undergoing regeneration or renewal. A third group of growing mainstream churches could be identified as 'niche'. These are churches that reach for gay and lesbian congregations, death congregations, churches for small racial or ethnic groups of various kinds, or maybe radical and avant-garde. The fourth and final group of growing mainstream churches, one which arguably provides a greater source of hope for denominations but which is struggling with the loss of identity and apparently experiencing decline in members, is that comprising spiritually orientated and liberal churches. Such churches are often involved in community ministry, with a clear focus on social justice. Yet at the same time, their work is rooted in deep and powerful worship experiences, which in many cases have transcended the established patterns set by their parent denomination.

Roozen and Hadaway recognize that Peter Berger's analysis (namely that there has been a turn away from the authority of tradition to experience as the focus of religious thought) does mean that liberal mainstream denominations are arguably particularly well suited to provide a reflexive and engaging spirituality that would lead to numerical church growth in the twenty-first century. Roozen and Hadaway suggest that churches that are spiritually alive, radically inclusive and justice-orientated have a real future, provided that those churches are clear about their identity and purpose, and willing to take risks. Moreover, they avoid the fear of revitalization if they are to become a spiritually orientated liberal church.

But what lessons can the diocese of Northfield, together with its congregations and parishes, learn from Mead and Mann? What would it mean to speak of 'church growth' in these situations? Several points need making here, which suggests that there are plenty of challenges, but also that much has already been quietly achieved. Arguably, the strategy as a whole turns on making the implicit far more explicit and learning to celebrate varieties of growth and transformation rather than colluding with a conservative culture that is suspicious of change.

First, Mead and Mann both suggest that congregations and churches need to rediscover their core spiritual message. This is not merely an exercise in cognition, let alone 'adopting' an agreed mission statement or motto. It is, rather, a task that is centred on the passion and energy that gave life to the church in the first place. Leaving aside all issues of maintenance, what are the core spiritual values that enable this congregation to cohere? What is its good news for the neighbourhood? What does it want to proclaim in word, deed and ethos? Only when this has been discerned can the congregation engage in collective outreach that is energetic and explicit.

Second, congregations need to identify and celebrate the different types of growth that occur within their life. Maturational, organic and transfer growth may be implicitly assumed to be commonplace. But can congregations learn to share stories of such growth in ways that are empowering and effective? Are there opportunities for congregations to offer feedback on how their spirituality has developed in recent years? Can such conversations be turned to engage the community, so that they see the church as a place of transformation and energy, rather than merely maintenance?

Third, mainline congregations must constantly confront the myth that only certain types of conservative church can grow. As we saw earlier, there are forms of conservativism that inhibit growth by curtailing questions and prematurely ceasing in exploration. Conservative cultures, ironically, attract large numbers of people who are effectively engaged in the business of maintenance, and seek transformation to that end. Liberalism, in contrast, has much to offer in terms of openness, questioning, freedom and fellowship that is no less attractive. Mainline liberal churches need continually to discover new ways in which this can be celebrated, and to remind the rest of Christendom that, they too can grow. The growth can occur in their depth of discipleship, in their connectedness to the community, in their spirituality and also in their numbers.

As if one needed reminding, some of the most effective forms of ecclesial witness in the world are actually numerically quite small. Numbers are something, to be sure. But they were never everything. The God of small things continues to smile on the marginalized and the overlooked. Mainline churches need to worry about size a little less, and concentrate on worship, discipleship and outreach just a little more. Whoever planted, and no matter who watered, it is only God who gives the growth.

Notes

1. James Hopewell, *Congregation: Stories and Structures* (London: SCM Press, 1987).

2. Northrop Frye, *The Anatomy of Criticism* (Princeton, NJ: Princeton University Press, 1957).

3. Hopewell, *Congregation*, p. 81.

4. Frye, *Anatomy of Criticism*, p. 207.

5. Hopewell, *Congregation*, p. 81.

6. Loren B. Mead, *The Once and the Future Church* (Bethesda, MD: Alban Institute, 1991).

7. Callum Brown, *The Death of Christian Britain* (London: Taylor & Francis, 2000).

8. Mead, *The Once and the Future Church*, p. 42.

9. Ibid., p. 20.

10. Ibid., p. 44.

11. Ibid., p. 46.

12. Ibid., p. 60.

13. Elizabeth Kubler-Ross, *On Death and Dying* (Riverside, NJ: 1970); *Questions on Death and Dying* (Basingstoke: Macmillan, 1979).

14. Loren B. Mead, *More than Numbers: The Way Churches Grow* (Bethesda, MD: Alban Institute, 1993).

15. Ibid., p. 40.

16. Ibid., p. 60.

17. Karl Barth, in *Church Dogmatics, Extension and a Wider Audience*, Vol. 4, Book 2 (Edinburgh: T&T Clark, 1958).

18. Alice Mann, *The In-between Church: Navigating Size Transitions in Congregations* (Bethesda, MD: Alban Institute, 1998).

19. Alice Mann, *Can our Church Live? Redeveloping Congregations in Decline* (Bethesda, MD: Alban Institute, 1999).

20. Alice Mann, *Raising the Roof: The Pastoral to Programme Size Transition* (Bethesda, MD: Alban Institute, 2001).

21. David A. Roozen and C. Kirk Hadaway, *Re-routing the Protestant Mainstream: Sources of Growth and Opportunities for Change* (Nashville, TN: Abingdon Press, 1995).

Chapter 8

SOCIAL JUSTICE AND CHURCH GROWTH IN THE AFRICAN-AMERICAN CHURCH

Benjamin K. Watts

Introduction

The African-American Church has a long history of social justice advocacy that began in slavery and has consistently been intertwined into the churches' growth and development. For this work social justice is defined as churches that are involved in community development, social uplifting and improvement to the general welfare of their constituent population. This chapter does not offer an assessment as to the quality or quantity of the social justice offered, instead it points without prejudice to what is currently taking place. Moreover, this chapter examines the two streams of consciousness that flow in the area of social justice and the African-American community. These streams of consciousness are best seen in tangential form between the greater and lesser-known local congregations that are at work at the grassroots level of soup kitchens, shelters and modest housing projects and popular fast-growing 'super-mega' churches. It should be noted that the predominantly African-American 'super-mega' membership (in excess of 20,000) churches differ not only in size but also in style from the large urban African-American churches of many denominations.

This chapter addresses the issue of rapidly increasing African-American congregations, and seeks to answer the following questions: are these congregations active in social justice ministries, and if so, to what extent? Are they primarily social-justice oriented, or are they focused on other areas of ministry and covering social issues as an aside? And, furthermore: are the congregations that use social justice as the central theme of their external work growing at the rate of congregations that are differently focused?

The chapter will take a case study approach, utilizing both urban and suburban (most of these churches have urban roots and have moved out of the city to get land for huge mega complexes) predominantly African-American congregations. All of the 'mega'-churches examined are to some extent multiracial, but they all have at least 70 per cent of their congregation listed as African-American. These congregations are thriving on different levels, utilizing methodologies that have suited the purposes of their leadership to facilitate growth as extension of the biblical mandate, and all, to varying degrees, have been active in social justice ministry. This chapter does not seek to answer a right or wrong question regarding methodologies, but rather to examine the state of African-American social justice ministry in the post-Civil Rights era. Finally, it should be noted that there are numerous examples of congregations that are not generating substantial growth that follow some of the models given in this chapter; why this should be so, however, is beyond the scope of this chapter.

History

Our churches are where we dip our tired bodies in cool springs of hope; here we retain our wholeness and humanity, despite the blows of death from the Bosses.[1]

It is essential to start our discussion with a sense of the ways in which the Black Church has been shaped by its distinctive history. The historical role of the Black Church has been to stand as a bulwark within the community while black people struggled for selfhood and empowerment. 'The black community, historically, has leaned heavily upon the church as that institution, peculiarly independent, which establishes its mores, determines its life-styles, formulates its opinions and articulates its societal needs.'[2]

From the time of the destructive, dehumanizing period of slavery, the Black Church has functioned as a citadel of strength. As the slaves fought their way through an environment of hate, they were forced to find a voice for their struggle. Something had to provide both protest and accommodation without afflicting them with further unnecessary pain. While many slaves rebelled and were killed, some ran away, and others fought to cope with their plight. '[T]hey longed for a place of refuge from racism which, for them, was and continues to be the paramount social evil.'[3] Although they were unable to eradicate racism and its attendant violence, they needed to have some power over their own lives and destinies. So they created the Black Church as a 'surrogate world' of their own.[4]

E. Franklin Frazier, in the *Negro Church in America*, described the Black Church as a 'nation within a nation'. The Black Church constituted the first independence movement in America among African slaves. Peter Paris describes the cooperative movement in this way:

Those nascent black churches evidenced the cooperative action of the slaves to build institutions and prove to themselves and others that they were capable not only of adapting to an environment but of constructing a world of their own. In time, the black churches were destined to become a surrogate world for black people in general. While the larger society sought to victimize blacks, the black churches aimed at socializing their members into creative forms of coping along with the development of imaginative styles of social and political protest, both grounded in a religious hope for an eschatological victory.[5]

In slavery, clandestine worship on the plantation became an 'invisible institution' that gave meaning to the lives of blacks.[6] With the African religious experience all but eradicated from their minds, the descendants of the first slaves found a home in Christianity. C.E. Lincoln, in his seminal work *Race, Religion, and the Continuing American Dilemma*, suggests that the potential of any African religions for being totally sustained is minimal; however, '[t]he transplantation of significant aspects of the African religious experience, or the Africanization of the host religion, was not absolutely precluded'.[7]

Nonetheless, no matter what the content of African religious experience, the historical evidence shows that the slaves had a predisposition toward religion that made their conversion possible.[8] However, rather than mimicking the behaviour of the white Christians from whom they learned of Christianity, the slaves formed a distinctive religious expression responsive to their particular needs and sensibilities. With religion as a source of strength, they fought oppression by attempting to redefine both their destiny and their identity. Using religious worship, they forged a way of protest and struggle and began to define themselves from their biblical teachings.

> [T]hey became a distinctive subculture, rooted in the African heritage, and developed in the black experience in America. They became Black Americans, and as the first expression of their new identity, they created a Black Church! Spiritually, theologically, idealistically independent of any previous cultural commitments which called it into existence.[9]

It was this development of the Black Church that provided slaves with the hope they needed to sustain their existence in this strange land. The Black Church began to take institutional form in 1758 when the African Baptist or 'Bluestone' Church was organized on the plantation of William Byrd in Mecklenberg, Virginia. During the same period in Augusta, Georgia, the Silver Bluff Baptist Church was established. Although records indicate that its organization was between 1773 and 1775, the cornerstone of the present edifice dates the founding to 1750.[10]

While Baptists in the South were developing independent churches, Methodists in the north were, for all practical purposes, integrated. Methodists, led by their founders John and Charles Wesley, had officially taken an anti-slavery position. Therefore, the Methodist Church became attractive to both slaves and freemen and -women.[11]

This relationship continued uninterrupted until 1787, when a group of black worshippers, led by Richard Allen and Absalom Jones, were pulled from their knees during worship at St George's Methodist Church in Philadelphia.[12] The group had been praying in a gallery that they did not know was reserved for white Christians only. Allen and Jones asked if they could finish their prayers. They were pulled from their knees. Ultimately, all of the black worshippers withdrew and, in the words of Richard Allen, 'they were no more plagued with [us] in that church'.[13]

Later, using the Free African Society they had founded for benevolent purposes, the blacks from St George's began to organize a religious meeting that met the spiritual needs of black Christians. In 1790 they began fund-raising efforts to build a meeting-house, which was eventually erected in

1794 as St Thomas African Episcopal Church. Absalom Jones became the first black Protestant episcopal priest and the church's pastor. Richard Allen, believing that Methodism was the best denomination for black people (prejudice, not theology, was the reason they had left St George's church), organized Bethel Church of Philadelphia in a refurbished old blacksmith shop that he owned. In 1816 Bethel became the mother church of the African Methodist Episcopal Church, a new denomination of black Methodists.

The Church institutionalized the deep devotion of free blacks who worked for racial solidarity, spirituality and the abolition of slavery. As the Black Church was being born, slavery persisted as a social evil. The institutionalized Black Church, by embodying the principles of the 'invisible Church', became the citadel of hope for a people in slavery.

The Black Church asserted itself as that institution at the heart of the community, as its 'institutional centre'. In 1903 W.E.B. Dubois described the Black Church as the centre of social life among American Negroes, calling it, in addition, 'the most characteristic expression of African character'.[14] The Black Church has stood as a barricade against every form of oppression, regression and depression that has attacked the African-American community. As Lincoln writes: '[T]he Black Church was the unifying force which made of a scattered confusion of slaves a distinctive entity. The church was the black man's government, his social club, his secret order, his espionage system, his political party, and his impetus to freedom and revolution.'[15]

As the property of their owners, slaves were treated like objects, things. This 'thingification' was legitimized by the laws of the land and perpetuated in every societal norm: religion, art and science. Upon the demise of slavery, the ethos and principle that had created this 'thingification' remained entrenched in the American psyche and was given full expression in the form of racism. America continued its subjugation of its former slaves through a system of Jim Crow laws, legalized by the *Plessy v. Furguson* court decision of 1896 that mandated 'separate but equal'. These laws forced segregation and were reinforced with intimidation by white citizen councils and their hooded cohorts, the Klu Klux Klan. 'As the experience of slavery clearly reveals, social systems that are shaped by the principle of racism aim at total human annihilation. In the process of achieving its aim, the impact of racism virtually ensures restrictive and crippling effects both on the race as a whole and on the personal development of its members.'[16]

The Black Church provided the social system and the extended family that had been wiped out by slavery. All of the needs of freemen and freewomen were met at the church. In 1899 Dubois wrote of this phenomenon in the *Philadelphia Negro*:

> As a social group the Negro Church may be said to have antedated the Negro family on American soil; as such it has preserved, on the one hand, many functions of tribal organization, and on the other hand, many of the family functions. Its tribal functions are shown in its religious activity. Its social authority, and general guiding and coordinating work; its family functions are shown by the fact that the church is a center of social life and intercourse,

acts as newspaper and intelligence bureau, is the center of amusements – indeed, is the world in which the Negro moves and acts. So far reaching are these functions of the church that its organization is almost political.[17]

In the words of William A. Jones, pastor of Bethany Baptist Church in Brooklyn, the Black Church has been bound together by 'four distinctions: blood, blackness, bondage, and the new birth'.[18] The nascent Black Church functioned as an extended family for slaves, and remains so for African-Americans to this day. The Black Church embraced the lives of its constituency; for every cultural norm of society and wholeness invested within its institutional walls, 'it was lyceum and gymnasium as well as sanctum santorum'.[19]

The Black Church is that institution that has emerged from slavery despite attempts by white Christians to dismantle it. This Church has been able to shine as a beam of light, radiating hope for the ultimate survival, existential and eschatological, of its constituency. C. Eric Lincoln calls the Black Church an 'authentic representation of what it means to be black in America'.[20]

For within the Black Church are all of the 'genius and emotion, hope and fear, projection and recoil which characterize the random gathering of people of West Africa who were fused in the black experience in America'.[21] As the surviving link to the past, the church has functioned in multifarious ways, including as mother and father to its community. At times political but always practical, it has stood as a hedge blocking the hatred of a cruel society. Even if it only gave momentary refuge, that moment was enough for the believers to gather strength and hope and to endure the lot of the outcast.[22]

> Black churches had the formidable job of restoring the damage done by the slave system to black families by emphasizing the infinite worth of every human personality in God's eyes, and by encouraging black men to assume the responsibility previously denied them as the head of families. Perhaps the most important contribution of black churches to the process of black economic survival was their stress upon acquiring an education and their establishment of educational institutions, often in the church themselves.[23]

The Black Church worked diligently to meet the needs of the former slaves by educating and enriching the lives of the newly free and by providing them with a means of survival. The church was responsible for the creation of schools and skill-training centres. Institutions of higher learning such as Wilberforce University, Morehouse College, Spellman College, Selma University and Tuskegee University are examples of Black Church involvement in education.

Without question, black pastors and their congregants have been on the front lines of the struggle for racial equality. The Black Church has been and will continue to be an instrument for change: '[i]t produced Nat Turner and it produced Martin Luther King, Jr. And ranged between their respective conceptualizations of Christian responsibility, the black church has been womb and mother to a vast spectrum of black leadership in every generation since its inception.'[24]

The Black Church served as the headquarters of the Civil Rights movement, which produced the greatest social change in America this century. Although the Black Church was not the sole support of the movement, it certainly provided both the leadership and moral impetus of the struggle.[25] The church served as the meeting centre where, within a revival type of atmosphere, the freedom-fighters were invigorated and inspired to continue their work. Wyatt T. Walker, an aide to Dr King and former pastor of the New Canaan Baptist Church, writes that '[t]he rallies were services of worship; the offering was the ammunition, the troops were the saints; it was chiefly a black church operation. A converse truth stands: if the black church were removed from the nonviolent movement in the south, there would have been no movement.'[26] The strong, contemporary Black Church is still the brightest hope for the crisis within the African-American community today.

The strength of the Black Church

The strength of the Black Church lies in three distinct areas: (1) economic (primarily from the charitable gifts of its members and the conservative stewardship of its leaders); (2) numerical (from the allegiance of the black community); and (3) ecumenical (from the long-standing informal relationship of pastors and churches across denominational lines). We shall now examine the three strengths in turn.

Economic strength
The economic power of the Black Church is a function of the tendency of African-Americans to give their charitable contributions to their churches. More than two-thirds of the money that blacks contribute to charity goes to the church.[27] In the Black Church, Lincoln and Mamiya estimate that the African-American community's annual church giving could easily surpass two billion dollars. If one were to include the monetary equivalency of time given by volunteers, the overall contribution would run into billions of dollars annually, 'giving significant clout to the area of religion in the black community'.[28]

In a survey of New York Baptist churches conducted by the office of the General Secretary of the National Baptist Convention, USA, Inc., W. Franklin Richardson revealed that 600 churches deposit approximately $6.8 million. Annually, these churches' banking deposits and loans total a staggering $327 million. Of this figure, less than 9 per cent is in loans.[29] The economic power is clear, particularly among large urban churches, many of which have already begun to make an economic and social impact within their respective communities.

At a 1992 conference of black seminarians and theologians in Dallas, Texas, Cecil Gray, director of the Church World Institute of Temple University in Philadelphia, informed the attendees of the opening of Unity Bank of Philadelphia that the purpose of Unity Bank is 'to serve African-Americans, Native Americans, women and other minorities' and 'to meet the needs of the poor'.[30] Unity Bank, with initial resources of about five million dollars, exemplifies the power of urban black churches to get its members to contribute to a common social cause.[31]

Many black churches have begun ambitious projects that until recently went unnoticed. *Black Enterprise*, in December 1993, highlighted a number of these church-based economic development projects. The examples that follow further demonstrate that the Black Church has not halted its active role in the liberation of black people.

Black churches like Hartford Memorial Baptist Church in Detroit, Michigan, have created a large economic base for community development. Hartford's projects include a McDonald's restaurant and a Kentucky Fried Chicken franchise: businesses that are part of a development project that transformed once-vacant land to productive prominence. The Hartford church has a master-plan that includes a 40,000 sq.ft commercial centre, a $17-million shopping centre, and a multi-million-dollar housing development. Initially, the church members paid $500,000 for the vacant properties now under development; today, the land is believed to be worth more than $5 million.[32]

The Allen African Methodist Episcopal Church in Queens, New York, has taken a blighted neighbourhood and given it new life. Under the leadership of Revd Floyd Flake, the Allen church has used $10.7 million in HUD grants to build a 300-unit senior housing complex. The Allen church has been involved in both the service and economic sectors of life. It has established not only a school but also a multiservice centre that provides prenatal and post-natal care for mothers. The church has purchased and rehabilitated more than fifteen storefront buildings that now provide badly needed goods and services to the community. The now eight non-profit subsidiary corporations of Allen church reportedly have over a thousand employees and an annual budget of $12 million.[33]

The Wheat Street Baptist Church of Atlanta, Georgia, formerly under the leadership of the Revd William Homes Borders, has amassed $33 million in real-estate holdings; it is among the wealthiest black churches in the country.[34] The Wheat Street Charitable Foundation (a non-profit-making organization within the church) owns two shopping plazas, two housing developments and several single-housing units. The church is helping to rebuild Atlanta's black community.

Job training, as well as economic development, has been the focus of Revd Leon Sullivan and the Zion Baptist Church of Philadelphia. Under Revd Sullivan's direction, the church set on a path to train people who were ill-prepared to enter the job market. Opportunities Industrialization Center (OIC), established in 1964, quickly spread across the nation. Within the first five years of operation, OIC training centres were opened in 70 cities, handling federal government contracts worth $18 million. According to Lincoln and Mamiya, OIC has depended for its expansion 'primarily upon the support of local ministers and churches in various communities, a pattern that is consistent with its origins. Although OIC does not have any formal ties with churches, four of the top five officers of the OIC National Board of Directors are ministers' and OIC is 'one of the more successful job training programs initiated by black church leadership'.[35]

In an interview with *Black Enterprise* magazine, Dr Adams, senior pastor of Hartford church, made a powerful point when he said:

> The church needs to concentrate on the business of creating economic institutions ... [T]he issue is jobs. People being laid off through this entire corporate downsizing are affecting every black community in this country. The church finds itself in a situation where it is the best continuing, organized entity in the black community for the acquisition and redevelopment of land, the building of business enterprises and the employment of people.[36]

The combined economic power and the creative genius of the Black Church makes its role seminal in the African-American community:

> Born of slavery and racism, the Black Church has been a spiritual refuge to heal the pain of an outcast people, and an instrument of liberation. The social conscience of the Black Church has been more overt and more pronounced at some times that at others ... However, the record is clear that the Black Church and its leaders have been active with varying degrees of effectiveness in both the political and economic spheres throughout the history of its existence ...The social ministry of the Black Church has been undergirded by a continuity of holistic theological perspectives that its ministry, caring for and serving people, ought to encompass all of life, including not only the spiritual but also the political and economic dimensions as well.[37]

Numerical strength

The Black Church not only has economic clout, it has numerical strength. This is the second strength. Despite all of the competing service clubs and social and fraternal organizations, the African-American community still identifies itself with the Black Church. This identification allows the Black Church the latitude to be prophetic (i.e. to speak against injustice) without fear of reprisal. The spirit of faithful struggle is the heartbeat of the Black Church, which empowers the African-American community.

> The Black Church has been and still remains the connecting rod between Black History and Black hope. It is the only institution on the island that has historic continuity. It is the largest base of numerical strength. It is the one place where [there is] the vision of nobler life as a perennial struggle by people in pilgrimage. And because of its non-dependence on the larger society, it is free to be prophetic.[38]

Although some mainline Protestant predominately white churches (Episcopal, Presbyterian and Lutheran) may be experiencing decline, the Black Church has not only maintained its membership but also in certain communities increased. Of the overall African-American population, 78 per cent, are church members, as opposed to 72 per cent of the general population.[39] The African-American community's propensity for religion is one of the factors that make the Black Church the ideal place for leadership and economic and social development within the community. The African-American community has remained steeped in religious tradition, its financial or economic condition notwithstanding. This devotion has made the church a viable link between suburban and urban African-Americans.

The Congress of National Black Churches, Inc. (CNBC) represents a partnership of eight black denominations: African Methodist Episcopal; African Methodist Episcopal Zion; Christian Methodist Episcopal; Church of God in Christ; National Baptist Convention of America, Inc.; National Baptist Convention, USA, Inc.; National Missionary Baptist Convention of America; and Progressive National Baptist Convention, Inc. Organized in 1978, CNBC boasts a membership of 65,000 churches, 250,000 church employees, and more than 19 million worshippers. Although these staggering numbers do not reflect the total black religious population, they provide a glimpse into the numerical strength of the Black Church. CNBC's only limitation on growth, in fact, is that its membership does not include black churches within the predominately white mainline denominations.[40] CNBC, which was the brainchild of AME Bishop John Hurst Adams, is an example of the ecumenism that takes place in the African-American community.[41]

Dean Emeritus Lawrence N. Jones of the School of Divinity at Howard University has been attempting to foster cooperatives and ecumenical projects with the National Congress of Community Economic Development (NCCED). NCCED has introduced a new programme for African-American churches called the African-American Congregations Project (AACP) and is actively educating pastors and lay people to develop community-based economic projects. In an article written for *Progressions*, a Lilly Endowment house organ, Dean Jones writes:

> What is required of the churches in the years ahead ... is a mixture of strategic development and selective application of financial and human resources. Black congregations alone cannot remedy epidemic pathologies in their communities. These urgent needs require coalitions of congregations so that their combined strengths and resources can more effectively serve their communities.[42]

Ecumenical strength

It is the mixture of planning and stewardship that provides the basis for ecumenism; which is the third strength of the Black Church. African-Americans have always practised informal ecumenism; the whole Civil Rights movement was, in its own right, an expression of that ethos within the community. Moreover, the ecumenism of the movement was formalized in the creation of the Southern Christian Leadership Conference (SCLC), organized in 1957 for developing strategy and communicating with various communities to set up mass meetings.

Chester Kirkendoll writes: 'For the last 50 years the black church has been a symbol of togetherness. This is a fact that is, without equivocation, irrefutable in every way. The rationale for the togetherness hinges upon the need for unity in the face of social and civil struggles that engulfed this country in these turbulent years.'[43] Kirkendoll concludes: 'Ecumenism is inherent, in one sense, in the very nature of the black Church.'[44]

There are already some programmes for stimulating interdenominational and interreligious ecumenism, such as a meeting in 1984 held in New Orleans by the National Assembly of Black Church Organizations. The meeting was 'more concerned with economic development than ecclesiastical or theological issues'.[45] Among the participants was Dr T.J. Jemison, then president of the National Baptist Convention, USA, Inc., and Minister Louis Farrakhan, leader of the Nation of Islam. The idea was to unite blacks of various religious affiliations in their efforts to make a difference in blighted communities.

The ecumenism currently being practised is localized to traditional African-American congregations primarily accustomed to coalescing their efforts of community advocacy. These churches have a long history of support for disenfranchised people and have made that mission paramount to their ministry. There appears to be a divide if not distrust between those traditional havens of hope and the new 'super-mega'-church developments. A review of three African-American 'super-mega'-church ministries demonstrates that a part of the divide is located in worldview. The 'super-mega'-churches engage in social justice in a different way from their counterparts. And their sheer numbers allow them to function independently and yet on a grand scale.

In Dallas, Texas, the 28,000-member Potter House Ministry of Bishop T.D. Jakes has been in the process of developing over a thousand homes in the greater Dallas/Fort Worth area. With over 59 different ministries addressing societal maladies, AIDS outreach, homeless shelter, prison ministry and economic development, the church has the ability to deliver social justice support in a macro form. While financially equipped to be fully independent Bishop Jakes does not linger in isolation, and has developed a network of churches – Potter's House International Pastoral Alliance. The difference between this alliance, as with most mega-church cooperative programmes, is that the affiliation is purposed around accountability and ministry development and not social justice.

Like the Potters House, New Birth Missionary Baptist Church, under the direction of Bishop Eddie Long, is one of the largest mega-churches in the country. New Birth, with a membership in excess of 25,000 members, covers the gamut of social justice delivery systems with multiple staff members dedicated to service. New Birth has every conceivable ministry already in place and has spent significant resources in creating a humongous campus inclusive of a 77,753-sq.ft Family Life Center replete with a state-of-the-art fitness facility, offering everything from massage therapy, aerobics and team sports. Furthermore, the ministry offers homeless shelters, housing development and treatment centres for addictions. It has a holistic approach to ministry that makes available a social service outlet for the greater Lithonia (GA) community. Bishop Long has practised his ecumenism through his involvement in the creation of satellite churches as well as the church's participation in the Full Gospel Baptist Fellowship.

The 23,500-member World Changers International Church, led by Dr Creflo Dollar has had a significant impact on its College Park (GA) community since 1981. WCCI offers over 60 programmes and ministries to meet the physical, financial, emotional and spiritual needs of its constituents and the community at large. The WCCI Career Center is a practical assistance training programme assisting people in obtaining employment opportunities: over half of their referrals obtain and maintain gainful employment. A food-distribution facility provides over 60 tons of food to needy families annually. Mentoring programmes for men and women are available to move people forward in their life quest. As with Potters House and New Birth, social justice ministry is done independently. Independence does not mean total isolation: Dr Creflo Dollar is president of International Covenant Ministries (ICM). This fellowship provides access to ministries seeking support for church growth and development. ICM works to assist ministers, pastors and churches large and small, with support services and ministry resources designed to optimize their effectiveness, including website development, workshops and conferences on ministry, organizational structure and logistical support.

The history of the Black Church makes a social justice ministry inescapable. Issues of racism and the economic struggle of African-Americans inevitably disturb the horizons of all black congregations. In so far as a commitment to 'social justice' is a defining mark of a 'liberal' or 'progressive' church, then the case can be made that many black churches are growing vibrant churches. However, two qualifications must be added to this statement immediately. The first is that the theology underpinning this social action is a traditional, orthodox, Trinitarian theology. It is biblical and incarnational. For many mainline Protestant churches, the theology of social justice is non-incarnational and Unitarian. For the Black Church, the theology of social justice is firmly incarnational and Trinitarian. Even in the emerging field of Black Theology, Christology remains central.[46] The second is that there is a changing emphasis between the traditional social justice churches and the mega-churches. The latter are more focused on meeting the 'spiritual' needs of the congregation, and less preoccupied with traditional social justice activism. And of course the churches that are growing dramatically are these socially and theologically conservative mega-churches.

Summary

Some conclusions are obvious in all this. First, social justice ministry has a long history within the African-American Church, and is likely to remain a part of the church, as a means by which the disenfranchised can seek support in a harsh world. Second, church growth in the African-American community does not appear to be tied to social justice ministries. People are not flocking to churches just because they are involved in community activities: the involvement is a legitimate reason to remain active, but is not the sole rationale. Most 'super-mega'-churches do not use their social justice ministry as a point of entry, as there is little, if any, advertising concerning their commitment. For the most part they appear to advertise and proselytize on the basis of their theological slant, offering a clear self-help, self-improvement, spiritual support-based message. Third, the large urban churches by mainline church standards are thriving, and African-American congregations maintain connectedness to the cause of amelioration of societal problems while ministering in a unique way. The conclusions drawn from this cursory look at three 'super-mega' churches are, however, generalized and a more extensive study would be necessary in order to determine both the impetus for growth and the full extent of the social justice ministry engaged in.

Notes

1. Richard Wright, *12 Million Voices*, (New York: Viking, 1951), p. 51.

2. C. Eric Lincoln, *Race, Religion, and the Continuing American Dilemma*, (New York: Hill & Wang, 1984), p. 62.

3. Peter Paris, *The Social Teachings of the Black Churches*, (Philadelphia, PA: Fortress Press, 1985), p. 5.

4. Ibid., p. 5.

5. Ibid., p. 6.

6. Albert Raboteau, *Slave Religion: The 'Invisible Institution' in the Antebellum South* (New York: Oxford University Press, 1978).

7. Lincoln, *Race, Religion*, p. 62.

8. See: Melville J. Herskovits, in Herskovits, *The Myth of the Negro Past* (Boston, MA: Beacon Press, 1990), 'The contemporary scene: Africanisms in religious life', pp. 207–60.

9. Lincoln, *Race, Religion*, p. 63.

10. C. Eric Lincoln and Lawrence H. Mamiya, *The Black Church in the African American Experience* (Durham, NC, and London: Duke University Press, 1990), p. 23.

11. Ibid., p. 50.

12. Ibid., p. 51.

13. Ibid., p. 51.

14. Dubois, *Souls* p. 213.

15. Lincoln, *Race, Religion*, p. 72.

16. Paris, *The Social Teachings of the Black Churches*, p. 4.

17. W.E. Bughardt Dubois, *The Philadelphia Negro* (Philadelphia, PA: University of Pennsylvania Press, 1899), p. 201.

18. Revd Harold A. Carter, Revd Wyatt T. Walker and Revd William A. Jones, Jr, *The Black Church Looks at the Bicentennial: A Minority Report* (Elgin, IL: Progressive National Baptist Publishing House, 1976), p. 123.

19. Lincoln, *Race, Religion*, p. 72.

20. Ibid., p. 73.

21. Ibid., p. 73.

22. See Frantz Fanon, *The Wretched of the Earth* (New York: Grove Press, 1968).

23. C. Eric Lincoln and Lawrence H. Mamiya, 'The black Church and social ministry in politics and economics: historical and contemporary perspectives', in Carl S. Dudley, Jackson W. Carroll and James P. Wind *Carriers of Faith: Lessons from Congregational Studies* (Louisville, KY: Westminster/John Knox Press, 1990), p. 67.

24. Lincoln, *Race, Religion*, p. 73.

25. Taylor Branch, *Parting the Waters: America in the King Years 1954–63* (New York: Simon & Schuster, 1988), pp. 695–6. Dr King spoke with 'blunt anger' about some Negro preachers who were unconcerned about the plight of the poor; suggesting they run the risk of making the church 'dangerously irrelevant'.

26. Carter *et al.*, *The Black Church Looks at the Bicentennial*, p. 58.

27. Emmett D. Carson, 'Survey dispels myth that blacks receive but do not give to charity', *Focus* 15.3 (March 1987): 5, as quoted in C. Eric Lincoln and Lawrence H. Mamiya, *The Black Church in the African American Experience*, (Durham, NC, and London: Duke

University Press, 1990), p. 261.

28. Ibid., p. 261.

29. 'Banking Practices of NBC, USA, Inc. Churches in New York State', Baptist Convention Supplement in *Minority Business Times* (September 1993), N9.

30. 'Faith and economics', *Christian Century*, 6 May 1992: 481.

31. Ibid.

32. 'The new business agenda of the Black Church', *Black Enterprise*, Special Report (December 1993): 54.

33. Lincoln and Mamiya, 'The Black Church and social ministry', p. 75.

34. *Black Enterprise*, p. 58.

35. Lincoln and Mamiya, 'The Black Church and social ministry', p. 79.

36. *Black Enterprise*, pp. 55–6.

37. Lincoln and Mamiya, 'The Black Church and social ministry', pp. 81–2.

38. Carter *et al.*, *The Black Church Looks at the Bicentennial*, p. 125.

39. Lincoln and Mamiya, 'The Black Church and social ministry', p. 261.

40. Jeremiah Wright, Jr, personal interview, 19 November 1993. Dr Wright, Jr, a United Church of Christ pastor, is frustrated at not being allowed to participate. He fears that this is 'tribalism', since he cannot join because he is not affiliated with one of the historically black denominations.

41. William D. Watley, *Singing the Lord's Song in a Strange Land: The African American Churches and Ecumenism* (Geneva: WCC Publications; Grand Rapids, MI: Eerdmans; Trenton: Africa World Press, Inc., 1993), p. 38.

42. See Revd Robert A. Clemetson and Roger Coates, *Restoring Broken Places and Rebuilding Communities A Casebook On African-American Church Involvement in Community Economic Development* (African-American Church Project National Congress for Community Economic Development, 1993), p. iv.

43. Chester Arthur Kirkendoll, 'Ecumenism in the Black Church', in Franklin Little, *The Growth of Interreligious Dialogue 1939–1989 Enlarging the Circle* (Lewiston, NY: Edwin Mellen Press, 1989), p. 206.

44. Ibid., p. 207.

45. 'Black Muslims, Christians unite behind economic development', *Christianity Today* 15 (June 1984): 64.

46. James Cone and Cornel, two seminal figures in this field, are both orthodox Christians.

Chapter 9

'OPEN AND AFFIRMING' OF GROWTH? THE CHALLENGE OF LIBERAL LESBIAN, GAY AND BISEXUAL-SUPPORTIVE CONGREGATIONAL GROWTH

Scott Thumma

This decision [to become an 'open and affirming' congregation] was preceded by a series of small 'Getting to Know You' groups whose membership was half straight, half lesbian/gay and who got together to talk about their similarities and differences. By the time the decision was actually made, very few of the older members were upset, and many new people found that they really had a spiritual home. Indeed, the congregation has flourished. Worship attendance hovers between two and three times what it was before [the new pastor] came.

(Ammerman 1997, p. 175)

Imagine a congregation that is theologically liberal, open to diversity and pluralism, driven by issues of justice, fairness, tolerance and an acceptance of the unwanted and outcast of society. Now, picture this church having a strong and well-articulated understanding of what it believes and also adamantly proclaiming this vision for the wider church and the world. Further envision this same congregation having engaged in a two-year intensive study of the substance of that vision – a study process that involved the majority of members in learning, working through theological and personal differences and coming to a unanimous conclusion about the direction of the collective body. Finally, assume that this firmly held stance is markedly liberal, controversial and prophetic within the congregation's larger denominational context. Given the previous sociological and theological analysis in this volume, as well as the bulk of more general findings regarding congregational growth, wouldn't it be assumed that this church should be an ideal candidate for growth?

The characteristics in the above paragraph describe the vast majority of churches that have associated with the lesbian, gay and bisexual-supportive congregational movements that have arisen within mainline denominations since the 1980s. These more than 1,600 churches in seven mainline denominations[1] made the intentional liberal (both progressive theologically and radically inclusive and welcoming) commitment to be 'Open and Affirming' (O&A) and 'Welcoming'[2] of gay, lesbian and bisexuals (GLB[3]) in their congregations. To come to this collective conclusion, the membership engaged in a process of study and debate, sometimes spanning several years. Once arriving at this decision, it often became one that profoundly shaped the identity and programmatic reality of these churches.

If there were a group of liberal congregations that would be expected to grow, based on the predictive models of growth in national studies of mainline churches, it should be these O&A congregations. Such is the hypothesis to be examined in this chapter. The hypothesis is that a congregation which takes a firm liberal stance for embracing an open and affirming stance for LGB acceptance and rights within a conflicted denomination should be one that would experience membership growth at a greater rate than other churches in the denomination. This congregation would have a clear vision, a distinctive mission and a concrete well-defined purpose as a result of its efforts to become an O&A church. This process (which often involves one to two years of study, numerous focus groups, congregational discussions, etc.) would theoretically increase its ability to deal with conflict, solidify unity and unanimity around this vision, as well as get a large number of members involved and participating in the visioning task. The effort to shape the congregation's life and public perception, at least in part, around this clear theologically and politically liberal, progressive stance, as well as a liberally welcoming and tolerant identity ('liberal in the sense of generous, engaged, committed to justice, and willing to learn from others', as Markham states in his chapter in this volume), should contribute to increased growth of a liberal congregation's attendance and/or membership. After describing the place of homosexuality in American society and mainline Protestant denominations, and outlining the process by which a congregation becomes O&A, the assumption of growth will be tested by looking at available data from the Presbyterian Church, USA, and the Evangelical Lutheran Church of America.

Unlike the previous chapters of this collection that show the correlations between certain characteristics and the congregations which have the greatest growth, this chapter focuses on those congregations which hypothetically should be likely to experience growth due to having many of these characteristics associated with liberal congregational growth. In part this exercise is mostly speculative, since very little data exists that could clearly test the hypothesis regarding O&A congregations. The vast majority of studies which have been done of O&A designated churches focus on stories of individual congregations engaging in the O&A process, rather than looking at the entire O&A population as a whole or even comparing a large number of cases on the necessary variables over time. However, the chapter also addresses a critique of the assumption that numeric growth of a liberal congregation should be an indication of its health and vitality, especially around such an important civil rights and human rights issue such as openness and acceptance of gay, lesbian and bisexual persons into liberal communities of faith.

The cultural/political significance of homosexuality

Before turning to a discussion of the place of O&A congregations in the religious context, it is essential to highlight the wider national, political and social climate in which this discussion is set. Judging from the emotionally charged rhetoric of the 2004 US presidential election, support of a 'homosexual agenda' is equivalent to a liberalism that is anti-family, anti-Christian and anti-American. As one journalist and commentator of popular American culture put it:

> [The] Republican Party faithful are already rolling up their sleeves and passing the collection plate. In church social halls, they are raising money for voter registration; issue advertising; and 'Christian scorecards,' which rate candidates on their positions on key cultural issues such as abortion and homosexuality. By contrast, there is little activity at the other end of the spectrum. Left-wing religious efforts at political mobilization, where they exist at all, seem puny, aged and marginalized. After decades of riding popular social movements such as civil rights, the left splintered and now seems unable to regroup. Conversely, the GOP has attracted many religious voters by focusing on cultural and lifestyle issues such as gay marriage.[4]

Given the almost daily public condemnatory attacks upon gay and lesbian rights and the homosexual presence in society, one might think that the vast majority of Americans neither know any gay person nor accept the 'homosexual lifestyle'. Yet, in a 2003 survey of US adults by the Pew Forum on Religion and the Public Life, nearly two-thirds of Americans say they have a homosexual friend, colleague or family member. In this study, women are somewhat more likely than men to say they have a gay acquaintance or relative (67 per cent vs 53 per cent). Additionally, the study found that more highly educated people, compared to those with less education, say they know or are related to someone who is gay. Almost three-quarters of college graduates say they have a friend or relative who is gay, compared with roughly half of those with a high school education. Democrats and Republicans differ very little in their scores on this question; however, those who self-identified as liberals (71 per cent) were far more likely to have contact with homosexuals than were conservatives (54 per cent) (Pew Forum on Religion and the Public Life survey, 2003). Judging from this information, it is apparent that a large percentage of Americans not only know about homosexuality from their reading of books, news reports and articles but also from personal contact.

Likewise, survey information related to opinions and attitudes regarding homosexuality show some increase in the level of acceptance of lesbian and gay persons in society and an interest in the protection of their civil rights. In 2000 a Gallup survey found 50 per cent of US adults agreed that 'homosexuality should be considered an acceptable alternative lifestyle'. The acceptance of gays and lesbians in society is even more pronounced when one looks explicitly at the youngest generations. Young adults as a group consistently register more supportive positions on homosexuality and the civil rights of gays and lesbians (Pew Forum survey, 2003).

It is interesting, however, that some of the support for gays and lesbians seems to have disappeared within the past few years, perhaps due to the same-sex marriage debates or to the Republican rhetoric leading up to the 2004 election. In the 2003 Pew Forum survey, slightly less than 40 per cent of respondents indicated a favourable opinion of gays and lesbians, while half of the public expressed an unfavourable opinion of gay men (50 per cent unfavourable) and lesbians (48 per cent unfavourable). Nearly one in three (29 per cent) have a very unfavourable opinion of gay men, and 26 per cent have a very unfavourable opinion of lesbians. Paralleling these figures, 55 per cent of Americans indicated on the survey that they believe homosexual behaviour is a sin; on the other hand, only 33 per cent of respondents disagreed with this condemnation of homosexual behaviour.

When religion is factored into the equation the divide is even more apparent between religiously conservative and liberal persons. Likewise, the Pew Forum surveys found that persons with high religious commitment were much more likely to hold negative views of homosexuals. While overall 55 per cent of respondents agreed that engaging in homosexual behaviour was a sin, over three-quarters of those with a high level of religious commitment thought it was a sin. Opinions were divided among white mainline Protestants and Catholics in the study, with 43 per cent of mainline Protestants and 46 per cent of Catholics having a favourable opinion of gay men; this is roughly the same for lesbians. Among the mainline Protestants the extreme response categories tell a significant tale: only 7 per cent held 'very favourable' opinions of gay men, while 22 per cent of this group selected the 'very unfavourable' response option. White evangelicals are even more negative, with 69 per cent unfavourable (including 47 per cent very unfavourable) and only 20 per cent expressing a favourable position. African-American Protestants also hold generally unfavourable views (62 per cent unfavourable, 27 per cent favourable). Nearly nine out of ten highly committed white evangelicals (88 per cent) said homosexual behaviour is sinful, and 64 per cent of committed white Catholics agree. Nearly three-quarters of black Protestants (74 per cent) see homosexual conduct as sinful. Just 18 per cent of the self-labelled secular respondents feel this way, however.

Several denominations have paid considerable statistical attention to this issue among their membership. This information shows that the national patterns are duplicated and perhaps even amplified in the majority of main-line denominations. Within the Evangelical Lutheran Church in America (ELCA), less than a third of members (27 per cent) agreed that 'homosexu-ality should be considered an acceptable alternative lifestyle', while 44 per cent disagreed. An examination of the votes taken by the participants at the most recent national gathering of the United Methodist Church showed a majority of the general conference attendees on the conservative right rather than on the liberal left of this issue. In these conference votes all but 1 per cent of participants voted to prohibit funding of 'pro-homosexual advocacy' within the institution, over three-quarters voted against gay and lesbian marriage rights, and, continuing a 30-year trend in the denomination, nearly three-quarters voted to deny ordination to practising, non-celibate gay people. In the Presbyterian Church (USA), a study by the Presbyterian Research Office found that 40 per cent of pastors, but only 28 per cent of members agreed that 'Homosexuality should be considered an acceptable alternative lifestyle.' Paul Djupe and Christopher Gilbert, in *The Prophetic Pulpit*, comment: 'The

discussion of gay rights ... has become very contentious in many denominations besides the ELCA and the Episcopal Church, with the very liberal
stances of clergy and denomination clashing against general congregational
discomfort or even hostility...'[5] Clearly, given this data, even within the
mainline denominations there is considerable resistance to the acceptance of
gays and lesbians as full members of congregational communities.

O&A as a liberal marker

Without a doubt, denominational and congregational acceptance of an
affirmative position on homosexuality, ordination of practising gay and
lesbian clergy, and the willingness to perform same-sex unions are marks of
a liberal position, even in moderate and liberal mainline denominations. The
denominations who have affirmed this position, at present only the
Unitarian–Universalist Association, the United Church of Christ (as a
denomination but not all individual congregations), the Religious Society of
Friends (Quakers), the United Church of Canada, the Moravian Church,
Reconstructionist Judaism and the Central Conference of American Rabbis
(Reform Judaism), (with the Episcopal Church officially in agreement with
most of these positions),[6] are often understood as the most theologically and
socially liberal in American society. Additionally, congregations which take
an O&A stance, whether affiliated with supportive national bodies or in
denomin-ations which reject homosexuality as a viable position, are seen by
most researchers and observers as both theologically liberal and also liberal
in their acceptance of all persons, welcoming and tolerant of diversity to the
point of taking a concrete public stance on a controversial religious issue.

And this issue is controversial. Since the early 1970s discussions regarding
homosexuality in America's religious bodies have been hotly contested.[7]
During the 1970s most major denominations drafted some official statement
about homosexuality, usually affirming the civil rights of gay persons but
denying that homosexuality was acceptable within their religious tradition.
At the same time, support and activist groups were being formed within most
of these denominations. These activist groups, while not directly affiliated
with the national organization, were occupied with the twin tasks of
supporting their gay and lesbian members while also pushing for greater
acceptance of LGB persons and agenda at the national level.

It wasn't until the mid-1980s and into the 1990s, however, that the debate
over homosexuality in many of the mainline denominations became highly
divisive and took on a political tenor. This issue became one of the two or
three markers in conflicted denominations such as the United Methodist
Church and the Presbyterian Church, USA (PCUSA) that conservatives
used to draw theological distinctions. There have been countless national and
state resolutions proposed, debated and voted upon in the past few decades
around this issue.[8] Several congregations in many of the major mainline
denominations have been forced to leave their denominations either because

of ordaining practising homosexual clergy, or because they performed same-sex commitment ceremonies. Not only have individual clergy and congregations been excised, from denominations, but there is also talk within several groups of actual schism. The Presbyterian Research Office released a study in 2001 that found that 73 per cent of ministers expected a split in the denomination along liberal–conservative lines due to this issue. These clergy affirmed that it was 'very' or 'somewhat' likely that in the next 50 years 'a large group will split off ... to form a new denomination'. Interestingly, 60 per cent of the lay respondents thought that a split was unlikely.

The considerable negative reaction at the national level to the initial push for increased gay and lesbian inclusion effected a slight shift in strategy away from national activism and efforts of major reform of the mainline denominations. Between the late 1970s and mid-1980s alternative efforts to create smaller pockets of acceptance at the congregational level were begun in earnest. As early as 1978 a Presbyterian minister at West Park Church in New York City wrote a statement of conscience that called for congregations who disagreed with statements or actions their denominations made around homosexuality to announce publicly their opinions and openly welcome gay men and lesbians into their congregations. This led to the More Light programme in the Presbyterian Church, which became a model for the Reconciling Congregation programme, as well as other O&A efforts (Cadge 2004). The local church efforts that followed have allowed many congregations to define themselves in a positive inclusive way as niche congregations with clearly defined identities of acceptance and tolerance over and against their denominations. Additionally, this identity as an O&A church is often held up as a banner of liberalism and progressive theological conviction in contrast to other congregations in their traditions.

O&A equals growth?

The willingness of certain congregations within non-accepting denominations to proclaim their commitment to welcome all persons regardless of their sexual orientation is a progressive and positive step toward a diverse and tolerant religious community. Few congregational actions in the life of a church are made with such care and intentionality as the prescribed procedure to become O&A. Within most religious traditions, the process by which a church comes to the decision about proclaiming its O&A status is a reasoned one, involving months of study, open debate, congregational meetings and eventually an overt decision by the entire membership. While the actual process churches use to arrive at their O&A decision varies, the description below of one such Methodist congregation is representative of many. It is also similar to what is encouraged by most O&A denominational groups, and thus is quoted at length from Wendy Cadge's excellent chapter on such churches (Cadge 2004, pp. 39–40).

First United Methodist Church of Germantown (FUMCOG), located in the Germantown area of Philadelphia, went through a lengthy process of discussion and debate before declaring themselves a Reconciling Congregation in 1990. While there is no 'typical' Reconciling Congregation, the majority have stories more like FUMCOG's than Bethany's. The process by which FUMCOG became a Reconciling Congregation was centred on education, followed by a congregational vote. It was slow and difficult at times, though gay and straight members of the congregation both report benefiting from it. For the next two years, the task force led the congregation in study and discussion about homosexuality. The senior pastor preached about the issue early in the process, and the congregation's approach was faith-based, with a deep concern about what God and the Bible had to say about homosexuality. Members of the congregation studied biblical passages, read medical reports, thought about the arguments made by theologians and heard from several gay and lesbian people about their experiences. The task force also staffed a table on Sundays after worship, distributed literature at the weekly coffee hour, wrote articles for the church newsletter and held classes about homosexuality as part of the adult Sunday School curriculum. Informal discussions were also held in people's homes. Child psychologists and experts from Parents and Friends of Lesbians and Gays spoke at the church, and several gay and lesbian people who were involved in the congregation but had not come out as lesbian or gay in a very public way also spoke. These personal narratives were particularly important, one member told me, 'when people had to put a face to the concept [of homosexuality] things changed. "Wait, this is someone I have known all my life."' Throughout the process, the task force members worked to 'encourage an environment where people could freely express their feelings', although this was sometimes difficult because people's feelings and opinions were strong.

At the end of the two years the task force submitted a report to the administrative board, which then voted unanimously to allow the congregation at large to vote. A Sunday was designated, and when the vote was taken five people dissented and the rest were in favour of becoming a Reconciling Congregation. A Reconciling Statement was adopted, the central portion of which reads: 'In becoming a Reconciling Congregation, we affirm the full participation of gay men and lesbian women in our church community and in the Church at large, including recognition of the gifts and graces they may bring to the ordained ministry in local congregations.'

Few internal church decisions are made with such intentional effort or result in such a distinctive identification, with profound implications for the larger world. The process involves a large number of a congregation's members working together to investigate serious theological and ideological issues. These members learn, discuss and argue as they wrestle with core issues of the congregation's identity and beliefs. In this process they determine collectively who they are as a community of faith and the central values of their fellowship. The end result of this process may be a reaffirmation of practices and values they already hold, or it may be an intensification of latent ideals. In either case the process results in a unity of purpose and a collaboratively derived mission and identity.

The entire process in many religious traditions is cast as a congregational stance for justice, openness and inclusivity as defined in Scripture. This is, in fact, the primary way all O&A organizations describe the need for the process. However, a careful look at the websites of various O&A organizations, as well as the accounts of O&A congregations which have gone through the process, show a tendency to describe additional more tangible and numerical benefits.

The website of Lutherans Concerned (the ELCA LGBT support group) and its O&A programme called Reconciling in Christ, describe the 'affirmation of welcome' which results from the O&A study process as primarily supportive of inclusivity and redemption, but it also hints of evangelism and numerical growth.

[The Affirmation of Welcome] is simple, yet powerful in its witness ... Making the Affirmation promotes a publicly inclusive ministry and helps heal the pain of doubt ... Hearing the experiences of GLBT people and their families often creates greater understanding and insights ... Experience shows that any changes in your church or group will happen slowly, opening up individuals to healing and deep spiritual reconciliation. Perhaps parents with a gay son may finally be able to feel they are not guilty of failure in raising their child. Maybe a closeted lesbian member will bring her partner to church for the first time. A bisexual or transgendered person, hearing of your congregation, might return to church after an absence of many years. It's amazing how the Holy Spirit works when we are willing to be an instrument of God's grace.[9]

Likewise, the site of the Presbyterian O&A organization, More Light Presbyterians (MLP), identifies their mission in a theological and socially just manner:

Since the 1978 General Assembly, our church has urged us to study sexuality, to take the initiative to know and listen to gays and lesbians, to respect their civil rights, and to see them as brothers and sisters in Christ. More Light Presbyterians provides resources, models and experiences to help that personal growth.[10]

In the section of the site on how becoming a More Light congregation makes a difference, this justice-mission focus continues; however, the tone also turns overtly more evangelistic:

More Light Presbyterians offers its member churches support in the struggle for a more inclusive Church. Participating in the connectional More Light movement will help our church know that we do not stand alone, and give us the opportunity to learn from and support others on the journey... Affiliating with the More Light Churches Network is an evangelistic move that will invite folks (not just lesbian, gay, bisexual and transgender people) who share our goal of an inclusive Church to visit us. Being More Light puts us on widely circulated lists people refer to when they are looking for a new church. The experience at churches like Mt Auburn in Cincinnati is that the public declaration is also important as an outreach tool to the LGBT community...[11]

It is hard to read the above passage and not perceive the implicit promise – become O&A because it is a positive inclusive action that gives the congregation a unique identity, which will then attract new like-minded persons to the church. Congregations are encouraged to use the O&A moniker to promote the congregation. It is suggested that churches should use the O&A identifier on all material and publications. Additionally, the websites of the various national denominational Gay and Lesbian caucuses, advocacy groups and O&A programmes include prominent lists of member congregations, their addresses and web-links – which are then 'widely circulated', as suggested in the above quote.

Proof of the effectiveness of the O&A path as evangelistic strategy is offered in written testimonials of congregations of all denominations who have gone through the O&A process. Two different chapters in the Alban Institute's *Congregations Talking about Homosexuality* (Gaede 1998) make this point. In one case a UCC congregation in Kentucky rose from 15 attenders in 1992 to over 100 by 1998 (Guess 1998, pp. 64–5). In the description of another church it was noted that 'One year after becoming Open and Affirming, the congregation recorded its greatest annual growth in nearly two decades' (Baldwin 1998, p. 56).

In one of the few books on the subject of the homosexuality debate within congregations, Gary Comstock reports that the small amount of early research related to the pro-gay stance and congregational growth tended to show a positive correlation. He quotes Harlan Penn as saying that 'adopting gay-positive stances and programs has not resulted in loss of membership for local Presbyterian congregations. A small number of people usually leave for another congregation, but a larger number join because of the newly stated inclusiveness' (Comstock 1996, p. 10). Comstock further reports that the coordinator of the Reconciling Congregations programme observed in a 1994 interview 'in spite of the general declining memberships of mainline Protestant denominations, these local congregations [after voting to declare publicly their acceptance and support of gays and lesbians] typically increase in size after taking such a stand' (Comstock 1996, p. 10).

If these anecdotal observations were indeed representative of all the O&A congregations, it would provide substantial evidence of the hypothesis that adopting such a liberal stance does promote growth in liberal congregations. It is to a body of more representative, and less anecdotal, data that we now must turn to investigate this claim further.

The tale of two denominations: homosexuality and growth factors

To date, no research is known to exist that analyses the membership or attendance patterns over time of the entire body of congregations that have declared themselves to be O&A in major US denominations. In an effort to begin to fill this information gap, the research offices of two large mainline denominations were contacted and attendance/membership data was obtained for their O&A congregations. These denominations, the Presbyterian Church (USA) and the Evangelical Lutheran Church of America, were chosen primarily because their research offices keep excellent records on their churches and both were willing to share their material for this project. Additionally, these two denominations have rich national trend material as well as recent congregational vitality reports from the *Faith Communities Today* (FACT) project[12] and the *US Congregational Life Study* (USCLS)[12] readily accessible. Both groups even created reports that analysed the characteristics of their growing congregations based on FACT and USCLS data. Furthermore, the two denominations have wrestled with issues of homosexuality over the past 30 years and their research offices have specifically surveyed their clergy and member attitudes on the topic. Therefore, while the selection of these two groups was out of necessity, both are ideal research candidates for exploring this issue.

The Presbyterian Church (USA)

The Presbyterian Church (USA) (PCUSA) is a moderate mainline denomination with approximately 11,000 congregations and 2.4 million members. Presbyterians have existed in the USA since prior to the founding of the country. The group's history is chequered with splits and mergers, with the largest schism occurring in 1861 during the American Civil War. The Northern and Southern branches of Presbyterianism created by that split reunited in 1983 to form the present Presbyterian Church (USA), currently the largest, but not the only, Presbyterian group in the USA. This Protestant Christian denomination holds a Reformed theology based on the thought of John Calvin and has a form of government that stresses representational leadership of both ministers and church members. Over the years, the denomination's beliefs have been codified into faith statements contained in the Book of Confessions.

The Book of Confessions contains numerous statements issued since the mid-1970s regarding homosexuality. This group's general stance is best summarized in one of the statements, 'On the basis of our understanding ... the practice of homosexuality is sin.' There are numerous variations and applications of this perspective related to civil rights, marriage ceremonies and clergy ordination which can be found on the PCUSA website.[14]

Currently there are dozens of cases pending in church courts in which clergy have been charged with violating the church's rules regarding homosexuality. Likewise, there is considerable discussion among groups of clergy on both sides of the issue contemplating schism. As a result of this tenuous situation, a 20-member task force on 'peace, unity and purity' was created to look into the homosexual issue, among others, in the light of the theological assumptions and core theological convictions of the church. This task force is to report to the 2006 national legislative assembly.[15]

All the members of the denomination, however, do not share the denomination's official position. Data from the Presbyterian Panel research[16] shows that four out of ten Presbyterian clergy surveyed agreed that 'homosexuality should be considered an acceptable alternative lifestyle'. Likewise, 28 per cent of members and 28 per cent of elders held this position as well. While a large majority within the denomination certainly affirmed the denominational policy, it is equally clear that a solid minority is of a different mind.

PCUSA has suffered a fate similar to many other mainline protestant religious groups over the past four decades in terms of denominational change. In fact, it shows the second largest percentage of decline of all mainline Protestant religious groups, second only to the Christian Church,

Disciples of Christ. Since 1965, when the denominational membership reached its peak at 4.25 million, PCUSA membership has plummeted, losing a total of 43.46 percent of members during that time. In the last decade the denomination declined by nearly 350,000 members to their current membership of 4.2 million.

Despite this general decline, a number of congregations show considerable increase. Between 1995 and 2000, according to the Presbyterian research office, '35 percent of congregations grew in membership, including 18 percent that grew by 10 percent or more.'[17] The research office's most recent data shows that 2,465 churches (21.7 per cent of all congregations) grew by 5 per cent or more in their membership from 1999 to 2003.[18] In 2001 Deborah Bruce and Cynthia Woolever identified 400 PCUSA congregations with at least 42 per cent growth in the previous five years.[19] From their research of 93 of these rapidly growing churches they found that these congregations 'provide a sense of community, educate people about the faith, share their faith with others, serve others in their congregations and communities, and convey "the sense that life has meaning"'. When all factors were controlled for, Deborah Bruce noted in an article in *Presbyterians Today* that only three congregational strengths actually turned out to be predictors of numerical growth. Those were (1) caring for children and youth, (2) welcoming new people and (3) getting people to participate in the congregation.[20]

The O&A organization within PCUSA is known by the name More Light Presbyterians (MLP). MLPs are 'people seeking the full participation of lesbian, gay, bisexual and transgender people of faith in the life, ministry and witness of the Presbyterian Church'.[21] The organization began not long after the denomination passed the resolution in 1978 declaring homosexuality to be a sin. It has grown to 519 or more member churches and many other local chapters and liaisons. The organization has a rich history of interaction with the denomination marked by considerable advocacy and activism in support of LGBT Presbyterians.[22]

The Presbyterian research office provided annual membership figures from 1990 to 2003 for 519 MLP congregations. Of these congregations that declared their O&A status, 17.4 per cent grew by more than 5 per cent between 1990 and 2003. During this same period 74.2 per cent of these congregations declined by more than 5 per cent of their membership. When compared to the growth and decline rates in the entire denomination it is apparent that the O&A churches were slightly less vital in terms of membership growth than the entire body of Presbyterian churches.

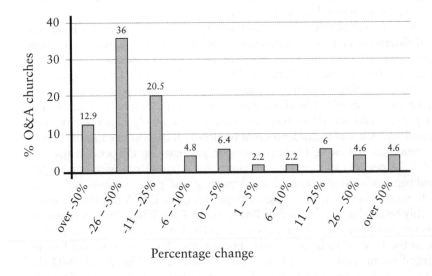

Percentage change

Figure 9.1: MLP membership change, 1990–2003

The Evangelical Lutheran Church in America

Churches within the Evangelical Lutheran Church in America (ELCA) trace their denominational origin to the Protestant Reformation in the sixteenth century and specifically to the German reformer, Martin Luther. German and Dutch Lutherans were among some of the earliest settlers in America. Much of the history of Lutheranism in the USA is marked both by ethnic influx through immigration and by mergers of smaller Lutheran church bodies into ever larger groupings. In 1988 the ELCA came into being as a result of the union of three church bodies: the American Lutheran Church, the Association of Evangelical Lutheran Churches and the Lutheran Church in America. The denomination is presently one of the five largest religious groups in the country, with a 2003 membership of 4,984,925 people and 10,657 churches.

The denomination has debated the issue of homosexuality in its national gatherings and policies for many decades. For most of this time the denomination explicitly encouraged the protection of the civil rights of gays and lesbians. For instance, at the 1991 national gathering participants agreed to affirm that gay and lesbian people, as individuals created by God, should be involved fully in Lutheran congregational life. Not long after this, however, the church's bishops voted in 1993 not to approve of ceremonies in affirmation of same-sex relationships. In 1999 church policies were further clarified to state that gay and lesbian persons actively expressing their sexuality could not be ordained or remain as clergy. An official church-wide study reporting in 2004,[23] recommended that there should be no change in church policy but did suggest that the denomination allow differences of opinion to coexist and that it should not punish those in violation of church policy.

There is no doubt that ELCA members are highly divided on the issue and real differences do exist. The denomination's research office found in a recent study that 27 per cent of members agree that 'homosexuality should be considered an acceptable alternative lifestyle', while 44 per cent disagree with the statement. Regarding the ordination of gay or lesbian pastors, 41 per cent reported they shouldn't be allowed under any circumstance and an additional 10 per cent said only if they were not sexually active. Only 23 per cent of those questioned felt that the ordination of homosexuals was acceptable under any circumstance. Likewise, 19 per cent support gay marriage (59 per cent against), while 28 per cent support gays in committed relationships with same rights and benefits as couples in traditional marriage (48 per cent against).[24]

In terms of denominational growth patterns, the ELCA has fared considerably better than most mainline Protestant groups. While the denomination also declined in terms of membership since 1965, its percentage of decline has been the least of eight major mainline groups. The denomination had its largest membership in 1965, when it reached 5,684,298. As of 2003 the ELCA listed a total of 4,984,925. This represents a decline of nearly 700,000 or a loss of 12.3 per cent of their 1965 membership.

Yet, whether a national denomination grows or declines generally, individual churches have their own patterns of membership change. It is apparent that within the ELCA many congregations are growing even as the overall denomination suffers decline. There are 47 ELCA congregations with over a thousand average attendees in weekly worship. The 1999 Faith Communities Today study of 832 Lutheran churches showed 22.7 per cent of these grew by more than 10 per cent over the previous five years, while another 16.4 per cent grew between 5 and 10 per cent.[25] Another research office report on attendance change in all ELCA churches between 1994 and 2003 identified 24 per cent of churches as growing by more than 5 per cent while, 46 per cent had declined by more than 5 per cent.[26]

Analysis of the 1999 Faith Communities Today study of ELCA churches[27] and an ECLA study in 2001 of 134 growing churches[28] led denominational researcher Kenn Inskeep to conclude that growing ELCA congregations possessed two key characteristics. These were (1) whether a church possessed a clear sense of mission and purpose and (2) if a congregation was able to welcome innovation and change. Inskeep stated that other factors were important but always in the context of these two key characteristics.

The sense that the congregation is vital and spiritually alive, that members are excited about the future of their congregation, the ease with which new members are incorporated into the congregation, and the ability of the congregation to deal openly with conflict are also important factors, but only within the context of the congregation having a clear sense of mission and purpose and an openness to innovation and change.

Within this changing context the extradenominational response to the issue of homosexuality in the denomination has been quite consistent. The Lutheran

LGBT advocacy group Lutherans Concerned/North America began in 1974 as an independent membership organization to work for full inclusion in the denomination. In 1984 Lutherans Concerned started the Reconciling in Christ (RIC) programme to recognize Lutheran congregations that welcome lesbian and gay believers. While there are presently approximately 240 churches in the RIC programme, there are a total of over 300 congregations, synods and other Lutheran organizations. The Reconciling in Christ programme 'seeks to make clearer the policy of churches where all people are welcome as full members, regardless of their sexual orientation, their gender identity or that of their children, siblings or friends'.[29] In 2002 the ELCA Division for Outreach passed a resolution which established a formal relationship between the group and the Evangelical Lutheran Church in America. However, the Lutherans Concerned organization was dismayed by the recent Lutheran task force report and recommendations.

Attendance figures from 1987 to 2003 for 241 Reconciling in Christ congregations were provided by the ELCA research office. During this period 26.9 per cent of these O&A congregations grew by more than 5 per cent. At the same time, 64.4 per cent of the RIC congregations declined by more than 5 per cent in their attendance figures. If these growth and decline rates are compared to the entire denomination, it seems clear that the growth and decline patterns of these O&A Lutheran congregations closely parallel the attendance growth-rates of the entire body of Evangelical Lutheran Churches in America, at least those from the more recent 2003 study showing 24 per cent with attendance gains of more than 5 per cent.

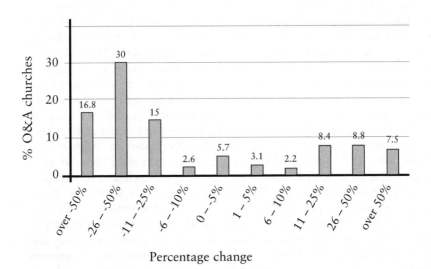

Figure 9.2: RIC attendance change, 1987–2003

Conclusions and implications

The growth data from the Presbyterian Church and the Evangelical Lutheran Church O&A congregations is quite conclusive. Some of these O&A churches are growing and many others are in decline in terms of participants. The growth patterns of these O&A congregations are either slightly less robust than, or roughly parallel to, the corresponding denominational trends. Judging from these findings, it is apparent that proclaiming an inclusive vision and adopting an Open and Affirming stance are insufficient liberal activities within the life of a church to guarantee congregational growth greater than that of the denomination as a whole. For these approximately 750 O&A churches espousing a firm liberal stance on a contested issue within a denomination, while creating a clear vision and sense of purpose related to that issue, and generating unity around that vision through study and discussion as an entire congregation, does not seem to increase the chance that a congregation's attendance or membership will grow. However, neither does this decision greatly hinder the growth of this examined group of churches. Voting to become an O&A congregation isn't the death-knell that certain contentious members often claim it to be. The O&A congregations examined declined at approximately the same rate as the total number of churches in a denomination.

Neither does the information presented deny or disprove the validity of the narrative cases. It should not be surprising that stories tell of considerable growth following the act of taking an O&A stance. After all, over a tenth of the congregations examined grew by more than 50 per cent. However, it is important to present these cases, as the weight-loss commercials do, with the disclaimer, 'these results may not be typical'.

Granted, this brief study is too tentative and speculative to argue the case conclusively. Much more study on the subject is required and hopefully will be undertaken. There are many variables left untested which might influence the growth or decline of attendance in these congregations. They may have inadequately or superficially followed the O&A recommended procedures. The issue may be too contentious in their community or there may be too many liberal-thinking congregations in the area for the option of another one to make a difference. Although a congregation makes a decision, it does not necessarily follow that they will likewise alter their organizational patterns and personal practices to embody fully the O&A position. Additionally, Ammerman (1997, pp. 130–33) has noted in her writing on 'niche' congregations that those with liberal views regarding the inclusion of gays and lesbians are often very small. They exist in urban, cosmopolitan cultural settings where the population has a higher degree of education and income. None of these characteristics is highly conducive to church attendance. Ammerman also points out the difficulty of maintaining a balance of gay and straight attendees, even though that balance is often what attracts persons from both groups. When the scale shifts, one or the other group may depart leaving the congregation as a different entity. Finally, within recent years many new avenues for LGBT spiritual expression have arisen apart from traditional denominational options (Thumma and Gray, 2004). Therefore, much more research needs to be undertaken before a conclusive answer to this issue can be proposed with confidence.

Nevertheless, these preliminary conclusions of no significant correlation between liberal church growth and an O&A stance should not hinder congregations from adopting an O&A position or exploring the process. However, this decision should be seen as a commitment to a liberal theological identity rather than a strategy of growth. It is also worth keeping in mind that though these congregations may not be experiencing numerical growth they may well have grown in vitality and spiritual depth due to the process of education and self-reflection over several years of intense study.

Therefore, if 'liberal growth' implies not just numerical growth but whether or not the congregation has a clearer sense of mission, is spiritually more vital and alive and increasingly helps members deepen their relationship with God, then O&A congregations collectively may well be 'growing' at a rapid rate. As the gay pastor of a UCC congregation in Kentucky affirmed, 'The public nature of our [O&A] study empowered us to state clearly among ourselves and for others the kind of church we intend to be and to choose between silence and justice. As in all such defining moments when bold professions are made, we found the beautiful depth of a gospel faith courageously witnessed and rightly lived' (Guess 1998, p. 72).

At this moment, around this issue, liberal congregations have an excellent opportunity for growth – if not in numbers at least in spirit and public presence. It is an ideal time for churches with a liberal spiritual under-standing of God's grace and an inclusive understanding of community boldly to profess this theology. Who but the liberal congregations within the Protestant main-line denominations will profess the theological position of liberal inclusiveness and tolerance? What other churches will open their doors to genuine public debate and offer a positive stance for inclusion and welcome of all God's people? Where else in our present social context could such a debate take place? The O&A liberal congregations in this study, whether growing numerically or not, became public spaces for such conver-sations (between gay and straight, between pro and con) to take place. More importantly, they covenanted together to be places of inclusion and interaction. They were willing, in contentious times, to take a stand so that LGBT persons are invited in to experience and participate in the love and grace of God and in the love and affirmation of a supportive Christian community. They are also open, as heterosexual persons, to learn about, get to know and engage in reconciliation and personal transformation across sexual difference and experience the multiplicity of God's creation. If not in liberal congregations, then where else will these conversations, these transformations, take place?

Glenn attended Bethany both because it was a United Methodist Church and because it was close to his home. He had visited Bethany on the two previous Easter Sundays, but it was not until his visit on Christmas Eve 1995 that he learned about the movement to welcome gay, lesbian, bisexual and transgendered people into individual congregations and the United Methodist denomination more generally. Glenn became involved in Bethany over the next few months, he told me, because he needed 'that personal self-love' and because he believed 'the resistance to gay and lesbian civil rights, the bedrock resistance to it, is in religion and Christianity' making the church 'central to the next stage of gay and lesbian civil rights'. Glenn believes in a God 'who cares very much about our lives and will be in our lives if we just ask', and in scripture that does not condemn gays and lesbians at base level: 'that notion [of scriptural condemnation] needs to be dispelled and can be dispelled if the people in power in the churches take a different position' (Cadge 2004, p. 38).

[The new pastor] brought new vitality and new life and new growth, but tied into all that is this change [to become O&A]… I think the congregation is coming to terms with it. It doesn't mean that we're becoming a gay church. It means that we are – as our tradition calls for – being active people in society, and this [the presence of gay and lesbian persons] is a societal issue right now. (Ammerman 1997, p. 176)

Notes

1.   By 'mainline Protestant' I am referring to eight Protestant denominations in the USA: the United Methodist Church, the Evangelical Lutheran Church in America, the Presbyterian Church (USA), the United Church of Christ, the Episcopal Church, the Christian Church, Disciples of Christ, the Reformed Church of America and the American Baptist Church. Of these, only the Episcopal Church does not have a parallel O&A or Welcoming Congregations effort, and so will not be discussed in this context. Only the United Church of Christ has a formal and official denominational tie to its ONA group.

2.   The various mainline denominational traditions have different names for their gay and lesbian-supportive congregations, including Open and Affirming/O&A (Disciples), O&A/ONA (United Church of Christ), Reconciling Congregations (United Methodist Church) and More Light (Presbyterian Church), Welcoming (American Baptist Church), and Reconciling in Christ (Evangelical Lutheran Church in America). For this chapter I will use the open and affirming, or O&A, designation as a generic label for all the efforts, unless talking specifically about one of the individual organizations.

3.   The majority of sample denominational O&A statements seldom talk about transgender persons, neither do most of the congregational statements I have read include reference to transgender, questioning or intersex persons in their O&A statements. However, this does not mean that they exclude them.

4.   Mark I. Pinsky, *Orlando Sentinel* www.philly.com/mld/inquirer/news/editorial/7735182.htm?lc

5.   Paul Djupe and Christopher Gilbert, *The Prophetic Pulpit: Clergy, Churches and Communities in American Politics* (Lanham, MD: Rowman & Littlefield 2003). (See Adair Lummis, Ch. 11 this volume.)

6.   See the works of Louie Crews for a detailed look at LGBT Episcopal Church issues http://andromeda.rutgers.edu/~lcrew/rel.html. The Ontario Consultants on Religious Tolerance website at www.religioustolerance.org/homosexu.htm has a wonderful and comprehensive analysis of the positions of all major American denominations and religious bodies on this position.

7.   Several notable religious activities in support of gay and lesbian religious freedom took place prior to the gay liberation movement, which began officially in 1969. See Comstock (1996, pp. 4–8) and D'Emilio (1983) for more detail and references to these early supportive efforts, as well as accounts of more recent decades of religious activities.

8. The denominational debate has been well researched and discussed in the United Methodist Church by James Wood. (See Wood 2000 and Wood and Bloch 1995.)

9. http://www.lcna.org/ric.shtm

10. http://www.mlp.org/index.php?topic=aboutUs

11. http://mlp.org/staticpages/resources/mldiff.html

12. http://fact.hartsem.edu

13. http://uscongregations.org

14. http://www.pcusa.org/101/101-homosexual.htm

15. http://www.pcusa.org/peaceunitypurity/

16. http://www.pcusa.org/research/panel/index.htm

17. http://www.pcusa.org/today/department/go-figure/past/gf-0702.htm

18. Email communication, 17 March 2005.

19. http://www.uscongregations.org/Growing_Presbyterian_Churches.pdf

20. http://www.pcusa.org/today/department/go-figure/past/2004/gf-1004.htm

21. http://www.mlp.org/

22. http://www.mlp.org/resources/history.html#mlcn

23. This report is available on the ELCA website at http://www.elca.org/faithfuljourney/. The 1993 statement by the Conference of Bishops on blessing of homosexual relationships is at http://www.elca.org/sr/bishopsblessings.html.

24. http://www.elca.org/re/uscongs/homosexuality.pdf

25. http://www.elca.org/re/reports/ccspwrsp1.pdf

26. http://www.elca.org/re/synoddata/avgatts.html

27. http://www.elca.org/re/reports/ccspwrsp1.pdf

28. http://www.elca.org/re/USCongs/ProfileFast.pdf

29. http://www.lcna.org/ric.shtm

References

Ammerman, Nancy T., 1997 *Congregations and Community* (New Brunswick, NJ: Rutgers University Press).

Baldwin, Frank, 1998 'First Congregational Church of Fresno', in Gaede 1998, pp. 49–56.

Burgess, John, 1999 'Framing the homosexual debate theologically: lessons from the Presbyterian Church, USA', *Review of Religious Research* 41:262–74.

Cadge, Wendy, 2002 'Vital conflicts: the mainline denominations debate homosexuality', in Robert Wuthnow and John H. Evans (eds), *The Quiet Hand of God: Faith-Based Activism and the Public Role of Mainline Protestantism* (Berkeley, CA: University of California Press), pp. 265–86.

———, 2004. 'Reconciling Congregations Bridging Gay and Straight Communities', in Thumma and Gray (2004), pp. 31–46.

D'Emilio, John, 1983 *Sexual Politics, Sexual Communities: The Making of a Homosexual Minority in the United States 1940–1970* (Chicago, IL: University of Chicago Press).

Gaede, Beth Ann (ed.), 1998 *Congregations Talking about Homosexuality* (Alban Institute).

Guess, J. Bennett, 'Zion United Church of Christ', in Gaede 1998, pp. 64–72.

Hartman, Keith, 1996 *Congregations in Conflict: The Battle Over Homosexuality* (New Brunswick, NJ: Rutgers University Press).

Olsen, Laura and Cadge, Wendy, 2002 'Talking about homosexuality: the views of mainline Protestant clergy', *Journal for the Scientific Study of Religion* 41.1:153–67.

Pew Forum Survey, 2003 Pew Forum on Religion and the Public Life.

Thumma, Scott and Gray, Edward, (eds) 2004 *Gay Religion* (Walnut Creek, CA: AltaMira Press).

Wood, James, 2000 *Where the Spirit Leads: The Evolving Views of United Methodists on Homosexuality* (Nashville, TN: Abingdon Press).

Wood, James and Bloch, Jon, 1995 'The Role of Church Assemblies: The Case of the United Methodist General Conference's Debate on Homosexuality', *Sociology of Religion* 56.2: 121–36.

Chapter 10

OLDLINE PROTESTANTISM: POCKETS OF VITALITY WITHIN A CONTINUING STREAM OF DECLINE

David A. Roozen

Introduction

Forty years ago a group of researchers gathered to plan the first set of empirical studies of mainline Protestant membership growth and decline since Dean Kelley's influential, *Why Conservative Churches are Growing*[1] and the more modest launch of the Fuller Seminary-centred, Church Growth Movement.[2] The eventual publication of the research, *Understanding Church Growth and Decline*,[3] pinpointed the mainline's membership dip into the red as occurring in 1965 and touted two major findings of special note here. First, that the mainline declines were primarily due to social demographic changes, the two most prominent being the dramatic value changes being carried into young adulthood by the baby-boom generation and population shifts out of geographic areas of traditional mainline strength. Second, that a combination of the social changes and membership declines were intimately related to a crisis of identity within the mainline. One topic not addressed in the research was the likely future direction of the declines; and one nuance not articulated was the possibility that the reason the external factors of social change appeared as the drivers of decline was the mainline's inability to adapt its internal style, programme and message to the changing world around it. The purpose of this article is to address these two issues. What has been the trend in formerly mainline, now oldline Protestant membership and vitality since the 1970s? What do the data show us now about the dynamics of oldline growth and vitality, especially about the internal, adaptive capacity of those organizations in which Protestants hold membership: namely, congregations.

One of the more helpful consequences of all the attention given in the late 1970s to the original research and commentary on the oldline membership declines was a questioning of whether or not membership trends were an appropriate gauge of the/a church's faithfulness. Although the debates were often clouded in abstractions and subtlety overlaid with the typical, academic deconstructive strategy of caricaturing one's opponent, two issues dominated. One was whether evangelism (pro-membership growth) or social justice (highlighting the costliness of discipleship) was the primary purpose of the church. A second was whether or not God would provide the blessing of growth to faithful congregations. The pro-growth position within the latter was that while membership growth per se was not the primary purpose of the church, God surely intended that faithful congregations should grow. Two generations (and two generations of continual membership declines) later the debates continue with two major differences. One is that they seem less intense and less direct, perhaps because after 40 years of losses few oldliners are against recruitment and/or development efforts that can be (correctly or incorrectly) passed off as evangelism, and social justice has lost its edge as denominational identities have become more diffuse and contested. Perhaps more importantly, the last decade or so has witnessed an increasing emphasis on multidimensional notions of congregational vitality, with an especially strong surge of interest and prominence being given to 'spiritual vitality'.

Hopefully other chapters in this book will explore the variety of possible definitions of vitality, including my own personal preference for the affinity between multidimensional approaches and postmodernity. The latter notwithstanding, the major thrust of my analysis here will focus on membership growth for three reasons. Most importantly and comforting, all empirical studies including multidimensional measures of congregational vitality of which I am aware show that membership growth is significantly related to other possible indicators of vitality. That is, congregations that show high levels of mission outreach, spiritual vitality, financial health, lay involvement, etc. also tend to experience numerical growth. More pragmatically, membership growth is the most concrete and statically robust measure of vitality available in the largest national sample survey of congregations (over seven times larger than its nearest rival) available for multivariate analysis. Finally, there is a much more substantial body of social scientifically informed literature on membership growth than for any other of the currently debated measures of congregational vitality.

Choosing a measure of congregational vitality is a debatable enough decision in itself, but it begs an equally vexing and even more foundational question. When dealing with theological, spiritual or religious matters, why bother with measurement and human statistics at all? It is a question that has haunted religious research since its outset;[4] and as Smilie has reminded church-growth researchers, Karl Barth presented as far back as 1948 a particularly clear and passionate argument against confusing membership trends with questions of faithfulness. It is beyond this essay to argue the case for the value of using human agency in general, or a social scientifically informed rationality in particular, as a vehicle for God's purposes.[5] Therefore let it suffice to note just two major dimensions of such an argument. One would build on the simple fact that the dismissal of human agency occupies an extremely minimal space in both the long history and contemporary currency of Protestant theology, especially that of Liberal Protestant theology. A second, more defensively deconstructionist tactic, and one more specifically in regard to the statistical measurement of changes in growth, would use Smilie's rejoinder to Barth as a point of departure: 'Some observers, unable to relieve themselves of "all quantitative thinking", might observe that Barthians in Europe have succeeded in lowering membership and participation without necessarily lifting the quality of life of the body of Christ.'[6]

So on to our empirical case! With the exception of one brief, introductory dip into denominational membership figures reported by the *Yearbook of American and Canadian Churches,* the data for my analysis come from the 2000 *Faith Communities Today (FACT)* national, interfaith survey of 14,301 congregations in the USA.[7] *FACT 2000* was a cooperative effort among agencies and organizations representing 41 denominations and faith groups – from Southern Baptist to Bahai, Methodist to Muslim to Mormon, Assemblies of God to Unitarian Universalist, Orthodox, Roman Catholic, Jew and all the usual oldline Protestant players. The groups worked together to develop a common, key informant questionnaire. Groups then adapted wordings to their respective traditions and conducted their own surveys, typically mailed during 2000 to a stratified random sample of a group's congregations. Return rates averaged over 50 per cent with independent congregations proving their independence with the lowest rate of return and the Church of Jesus Christ of Latter-day Saints demonstrating one of the virtues of hierarchy with a 98 per cent return rate. Data from the total of 14,301 returns from the various group samples were sent to the Hartford Seminary Institute for Religion Research for aggregation. Zip-code-level census data was added to each congregational case and the cases in the aggregated dataset weighted to provide proportionate representation of each denomination and faith group.

Hope or reality

For those who value oldline Protestantism, it is undoubtedly refreshing to hear all the hints and rumours of vitality that have been swirling around for the last decade or so. Some proponents, including contributors to this volume, have even suggested that oldline Protestantism is currently the most vital stream of Christianity. With all due respect for the strength of the latter's imagination and depth of hope, and while there certainly are identifiable pockets and sources of oldline vitality, any claim to the oldline's dominance of the religious vitality market, at least in the USA, unfortunately flies in the face of empirical reality. In their editing of the 1993 follow-up to *Understanding Church Growth and Decline,* Roozen and Hadaway charted the membership trends for every denomination with consistently reliable data for 1950 through to 1990 in the *Yearbook of American and Canadian Churches.*[8] Among others, this included eight denominations that would be considered oldline Protestant and fifteen that would be considered conservative Protestant. Figures 10.1 and 10.2 update the Roozen and Hadaway figures to 2000.[9]

Figure 10.1 makes one point clear and suggests another of note. What is clear is that the mainline-now-oldline membership decline that began in the mid-1960s continues to the present, and that this contrasts sharply with continual conservative growth. What is suggested, although not decisively shown, is that conservative Protestants now outnumber mainline Protestants.

Figure 10.2 presents the same data, except it charts the rate of growth/decline rather than the actual number of members. For those with a desire for an

Why Liberal Churches are Growing

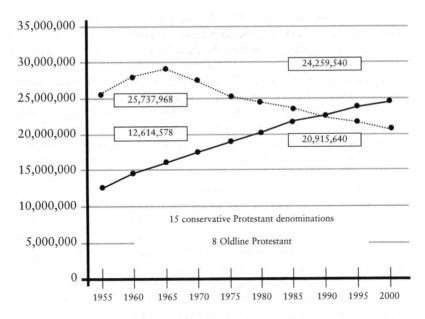

Figure 10.1: Oldline and conservative Protestant trends in membership: 1955–2000

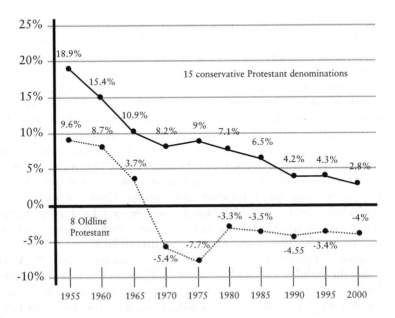

Figure 10.2: Percentage change in membership over previous five years

	Oldline Protestant	Conservative Protestant

Considerably stronger*	Ecumenical worship
	Interfaith worship
	Ecumenical social ministry
	Interfaith social ministry
		Clear sense of mission and
		  purpose
		Deepen members'
		  relationship with God
		Expressing denomination
		  heritage
		Moral beacon in the
		  community
		Excitement about future
		Emphasis on:
		  personal spiritual
		    practices
		  family devotions
		  keeping the Sabbath
		membership growth

Moderately stronger**	Emphasis on social justice
	Number of social
	  outreach programmes
	Physical condition
	  of buildings
		Inspirational worship
		Sense of spiritual vitality
		Close-knit family feeling
		Trying to increase
		  racial/ethnic diversity
		Welcomes innovation and
		  change
		Dealing openly with conflict
		Assimilating new members
		Number of member-oriented
		  programmes
		Financial health

No meaningful difference***	Well organized Amount of serious conflict	

Key
* More than a 10 per cent difference in congregations falling into the positive extreme response category
** A 2–10 per cent difference in congregations falling into the positive extreme response category
*** Less than 2 per cent difference

Figure 10.3: Comparative strength of oldline and conservative Protestant congregations

Source: Based on the *Faith Communities Today 2000* national survey of 14,301 congregations: fact.hartsem.edu

oldline spin, it presents a somewhat more optimistic assessment than Figure 10.1. It shows, for example, that the oldline rate of decline is currently only about half of what it was at its worst in the mid-1970s. It also shows that during this very same time that the oldline decline was easing, conservative growth progressively slowed, so that the conservative advantage in 2000 was only about a third of what it was in the mid-1970s. Unfortunately for the vitality of the oldline cause, the closing of this gap over the last twenty years has come solely from the decreasing strength of conservative Protestant denominations, rather than from any overall gain in strength in the oldline. Indeed, it has to be noted that the rate of numerical membership decline within oldline Protestantism has held steady at just under 1 per cent a year for the past two decades.

One could object that, given conservative Protestantism's strong theological and practical investment in evangelism, the use of membership growth as one's sole measure of vitality in a comparison with oldline Protestantism stacks the deck in favour of the conservative. Figure 10.3 suggests that such an objection is partially correct. It uses data from *FACT 2000* to compare oldline and conservative on a rather broad array of conceivable measures of vitality.[10] Most importantly for oldline advocates, it does show that for measures of ecumenical and interfaith involvement, and for social outreach and social justice, and for the physical condition of a congregation's property, the oldline outscores its conservative counterparts. Nevertheless, the figure also shows that on balance, indeed by a margin of more than 2 to 1, conservative Protestantism leads the way in a much more extensive and wider set of measures than does oldline Protestantism, including for example, spiritual vitality, inspirational worship, purposefulness, welcoming change, extent of congregational programming and financial health. Additionally, if one were to add in the *FACT 2000* data for congregations in the historically black denominations, oldline Protestantism loses its lead in social outreach and social justice. Then if we add in the *FACT 2000* Jewish congregations, oldline Protestantism loses its lead in the area of ecumenical/interfaith relations. The net result: oldline Protestantism only leads the Judaeo-Christian tradition in the USA in the physical condition of its buildings.

Fortunately, the rumours of vitality in oldline Protestantism are not totally unfounded and pockets of strength are clearly evident.[11] One finds in *FACT 2000*, for example, that 45 per cent of oldline Protestant congregations report membership growth between 1995 and the year of the survey. Among other things, this means we have ample numbers of such congregations in the *FACT 2000* dataset for an in-depth exploration of the sources of growth: the task to which we now turn.

Oldline sources of adaptive vitality and growth: the theory

Religion and the social sciences merged just before the turn of the twentieth century in the USA as the Social Gospel movement emerged in response to waves of economically marginalized immigration that washed across established urban neighbourhoods in costal northeastern cities. By the time this initial flourishing of religious research had differentiated itself and reached its zenith with the publication of Douglass and de Brunner's *The Protestant Church as a Social Institution* in 1935, it had established what would be the common wisdom of church-growth studies for the next 50 years: As goes the neighbourhood, so goes the church.[12] Kelley's presumption that strictness was the reason why conservative churches were growing and liberal churches declining was the only major, social scientifically argued alternative to the demographic or contextual captivity of church-growth studies through the 1980s.[13] Next to strictness the only other internally focused explanation for oldline declines that gained significant currency at the time was the divisive support for social justice voiced by many oldline pastors and denominational leaders. Neither found significant empirical support in *Understanding Church Growth and Decline*, the latter highlighting the primacy of neighbourhood population changes as the leading predictor of congregational growth.[14] The affinity of demographic change explanations for mainline decline with the homogeneity principle of the Fuller Church Growth Movement sweeping conservative Protestantism at the time, kept church eyes focused outward.[15]

The rumour or hope that congregations were not totally captive to their context received new energy in the late 1980s as a group of economists interjected supply-side, rational choice arguments into the sociology of religion. The foundational presupposition of this approach is that the more individuals sacrifice on behalf of their religion, the more benefits they receive, hence the applicability of rational choice models. One implication of this for present purposes is that churches are in control of how much sacrifice they demand of members, hence the 'supply'-side emphasis.[16]

This may seem like Kelley's 'strictness' thesis being recast in economic terms, which indeed it is; and that is exactly how the new socioreligious economists presented it. But instead of Kelley's appeal to the sociology of knowledge and plausibility structures, the new socioreligious economists drew on the extensive economic literature on *free riders*. Truly rational actors will not pay for something when they can get it for nothing. Free-riding churchgoers take worship and other religious goods without further investment of time or talents. Strict religion, accordingly, strengthens a church for two reasons. Sacrifice increases the individual commitment of those who stay and drives away those unwilling to contribute to congregational life.

Applying this argument on a more societal scale, the new socioreligious economists provided a wonderfully parsimonious answer to one of the more perplexing problems of classical sociology of religion. Why has not religion withered away in arguably the most secularized society in the developed world, namely the USA? There are two main reasons. First, the separation of Church and state allows for a free-market religious economy. Second, because of this, and while it is true that established religions tend to get less strict over time, new religious groups appear which present new and contextually adaptive forms of strict religion.[17]

Innovation in religious product is what has kept religion vital in the USA, and this innovation arises through entrepreneurial new firms (movements or denominations). The good news in this for religious establishments is that it recognizes the reality and centrality of a continuing 'demand' for religion and of innovation in a vital religious marketplace. The bad news is that it seems to preclude the possibility that significant innovation can come from within established religions to produce the religious product that the customers want to buy.

Was there nothing identifiable in the empirical research, beyond the testimony of a few seemingly idiosyncratically successful pastors, that oldline Protestant congregations could do to stem membership decline? With the help of a new emphasis on congregational surveys, in contrast to the limitations of yearbook statistics and extrapolations from individual surveys, the 1990s seemingly ushered in a hot pursuit of this question among religious researchers. One of the first compilations of such research, *Church and Denominational Growth*, reached two noteworthy conclusions in this regard. First, 'Growing [oldline] churches emphasize outreach and (or) evangelism ... [T]he key is an "outward orientation". Churches that are primarily concerned with their own needs are unlikely to grow.'[18] Second, at least for oldline congregations, the studies concluded that 'There is no clear relationship between strictness at the local congregational level and church growth.'[19] And indeed, in contrast to Kelley's conservative strictness, the studies showed that if anything, again among oldline congregations, there was a small association between growth and liberalism.

But it wasn't until almost a decade later, and the *FACT 2000* national survey of American congregations, that the empirical research really began to get interesting for those looking for an adaptive capacity within oldline congregations. Two initial explorations of this terrain using *FACT 2000* followed from hints from research centred on slightly different issues. One focused on the apparent importance of new forms of, especially, contemporary worship within the currently most vibrant streams of conservative Protestantism.[20] The other took a look at the seeming preference of baby-boomers for spiritual practices.[21]

In my 2001 H. Paul Douglass Address to the Religious Research Association I used a comparison of the ground-breaking work in congregational studies from Douglass's Institute for Social and Religious Research with the data from *FACT 2000* to ask how what we know about congregational vitality may have changed over the course of three-quarters of a century.[22] Of particular interest was whether the reality or our understanding of the dynamics of congregational change had moved from the demographic determinism typical in Douglass's writings to a greater appreciation of internal adaptiveness. Accordingly, I looked at the relationship of four variables to membership growth for Protestant congregations. The four included: (1) 1990–2000 zip-code population change (as a typical measure of demographic influence); (2) the breadth of internal programming (one of the few internal factors noted by Douglass as holding potential for adaptation); (3) strictness (in appreciation of Kelley's[23] work and its reformulation by the socioreligious economists); and (4) the use of electric guitars in worship (*FACT 2000*'s best single measure of contemporary worship). Not surprisingly, with over 11,000 Protestant cases, I found that all produced significant, zero-order Pearson correlation coefficients. They ranged from a low of 0.118 to a high of 0.272. None of these are particularly large, but at least the top two are strong enough to warrant attention. Perhaps most surprisingly, population change was at the bottom (0.118) and breadth of internal programming at the top (0.272). Strictness ranked second lowest (0.158) and electronic guitars ranked second highest (0.206). In further reflection on these findings I noted:

> I have argued elsewhere that contemporary forms of worship, whose positive correlation with growth is even stronger in oldline Protestantism than conservative Protestantism, may be the first generally applicable adaptive strategy appearing in oldline Protestantism for the generationally carried social changes that have driven membership declines for over a quarter of a century. (Roozen 2001, forthcoming) To the extent that I am correct, I think that Douglass would be pleased to learn that two adaptive strategies sit at the top of our growth correlates. Social change may be the driver, but congregations are capable of adaptive responses. While strictness may have to be downgraded a notch, supply-siders and church leaders should nevertheless be pleased with the dominance of institutional factors. Those given to market models, however, should note as Douglass showed 70 years ago that supply can change through the adaptation of existing firms as well as the entry of entirely new firms.[24]

In a return engagement with the Religious Research Association in 2003 I used the *FACT 2000* data to see if there was a congregational equivalent to the apparent surge in individual spirituality.[25] Starting with one of the many end-of-the-millennium polls that found that 52 per cent of all Americans pray every day and that 56 per cent report that someone in their family usually says grace at family meals,[26] I discovered in the *FACT 2000* survey that a nearly equal 51 per cent of all US congregations reported giving 'a great deal' of emphasis to personal devotional practices in their preaching and teaching and that 54 per cent of US congregations reported giving 'a great deal' or 'quite a bit' of emphasis to family devotions. The *FACT 2000* data also showed that oldline Protestants were less likely than people from other faith groups to pray every day, less likely to engage in family devotions and, indeed, less likely to engage in any of the home or personal religious practices mentioned in the *FACT* study. More importantly for present purposes, the *FACT 2000* data indicated that the more emphasis a congregation gives to the values of home and personal religious practices the greater its vitality, and the more likely it is to be growing in membership. The *FACT* data also showed that these results were evident within oldline Protestantism as well as within other faith groups.

Most recently, Diana Butler Bass's *The Practicing Congregation* combines an emphasis on spiritual practices with the intentionality of mega-church pastor and bestselling author Rick Warren's *The Purpose-Driven Church* to argue that the purportedly new form of church she describes may well constitute 'the "most faithful and most hopeful" possibility for renewal, vitality, growth, and spiritual and theological deepening' for oldline

Protestantism.[27] In so arguing, she highlights the value of intentional churches in general, but worries that much of what has recently been written about under this banner was too conservative to be genuinely oldline. In contrast she argues that the intentional 'retraditioning' of Christian practices she has observed in some liberal congregations is the sub-type of purpose-driven churches that 'is most native to mainline Protestants, the pattern that grows from the soil of their experience, history, and traditions'.[28] She is especially direct in claiming that her practising congregations are a necessary adaptation to the now-failing, full-service, programme-model of congregation that church historian Brooks Holifield argues came to dominance in oldline Protestantism in the post-Second World War period.[29]

Oldline sources of adaptive vitality and growth: the empirical test

Bass's *Practicing Congregation* provides a wonderful, substantive starting point for guiding an empirical search for current, institutional sources (those internal to and therefore more under the control of a congregation) of oldline vitality and growth because, especially if one makes explicit the centrality of contemporary forms of worship in many of her 'seeker' and 'new paradigm' types of intentional congregations, she summarizes what can only be taken as the leading contenders. Specifically one finds internationality, contemporary worship, spiritual practices and the apparently now disposed-of former champion, the programme church.

As good fortunate, or insightful foresight, would have it, questions dealing with each of these areas were included, along with a measure of membership growth, in the *FACT 2000* national survey of American congregations. In addition to the substantive match of the survey to current interests, the huge overall number of responding congregations (14,301) provides a proportionately large number of responding oldline Protestant congregations (around 4,500), which makes this data set absolutely unique in its ability to sort out newly emergent types of congregations which may currently only exist in very small numbers.

As an initial foray I have combined the above-named characteristics into the following sixfold typology of oldline Protestant congregations and then simply looked at the percentage of each type that was growing:

- congregations that reported high intentionality, regular use of contemporary worship and a strong emphasis on personal and familial spiritual practices (Hi Int, Hi CW and Hi Pract in Figure 10.4);
- congregations that reported high intentionality and a strong emphasis on personal and familial spiritual practices, but did not report regular use of contemporary worship (Hi Int and Hi Pract);
- congregations that reported high intentionality and the regular use of contemporary worship but did not report a strong emphasis on personal and familial spiritual practices (Hi int and Hi CW);

- congregations that reported high intentionality but neither a regular use of contemporary worship nor a strong emphasis on personal and familial spiritual practices (Hi Int only);
- congregations that were highly programmatic, but did not report high intentionality (Hi Prog only);
- congregations that were neither highly programmatic nor high intentionality (No Int and No Prog).

For the specific measurement of each of the variables that were combined to form this typology and the specific question used to measure membership growth, see the Appendix.

Figure 10.4 shows the percentage of growing, oldline Protestant congregations for each type. Two findings jump out of the graphic. Those congregations that are not distinguished by either intentionality or a strong programmatic thrust are considerably less likely to be growing (only 38 per cent) than any of the other types. Those congregations distinguished by both high intentionality and high contemporary worship (with or without the further feature of high practices) are most likely to be growing (indeed nine in ten of such congregations). High intentionality and High programme by themselves are an improvement over nothing, but lack the added boost provided by practices, and especially by contemporary worship.

Figure 10.4 does not show how many of each type there are. Perhaps most disconcerting from the perspective of the adaptive capacity of the qualities captured in the typology is that the *FACT 2000* survey finds that a full 75 per cent of oldline Protestant congregations report being neither highly programmatic nor highly intentional. The comparable figure for evangelical congregations is 63 per cent. Next most frequent are congregations which are highly programmatic but not highly intentional – about 12 per cent with both oldline and evangelical Protestantism. Then, highly intentional with a strong emphasis on spiritual practices – 7.5 per cent within the oldline, but nearly double that (13.4 per cent) within evangelical Protestantism. Highly intentional congregations that regularly use contemporary worship are least frequent within the oldline (only 1.3 per cent), but almost 9 per cent within evangelicalism. The greater propensity of the oldline toward high intentionality and practices than toward high intentionality and contemporary worship lends some support to Bass's contention that her practising congregations may be the most natural path of oldline renewal. However, one has to wonder if (or how many of the) 7.5 per cent of oldline Protestant congregations are highly intentional and practising because of a recent retraditioning (*à la* Bass's perspective) or because they have always been that way, and whether it makes a difference. The data also indicates that while there is a slight skew toward the social justice extreme among highly intentional, practising oldline congregations, one finds such congregations represented along the entire social justice continuum. Since 'liberal' is an explicit component of Bass's characterization of her practising congregation, one has to wonder what difference this makes and about the extent to which she does this from a normative or an empirical perspective.

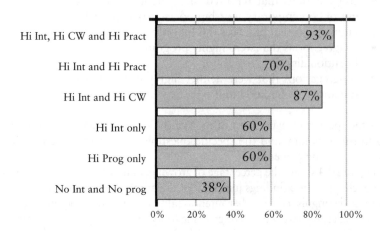

Figure 10.4: Percentage of growing congregations by congregational type (oldline Protestant)

It appears that all of the recently distinguishing characteristics examined in Figure 10.4 (internationality, contemporary worship, spiritual practices and the programme church) can be sources of oldline Protestant vitality and growth. But how do they compare with previously identified sources of growth and vitality? Among those for which we have measures in the *FACT 2000* are the following:

- a highly relational ethos (as measured by close-knit family feeling)
- how welcoming a congregation is of innovation and change
- inspirational worship
- the size of the membership
- population change in the congregation's neighbourhood (as measured by 1990–2000 percentage change in the total population in a congregation's zip-code area)
- the presence or absence of serious conflict
- the number of social outreach programmes
- evangelistic outreach (as measured by having 'special evangelistic' programmes)
- strictness (measured by expectations of members).[30]

Multiple regression is a common statistical method for assessing the relative influence of multiple factors. It provides a host of measures of association, and the one I report here is called the 'part correlation'. It is a standardized measure of the unique effect of a particular variable on (in our case membership) change, when the confounding influences of all the other variables in the regression have been removed from the total (zero-order) association between the particular variable in question and membership growth (the higher the part correlation the greater the unique effect). For example, we know large congregations are more likely to be growing than small congregations. We also know that congregations with lots of programmes are more likely to be growing than those with little programming, and that large congregations are most likely to have lots of programmes. Question: Are large congregations more likely to be growing because they have lots of programmes, or is there something about large size itself that is conducive to growth. The 'part correlation' statistic generated by a multiple regression analysis tells us whether or not size matters independent of the influence of number of programmes.

Figure 10.5 charts out the part correlation when the thirteen above noted variables are 'regressed' on membership growth using oldline Protestant congregations. One immediate observation is that there are only nine variables (bars) in the chart. This is because four of the thirteen variables entered into the analysis did not have a statistically significant relationship with membership growth when the confounding influences of other variables were controlled. These four included: close-knit family feeling; special evangelism programmes; number of social outreach programmes; and strictness. The latter is, of course, consistent with past research – strictness may differentiate oldline from evangelical congregations, but does not seem to be related to growth and vitality within the oldline. In contrast, the insignificance of outward orientation (whether evangelistic or social ministry) calls into question a pet theory from little more than a decade ago.

A second immediate observation is that number of programmes is one of the leading sources of growth (fifth of the top five) and that size appears to have a statistically significant, although small, influence independent not only

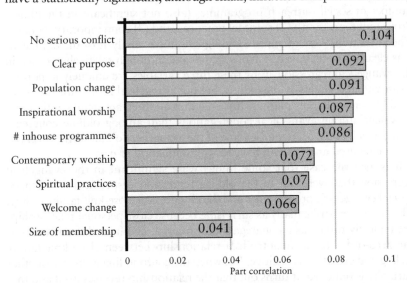

Figure 10.5: Multiple regression with membership growth (oldline Protestant)

of number of programmes but also of the quality of worship – this being another reason typically given for why large congregations have a growth advantage.

Then perhaps the most visually pronounced feature of Figure 10.5 is that the absence of serious conflict not only has the strongest relationship to growth, but is notably stronger than the next most important factor: namely, having a clear purpose, which is our measure of Warren and Bass intentionality. Rounding out the top five are population change and inspirational worship. Demographic change may not be as strong as it was 40 years ago, but it is still a significant consideration.

Following the top five, although with yet another 'step down' in strength of relationship are our two most 'contemporary' factors – with contemporary worship nosing ahead of spiritual practices. Two things to note in the data about worship are that the inspirational quality of worship is slightly more important than having a contemporary style of worship, but that even allowing for the inspirational quality of a congregation's worship, a contemporary style of worship still has a significant independent relationship to growth.

For a comparative perspective I ran the same multiple regression for the evangelical Protestant congregations in *FACT 2000* (see Figure 10.6). Perhaps the most striking visual cues in Figure 10.6 are, (1) the absolute and relative strength of the absence of conflict (both considerably greater than for oldline Protestant) and (2) the general weakness of the rest of the relationships, especially in comparison to the oldline (i.e., it is less clear what prompts growth in evangelical than in oldline congregations).

As was the case for the oldline Protestant results in Figure 10.5, some of the thirteen regressed variables do not appear in the evangelical results shown in Figure 10.6 because they were not statistically significant. There are three: (1) number of social outreach programmes (also not significant in the oldline Protestant regression); (2) spiritual practices; and (3) contemporary worship. The latter two, were of course, highlighted in our analysis of the oldline, as was clear purpose, which remains significant, although relatively weaker, in the evangelical regression. Why these three variables are uniquely important to growth and vitality in the oldline, but not evangelical Protestantism, is not readily evident in our analysis. It is true that all three are significantly more prevalent among evangelical congregations than among oldline congregations, which could account for some of the evangelical/oldline difference. But a more focused analysis will have to wait until another day.

It is also the case that some things were significant in the evangelical regression that were not in the oldline regression – specifically strictness, special evangelistic programmes and the absence of a close-knit family feeling. The latter may strike many as surprising because close personal relationships are typically touted as a congregational strength; and indeed if one looks at the zero-order (i.e., uncontrolled) relationship between close-knit family feeling and growth it is positive. But when the confounding influence of other variables is removed, it turns out that the relationship reverses itself and that the flip side of 'warm fuzzies' asserts itself, namely the sharp and impenetrable edges of cliquishness. One sees the same reversal in the oldline regression, except that although negative, the part correlation never reaches statistical significant. That special evangelistic programmes should be positively related to membership growth hardly seems surprising, and indeed the only apparent puzzle is why this only appears to be true for evangelical congregations and not for oldline congregations. Could it be the Protestant equivalent of 'white men can't jump?' Or perhaps it remains true that oldline congregations only turn to such kinds of programmes when they are in a desperate state of decline (that is, being in decline causes one to try special evangelistic programmes)? Why evangelism programmes don't appear to be a clear source of growth for oldline Protestant congregations remains to be answered, but mine is not the first study to report the same absence of relationship.[31]

Oldline sources of adaptive vitality and growth: the why

There are many perspectives from which to address the question of why the things identified in our oldline regression are sources of vitality and growth in the USA at the beginning of the twenty-first century. The limited space of a conclusion is not the place for an encyclopaedic rending of either the possibilities or the specifics. But it does appear appropriate to remind ourselves as we come to the end of our analysis of the main theme that emerges from the research, and then to suggest briefly how each of the sources connects to it.

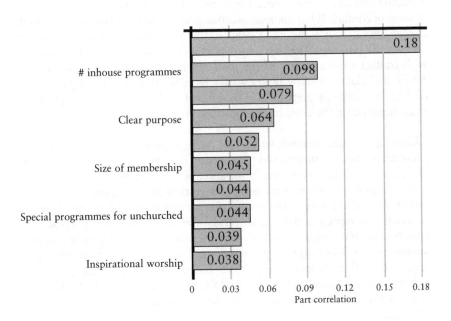

Figure 10.6: Multiple regression with membership growth (evangelical Protestant)

The main theme is that there has been a change in both the rhetoric and the empirically verifiable reality about the fortunes of oldline Protestant congregations from *demographic* captivity to *adaptive* capacity. Yes, the social context of the USA has changed dramatically in the last half-century, continues to change, and it is absolutely clear that this change is culpable in the now 40 continual years of oldline decline. But the good news is that, unlike past theory and research that stressed the oldline as helpless victim, the most recent research (including that of this chapter) strongly suggests that there are things a congregation can do to adapt to the contextual changes. The contextual changes are complex and obviously vary in intensity by specific locale. But there is nevertheless a general agreement among social analysts that we are somewhere in the early stages of a major socio-economic, cultural transition, variously labelled as late or postmodernity. Among other things it is a merging of the demographic and value changes carried in and by the postwar generation, with the electronic, economic and cultural changes of globalization.[32] Assuming this to be the case, then my concluding reflections briefly, but specifically, address the question of how each of the major, institutionally controllable sources of vitality and growth identified in Figure 10.5 (the oldline Protestant regression) might be adaptive to late or postmodernity.

Absence of serious conflict: Postmodernity is characterized by an increasing awareness of and affirmation of diversity, and correspondingly an increasing politicization of institutional decision-making in all major sectors of society including religion.[33] One implication of this for congregations is an increasing amount of conflict. What our regression suggests is that a near necessity for vital congregations today is the ability either to contain conflict or channel it toward constructive purposes. That it is more a matter of a congregation's ability to deal with conflict than a matter of the total absence of conflict is supported by *FACT 2000* data that show almost no difference between growing and declining oldline Protestant congregations in the amount of low levels of conflict, but a huge difference in the amount of *serious* levels of conflict.

Clarity of purpose (intentionality and purposefulness): From a marketing perspective, the postmodern world is a world of niches and a world of choice. Uniqueness sells at a premium, to be sure, but minimally; a consumer with options is going to gravitate toward products that clearly address her interests rather than those where the connection is vague or ambiguous. From a production perspective, the organizational advantages of a clear purpose that have long been recognized in the field of organizational development and well summarized in *The Purpose-Driven Church*[34] (not the least of these being in regard to conflict management) take on added significance during periods of cultural unsettledness precisely because the comfortable and often taken-for-granted patterns of the past can no longer be counted on.

Inspirational worship: Given the centrality of worship for congregations, it hardly seems worth noting that the quality of worship might be a source of vitality. But there is a growing awareness that either a taken-for-grantedness about or other priorities distracted oldline Protestantism from this seeming truism during much of the last 40 years.[35] The connection of this distraction to postmodernity is probably less direct than for other sources on our list. However, both quality and 'inspiration' attract a premium in the postmodern world, so to the extent that the distraction led to a fall in quality and/or that more habitual 'pedagogical' models of worship dominated more 'inspirational' emphases, one can see postmodern implications.

Extensiveness of programme: In a world of difference, diversity and choice, it seems self-evident that the broader array of options a congregation has to invoke participation and express commitment, the greater the number of constituencies that the congregation can attract and sustain. This was the genius of the modern programme church; its genius is geometrically amplified in a postmodern world and the mega-churches have taken the expression of programme church to a new level.[36]

Contemporary worship: Contemporary worship is typically characterized by an informality and style of worship music that takes its cues from the baby-boom generation. The research of the 1970s was absolutely clear that the onset of the oldline declines in the mid-to late 1960s was primarily due to an inability of congregations to retain or attract baby-boomers as young adults. The reasons for this are too complex to elaborate here, especially since work on the subject is readily available.[37]   But the more important and related question for present purposes is whether or not oldline congregations that use a contemporary style of worship are able to attract and/or retain younger members. Certainly the antidotal evidence of this is plentiful, and the *FACT 2000* data confirm it. Of the six 'Programme–Intentionality–contemporary worship–spiritual practice' types of oldline Protestant congregations analysed in Figure 10.4, those regularly using contemporary worship have the largest numbers of young adults and lowest number of older adults. The programme type is the second (albeit a distant second) most likely to have large numbers of young adults. Those congregations emphasizing spiritual practices are next, with those congregations not distinguished by any of the traits given in Figure 10.4 representing the opposite extreme – the least numbers of young adults and largest number of older adults.

Spiritual Practices: I have recently argued that the most profound of the religious transitions related to postmodernity is the change in religious expression from a grounding in the 'Word' to a grounding in the 'Spirit'.[38] In making this argument I demonstrated the significance of the shift by showing that even when we separately examine oldline and conservative Protestantism, for example, we find higher levels of vitality among the more expressive denominations (e.g., Episcopal and Unitarian–Universalist with oldline Protestant) than among the more cognitive (e.g., Presbyterian and United Methodist with oldline Protestantism). The importance of spiritual practice as a source of vitality in oldline Protestant congregations found in the empirical analysis presented above is a further manifestation of this consequence of postmodern adaptability.

I concluded my 2003 article signalling the importance of home and personal spiritual practices by noting: 'the *FACT* data clearly report that vital congregations not only practice what they preach – they also preach about home and personal religious practice'.[39] Preaching, of course, is an exercise in internationality, so unwittingly I further signalled another of the key contemporary sources of oldline vitality. The research presented above adds two further images to this appropriately postmodern montage on oldline vitality. Vital oldline congregations not only are practised at programming; they also programme their practices. And, a very small but growing segment of the most venturesome experiments in oldline vitality seek to praise God and inspire themselves not with an organ-guided rendition of 'Rock of ages', but an electronically amplified 'We will Rock you!'

Notes

1. Dean M. Kelley, *Why Conservative Churches are Growing* (San Franscisco, CA: Harper & Row, 1972).

2. Two of the foundational publications of the movement include: Donald A. McGavern, *Understanding Church Growth* (Grand Rapids, MI: Eerdmans, 1970); and C. Peter Wagner, *Your Church Can Grow* (Glendale, CA: G/L Regal Books, 1976).

3. Dean R. Hoge and David A. Roozen (eds), *Understanding Church Growth and Decline: 1950–1978* (New York: Pilgrim Press, 1979).

4. See, for example, the apologetic included in H. Paul Douglass and Edmund de Brunner, *The Protestant Church as a Social Institution* (New York: Harper, 1935).

5. James H. Smylie, 'Church growth and decline in historical perspective: Protestant quest for identity, leadership and meaning', in Hoge and Roozen (eds), *Understanding Church Growth and Decline*, pp. 69–93.

6. Ibid.

7. *Faith Communities Today* (*FACT*) survey. The survey was funded by the Lilly Endowment and the participant groups. For more information see the *FACT* website: http://www.fact.hartsem.edu

8. David A. Roozen and C. Kirk Hadaway (eds), *Church and Denominational Growth* (Nashville, TN: Abingdon Press, 1993).

9. Oldline Protestant denominations included in Figures 10.1 & 10.2: Episcopal, Presbyterian-USA, United Church of Christ, Christian Church-Disciples, Church of the Brethren Evangelical, Lutheran–ELCA, Reformed Church of America, United Methodist. Evangelical Protestant denominations included in the figures: Baptist General Conference, Christian and Missionary All, Cumberland Presbyterian, Evangelical Covenant Church, Lutheran Church, Missouri Synod, North American Baptist Conference, Seventh-Day Adventist, Southern Baptist Convention, Wisconsin Evangelical Lutheran Synod, Assemblies of God, Church of God, Anderson, Church of God, Cleveland, Church of Nazarene, Free Methodist of North America, Salvation Army.

10. See Appendix to this chapter for the *FACT 2000* list of oldline and evangelical Protestant denominations.

11. Unfortunately, trend data over any significant time period for any measure of vitality at the congregational level other than membership growth are not readily available, so that

any claim to more or less at the current time in any of these other areas is, at best, impressionistic.

12. Douglass and de Brunner, *The Protestant Church as a Social Institution*.

13. Kelley, *Why Conservative Churches Are Growing*.

14. McGavern, *Understanding Church Growth*.

15. Wagner, *Your Church Can Grow*.

16. Laurence R. Iannaccone, 'Why strict churches are strong', paper presented to the annual meeting of the Society for the Scientific Study of Religion, Salt Lake City, UT, 1989.

17. Roger Finke and Rodney Stark, *The Churching of America, 1766–1990: Winners and Losers in Our Religious Economy* (Piscataway, NJ: Rutgers University Press, 1992).

18. Roozen and Hadaway (eds), *Church and Denominational Growth*, p. 129.

19. Ibid., p. 133.

20. Donald E. Miller, *Reinventing American Protestantism: Christianity in the New Millennium* (Berkeley, CA: University of California Press, 1997); C. Kirk Hadaway and David A. Roozen, *Rerouting the Protestant Mainstream: Sources of Growth and Opportunities for Change* (Nashville, TN: Abingdon Press, 1995).

21. Wade Clark Roof, *A Generation of Seekers: The Spiritual Journeys of the Baby Boom Generation* (San Francisco, CA: Harper, 1993); Peter A. R. Stebinger, 'Congregational paths to holiness', Hartford Institute for Religion Research Working Paper, 95-1, 1995; Nancy T. Ammerman and Adair Lummis, *Spiritually Vital Episcopal Congregations* (Report to Trinity Grants Board, 1996).

22. David A. Roozen, H. Paul Douglass Address to the Religious Research Association, Columbus, OH, 19–21 October 2001. Subsequently published as '10,001 congregations: H. Paul Douglass, strictness and electric guitars', in *Review of Religious Research*, 44.1 (2002): pp. 51–121: Also available online at: http://hirr.hartsem.edu/bookshelf/roozen_article3.html

23. Kelley, *Why Conservative Churches are Growing*.

24. Roozen, '10,001 congregations'. (Roozen '2001' reference is to David A. Roozen, 'Worship and renewal: surveying congregational life', *The Christian Century*, 5–12 June 2002:10–11).

25. David Roozen, 'FACTs about personal religious practice: meeting evangelicals halfway', Norfolk, VA, 24–26 October 2003. Subsequently published online: http://fact.hartsem.edu/topfindings/topicalfindings.htm

26. Cited in '75% say God answers prayers', by Thomas Hargrove and Guido H. Stempel III, distributed by Scripps Howard News Service, 28 December 1999. www.shns.com.

27. Diana Butler Bass, *The Practicing Congregation: Imagining a New Old Church* (Herndon, VA: The Alban Institute, 2004), p. 19; Rick Warren, *The Purpose-Driven Church: Growth without Compromising Your Message and Mission* (Grand Rapids, MI: Zondervan, 1995).

28. Bass, *The Practicing Congregation*, p. 19.

29. E. Brooks Holifield, 'Toward a history of American congregations', in James P. Wind and James W. Lewis (eds), *American Congregations, Vol 2: New Perspectives in the Study of Congregations* (Chicago, IL: University of Chicago Press, 1994), pp. 23–53.

30. See Appendix to this chapter for specific measures used.

31. Marjorie H. Royle, 'The effect of a church growth strategy on United Church of Christ congregations', Roozen and Hadaway (eds), in *Church and Denominational Growth*, pp. 149–54.

32. See, for example: Wade Clark Roof, Jackson W. Carroll and David A. Roozen (eds), *The Post-War Generation and Religious Establishments: Cross-Cultural Perspectives* (Boulder, CO: Westview Press, 1995); and N.J. Rengger, *Political Theory, Modernity and Postmodernity* (Oxford: Blackwell, 1995).

33. For a brief elaboration of this in relationship to oldline Protestantism see the section on 'From prophetic to the political', in David Roozen, 'Four mega-trends changing America's religious landscape', presentation at the Religion Newswriters Association Annual Conference,

22 September 2001. (Available online: http://hirr.hartsem.edu/bookshelf/roozen_article4.html.) For a more extended discussion of this reality at the national denominational level, see David Roozen, 'National denominational structures' engagement with postmodernity: an integrative summary from an organizational perspective', in Roozen and Nieman (eds), *Church, Identity, and Change: Theology and Denominational Structures in Unsettled Times* (Grand Rapids, MI: Eerdmans, 2004).

34. Warren, *The Purpose-Driven Church*.

35. See, for example, the section 'From Mission to Worship', in Roozen, 'Four mega-trends'.

36. See, for example, two online articles by Scott Thumma: 'Megachurches Today: a summary of data from the Faith Communities Today Project': http://hirr.hartsem.edu/org/faith_megachurches_FACTsummary.html; and 'Exploring the megachurch phenomena': http://hirr.hartsem.edu/bookshelf/thumma_article2.html

37. See, for example, McGavern, *Understanding Church Growth* and Roof, *A Generation of Seekers*.

38. Roozen, 'Four mega-trends'.

39. Roozen, 'FACTs about personal religious practice'.

Appendix

FACT 2000 *oldline and evangelical Protestant denominations*
The following denominations are included in the *FACT 2000* data:

> *Oldline Protestant*: Episcopal, Presbyterian, Unitarian–Universalist and United Church of Christ; American Baptist, Disciples of Christ, Evangelical Lutheran, Mennonite, Reformed Church in America and United Methodist.
> *Evangelical Protestant*: Assemblies of God, Christian Reformed, Nazarene, Churches of Christ, Independent Christian Churches (Instrumental), Mega-churches, Nondenominational Protestant, Seventh-Day Adventist and Southern Baptist.

The following denominations and faith groups were also included in the *FACT 2000* survey, but their data are not used in the articles' multivariate analyses: the Historic Black Protestant denominations, Roman Catholics, Orthodox, Bahai, Mormon, Jewish and Muslim.

FACT 2000 *measures*
1. How well does each of the following statements describe your congregation?

1 Very well
2 Quite well
3 Somewhat
4 Slightly
5 Not at all well

A. Our congregation feels like a (large) close-knit family. _____
H. Our congregation welcomes innovation and change. _____
O. Our congregation's worship services are spiritually uplifting
    and inspirational. _____

Size of membership: Approximately how many persons – both adults and children – would you say *regularly participate* in the religious life of your congregation – *whether or not* they are officially members of your congregation?

A.   Number of *regularly participating* adults (18 and over)   _____

Presence or absence of serious conflicts: During the last *five years* has your congregation experienced any serious disagreements or conflicts in the following areas?

A. Theology
B. Money/finances/budget
C. How worship is conducted
D. Program/mission priorities or emphases
E. Who should make a decision
F. Pastor's leadership style
G. Pastor's personal behavior
H. Member/participant's personal behavior
I. Other: _____

Number of social outreach programs: In the past 12 months, did your congregation directly provide, any of the following services for your own members or for people in the community? (Sum of 'yeses' to following):

A. Food pantry or soup kitchen   ___
B. Cash assistance to families or individuals   ___
C. Thrift store or thrift store donations   ___
D. Elderly, emergency or affordable housing   ___
E. Counseling services or 'hot-line'   ___
F. Substance abuse programs   ___
G. Day care, pre-school, before/after-school programs   ___
H. Tutoring or literacy programs for children and teens   ___
I. Voter registration or voter education   ___
J. Organized social issue advocacy or community organizing   ___
K. Employment counseling, placement or training   ___
L. Health programs/clinics/health education   ___
M. Hospital or nursing home facilities   ___
N. Senior citizen programs (other than housing)   ___
O. Program for migrants or immigrants   ___
P. Prison or jail ministry   ___

Evangelistic outreach: Did your congregation do any of the following during the past 12 months to reach out to new or inactive participants, or to make your congregation better known in your community? 'Yes' to:

Special programs (e.g., parenting classes, young single nights, art festivals, street ministries) especially intended to attract unchurched persons or non-members in your community.

Strictness: Which *one* of the following three statements best describes your congregation?

• Our congregation has explicit expectations for members that are strictly enforced.

• Our congregation has fairly clear expectations for members, but the enforcement of these expectations is not very strict.

• Our congregation has only vague expectations for members that are seldom, if ever, enforced.

Part 4

CLERGY AND GROWTH

Chapter 11

THEOLOGICAL MATCH BETWEEN PASTOR AND CONGREGATION: IMPLICATIONS FOR CHURCH GROWTH

Adair T. Lummis

> Ever since the publication of *Why Conservative Churches are Growing* in the 1970s issues of 'strictness' and theological conservatism have created controversy. Are strict churches stronger than more lenient churches and can churches that take a more theologically liberal position grow and prosper in the current religious 'marketplace'? As with most things, the answers are not simple.
>
> (Hadaway 2002, p. 37)

The varieties both of definitions of theological conservatism/liberalism and of church growth cause problems in making definitive statements on whether and how theological orientations relate to church growth. The complexity of this relationship is further compounded by the variety of other contextual, institutional and individual factors that are related to assessments of growth in congregations. The probability that interactions among these factors will change as one or more become ascendant in the life of the congregation further makes it very difficult to either include all that are possibly relevant or assesses the relative importance of each in an empirical study of church growth.[1] This chapter will not attempt such a feat.

Instead, the relationship between theological liberalism and congregational growth will be explored in one denomination, the Episcopal Church, taking into account a limited number of other factors considered pivotal in growth or decline of membership. Congregational size has been noted as one of these factors. This chapter addresses how the degree of theological liberalism within local churches relates to their growth as perceived by congregational leaders and members within congregations of different sizes. Clergy leadership can be another pivotal factor. Clergy may or may not be in agreement with the majority of members in their theological views. The major focus of this chapter is on how the match or mismatch between priests' own degree of theological liberalism and that of the majority of their members may affect congregational growth. To paraphrase Hadaway above, most of the answers though not simple, are interesting and consequential for local church and denominational development. These queries and responses may also have broader implications for religious dialogue and community.

What can be considered 'liberal' or 'conservative' theological positions and what is understood by 'church growth' can differ considerably. Several different interpretations of the above concepts are discussed next, and the way in which they are defined empirically for this chapter described.

Theology, church growth, leadership and their relationships

Defining conservative–liberal theology

In defining theological conservatism–liberalism as it applies to churches, there seem to be several different facets singled out by scholars which are variously interconnected. First, the amount of authority accorded biblical scriptures is certainly an element in defining the degree of theological conservatism espoused by individuals, congregations or denominations, as Ian Markham (2003, p. 21) predicates; and conversely, the amount of willingness to revise traditional biblical teachings indicates degrees of theological liberalism. Revised understanding of biblical imperatives in the light of new learning, interfaith dialogue, contemporary social justice values or even human reason, is typically considered a liberal theological stance. Reliance on traditional creeds or direct communications from the Holy Spirit as sources of authority, however, are considered more in the conservative theological camp because of their closer association with the importance of biblical authority, as indicated by Dudley and Roozen's (2001, pp. 18–19 and *passim*) multidenominational *FACT* data. 'Foundational' reliance on biblical authority is far higher among conservative denominations than mainline denominations, particularly in the Episcopal Church.[2]

A second definitional element in the degree of theological conservatism/liberalism in church organizations refers to the amount of 'strictness' in what is expected of members in terms of beliefs and behaviour. 'Strictness' in this sense is conceptually distinct from how much theological authority is accorded biblical scriptures, although since the two are usually related within religious institutions, measures of 'strictness' are often taken as indications of theological conservatism/liberalism. Over half the congregations of the Episcopal Church and other mainline denominations in the *FACT* study, compared to only slightly over a quarter of congregations of the conservative denominations, are very liberal in the sense of having only implicit expectations for members that are seldom, if ever, enforced.[3]

A third definitional element in theological conservatism/liberalism in church systems, sometimes a combination of the first two, is the degree to which the theological beliefs and traditional practices are *negotiable* within and among congregations of a denomination. Martyn Percy advocates churches' adopting a reflexive approach in combining some of the traditional with the new in congregational theology, liturgy and ministry to reach people in the twenty-first century. However, he also notes that churches typically have some aspects that they see as theologically non-negotiable (Percy 2000, pp. 160–61, 190). From a historical review of denominational development, Roger Finke argues that some non-negotiability in theological precepts is advisable: to grow and remain strong religious organizations must continually innovate, but not to the extent that in trying to make their theology palatable to many, they lose their special, historical 'core teachings' (distinctive beliefs and practices).[4] The choice of *which* core teachings to retain and which to alter or drop, is of course crucial to church survival and growth.

The dual approach of a strong emphasis on biblical authority combined with lowering of 'strictness' gates to new people becoming church members appears to be the combination most important for sustained growth in many congregations. The largest, fastest growing congregations currently, the postmodern or new paradigm recently founded evangelical churches, according to Jackson Carroll (2000, p. 81), are 'seeker friendly but theologically conservative'. While these congregations allow leeway in members' lifestyles, worship preferences and some interpretation of biblical passages, they lift the Bible as the ultimate authority and uphold the Trinity, the divinity and physical resurrection of Christ, and justification by faith as core teachings. Although such congregations relate to the surrounding society, they also make a clear demarcation between Christianity and the wider culture (Carroll, pp. 39, 95 *passim*). The theological emphases of these thriving evangelical congregations would not, however, appeal to those who prefer their theology with more shades of grey, to use Markham's terminology (Markham 2003, pp. 170–89).

This raises a fourth element in defining theological conservatism/liberalism in church systems: the designation of particular beliefs or practices as evincing particularly conservative or liberal theological stances *within* a denomination. National executives of Protestant denominations are currently wrestling with questions of how accepting of different theological premises they can or should be in attracting the unchurched and converts, and yet still maintain a denominational identity based on core denominational beliefs and practices (Lummis 2004b, pp. 7–8). Allowing, if not encouraging, congregations of a denomination to draw somewhat different theological lines depending on their preferences, is one adaptation particularly characteristic of the mainline denominations. Within one denomination, for example, it can be negotiable for some congregations to teach only a literal understanding of the virgin birth and bodily resurrection, while other congregations accept a more symbolic interpretation of these events. From this vantage point, the theological shades may apply equally to the theological location on a black–grey–white continuum of individual congregations within one denomination, as well as to the *modal* theological shade of its total congregations, with reference to the whole denomination.

Denominations characterized by a greater acceptance of theological shades *among* their congregations (i.e., with some very conservative congregations, some moderately conservative, some of very mixed theological shades, some moderately liberal and some very liberal) may have some advantage over more theologically monochromic denominations in gaining new members. However, this is likely to hold mainly where there are several congregations of different theological shades of the denomination relatively close to one another;

otherwise congregations of other denominations may reap the new-member advantage. There is also the possibility in denominations with many theological shades that a theologically argued policy or practice may become so divisive an issue that the unity of the denomination is severely jeopardized.

Although the theological rectitude of having ordained women in top church leadership positions is less divisive than it was two or three decades ago in the mainline Protestant denominations, the issue has not disappeared. Currently, however, whether sexually active homosexual persons should be ordained and lead churches rates as the most theologically divisive issue in the mainline denominations because it is non-negotiable to different factions. In terms of these two issues alone, congregations in the Episcopal Church can be arraigned from very liberal to very conservative. This does not mean that Episcopal congregations are presently in conflict as a whole over these issues; other studies suggest that most members do not want their clergy or congregations to address such issues as homosexuality, precisely so their congregation will not be divided.[5] Nonetheless, these issues can burst forth and divide a congregation. Further, a high proportion of members can probably make a rough estimate of where others in their church stand on these issues, based on their observations, informal conversations and gossip.

In the following analyses, survey respondents' answers to these questions regarding their own opinions and those of most in their congregations on these characteristics as acceptable for church leaders and officials will define the degree of theological conservatism/liberalism of both individuals and their congregations.

Church growth

It is heresy to some, but I must say it: Many congregations will never grow in numbers.
(Mead 1993, p. 40)

Loren Mead follows this statement with a discussion of how churches can grow in several ways using the framework of: maturational growth, organic growth and incarnational growth, as well as numerical growth.[6] Kirk Hadaway empirically defines Episcopal congregations' overall strength not simply in terms of numbers attending worship but also as to whether the congregation has a clear sense of mission, is in good financial health, is spiritually vital and alive, and helps members deepen their relationship with God (Hadaway 2002, p. 37 and *passim*). Sachs and Holland (2003, p. 307) report that by *church growth* Episcopal lay members meant both 'increase in the congregation's membership and an enhanced quality of congregational life'.

The definition of growing congregations used both by most denominational leaders and sociologists, however, is increase in numbers of members (and presumably members who contribute their presence, time or money to the congregations to some degree, other than just allowing their names to be listed). However, sociologists and denominational leaders would concur that these other types of congregational growth are at least correlates and often causes of congregational numerical growth. Dudley and Roozen (2001, pp. 26–9) report that across denominations, congregational growth is empirically associated with inspiring worship, programmes which promote congregational vitality, focused vision, community outreach, care of and some regulations for members, and cultural affinity among members. Episcopal congregations which informants describe as growing are also perceived as spiritually vital and offering a variety of music and forms of worship, as found in two different studies. (Ammerman and Lummis 1996; Hadaway 2002, pp. 63–5). Woolever and Bruce (2004, p. 43) state that the higher the proportion of members participating in the congregation, the greater its growth. Indeed, Dougherty argues that good worship and programme resources affect congregational growth indirectly through increasing current members' *sense of belonging* to and subsequent greater participation in their congregations. Members give more of their money and time to increase their congregations' programmes and membership.

Perceptions of whether or not a congregation has grown in members alone can be affected by members' perceptions of what should be possible for their church, given what other churches in the area are experiencing, or simply the population growth of the region. Nonetheless, there is typically a fairly good relationship between perceptions of growth and actual church growth, as found by Hadaway (2002, p. 59) who used both survey respondents' reports and actual church membership statistics in analysing the *FACT* data on Episcopal congregations.

Congregational growth: importance of congregational size and location.
In order to attract the unchurched, Percy (2001, pp. 188–90) notes that churches are offering a substantial number of different activities, in addition to a variety of worship services. Small churches of under 100 worshippers cannot offer anywhere near the same number of services or variety of activities that a larger church of 400, 800 or 1,600-plus can. Carroll (2000, pp. 7, 38 and *passim*) reports that one factor in the continued success in attracting and retaining new members of the larger Catholic and Protestant congregations and new paradigm mega-churches is that the larger their size, the more personnel, money and space they have to mount a variety of programmes, that will attract people with different interests.

Becoming a numerically large and still growing congregation, however, also depends on the area in which a congregation is located. There have to be people in the vicinity of the congregation to attract. This is why larger congregations and growing congregations of any size are more likely to be found in populated areas, particularly the newer suburbs which have an influx of residents who are not long-standing members of one congregation.[8]

The area of the country in which a congregation is located, often in conjunction with the total population in its vicinity, can also be important not only in overall church growth, but also in the types of people who join congregations. In illustration, Dougherty (2003, pp. 65–85) found that congregations are more likely to be multiracial not just if they are located in areas where there is racial diversity (typically urban areas) but also if they are where the culture of the region promotes racial integration. This was least often the case in the US South. Ammerman similarly found that the majority of congregations with a programmatic concern for bridging racial differences are most often located in larger northern and Midwestern cities, but seldom in the South (Ammerman 2005, pp. 128–31 and *passim*).

The South, even if it has few multiracial congregations compared to other parts of the country, is where there is most church growth. The South has long been noted to be the most socially, politically and theologically conservative area of the USA. The southern hemisphere countries exhibit the greatest church growth. Jenkins, in describing the expansion of Christianity globally, comments: 'Not even Anglicans and Episcopalians are looking South, although that is where virtually all the growth is occurring in their Communion.' He further observes that the denominations that are triumphing all over the global South are stalwartly conservative theologically, interested not in liberation theology but rather in personal salvation and in a clear, scriptural authority (Jenkins 2002, pp. 7–8).

Church growth and theology
Congregations are more likely to grow and flourish if they attract a majority of members whose orientations and interests coalesce, even if these congregations are racially diverse. Emmerson and Kim (2003, pp. 217–27) found that successful multicultural/multiracial congregations had the mission and programmes that drew people who feel socially comfortable with one another. Those whose theological beliefs differ sharply from most others in their congregation are unlikely to feel comfortable, whatever other status and attitudes they may share with others. This is one probable factor in Dudley and Roozen's finding that congregations grow in locations where they find like-minded people in the demographics of their communities (2001, p. 26).

Because geographical region, rural/suburban location and present size of the congregation are such important determinants of church growth (however defined), it is understandable why there has been no consistent linear relationship reported between measures of congregational growth and its degree of theological conservatism/liberalism.[9] To explore this connection between theology and church growth, taking into account these other determinants, this chapter will focus mainly on the kind of growth most often meant by church growth: that is, growth in numbers.

Clergy leadership, church growth and theology

Pastors of congregations can impact on church growth through the style of leadership which they exert. The best pastoral leadership will be the reflexive, transformational style, as in Carroll's description, in which the clergy listen to members and try to respond to their needs, but at the same time set forth a vision which mobilizes members to work toward congregational growth.[10] Bishop Charles Bennison also describes the importance of clergy being true spiritual leaders in providing transformative leadership to congregations: that is, helping members adapt to changing neighbourhoods in ways that lead to their spiritual growth and to church revitalization (Bennison 1999, pp. 215–39 and *passim*).

Divisive conflict is least likely to occur in the theologically more conservative congregations where there are explicit and strict expectations for members (Dudley and Roozen, 2001, pp. 62–3). In more liberal congregations with relaxed expectations, however, a pastor who tries to exert autocratic leadership is very likely to incite congregational conflict (Lummis 2003, pp. 20–21). One of the most decisive factors militating against church growth is where the clergy cannot effect an open discussion of conflicts and disagreements that arise in their congregations. Hadaway (2002, p. 56) found that in Episcopal congregations, conflicts over the priest's leadership style is the greatest impetus for church fights and the kinds of conflicts that result in congregational membership decline.

The match of the pastor to the particular congregation is a pivotal area of denominational attention in clergy deployment. In most of the mainline Protestant denominations, however, race, gender, marital status and age of the clergy applicant are not considered appropriate characteristics in matching with a pastoral opening. Even so, congregational search committees typically still want a young, married white man (Lummis 2003, pp. 16–20), particularly if they are in the larger, wealthier and often growing congregations. An ordained woman, regardless of how well she may fit with the congregation in many ways, may be seen not be seen by some lay leaders as an appropriate pastor of their congregation because of her gender. Female clergy across denominations are more likely than male clergy to pastor the smaller churches at every stage of their careers (Zikmund, Lummis and Chang 1998, pp. 70–91; Nesbitt 1997, pp. 57–88 and *passim*). In the Episcopal Church it is still the case that among the clergy, women are more likely than men to be the rectors or vicars of smaller congregations (Hadaway 2002, p. 69). In part this is because lay respondents in smaller Episcopal parishes are more likely to be 'very willing' to have a woman as rector than those in larger parishes (Committee on the Status of Women, 2003, pp. 27–8).

There is another characteristic of clergywomen, other than their gender, which may antagonize lay leaders in the more theologically conservative churches. Clergywomen in mainline denominations tend to be more theologically and socially liberal and activist than clergymen on a variety of areas, including acceptance of homosexuality (Deckman *et al.* 2003, pp. 621–31). Episcopal clergywomen are more approving of the use of inclusive language in services than clergymen and especially more approving than lay members of either gender (Committee on the Status of Women, 2003, pp. 13–14). It follows that clergywomen are more likely to be pastors of fairly liberal than conservative congregations even within the same denomination.

Clergy leadership: theology and congregational growth in the Episcopal Church

In 2002 the Committee for the Status of Women, Executive Council, Episcopal Church commissioned a study of samples of clergy and lay members of congregations in eighteen regionally distributed dioceses. In this section we shall further analyse the data that went into the committee's report.[11]

The measure of theological conservatism/liberalism for individuals and for congregations is centred around eight questions about the acceptance of women in different levels of church positions in the respondent's own congregation and diocese. This series includes three issues on women as rectors of their congregation: (1) acceptance of a woman as rector *qua* woman, (2) if she has young children; and (3) if she is lesbian and living with a partner. On each of these eight questions, respondents were asked (a) how willing they personally would be to have a woman as a rector, and (b) how willing they thought most people in their congregation would be to have a woman as a rector. Through these measures, two indices were constructed: an index of personal theological liberalism and an index of their congregation's theological liberalism. Scores on the theological liberalism scales could range from 8 (highest) to 40 (lowest).[12]

Findings

On the measure of theological liberalism used it appears that Episcopal congregations are on the liberal side in accepting women in church leadership positions. Out of the total sample, only a minority of 13 per cent indicates that their congregations is *very liberal* (scores 8–10) from individuals' reports that 'most' in their congregations are very willing to have a woman (including a lesbian) in all eight offices. Slightly under a third, 30 per cent, say their congregations are quite to moderately liberal (scores 11–16), in that most members are usually willing to have a woman in a church leadership position, but more mixed about having a woman bishop and quite ambivalent or opposed to having a lesbian be their rector. Almost a third 31 per cent see their congregation as less liberal and more mixed toward the conservative side (scores 17–22), and over a quarter (26 per cent) report that most in their congregations are somewhat to fairly conservative (scores 23–40), preferring men in the top positions of congregation and diocese.

Measure of church growth: Respondents were asked about their congregation: 'In terms of membership, compared to five years ago, would you say this congregation is growing, staying about the same, or declining?' Slightly over half of those surveyed (52 per cent), said their congregation had grown over the last five years; 34 per cent reported it had stayed the same, and 14 per cent saw their congregation as having declined in numbers. So the answer to the question 'Are liberal or conservative Episcopal churches more likely to have grown?' is neither, necessarily. There is *no* direct correlation between the degree of congregational liberalism and church growth.

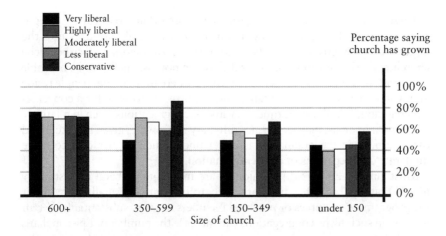

Figure 11.1 Church liberalism and church growth in different locations

Church growth in churches of different sizes and locations: The larger the congregation to which those surveyed belonged, the more likely they were to say that it had grown in the last five years,[13] so confirming the findings of many studies mentioned. Similarly, the larger the church the more likely clergy and lay respondents were to report that 'members are active in making this a vital parish',[14] thus further supporting previous research that large churches have more programmes and resources to involve their members more actively. Additionally, the relationship between present church size and its perceived growth over the last five years holds true regardless of whether the church is in a megatropolis, city, suburb or less populated area. At the same time, theologically liberal churches are just as likely to grow as conservative churches in each church size range. Within smaller to medium-sized churches (those under 600), liberal churches appear slightly more likely to have grown over the last five years than conservative churches, although the results are not statistically significant.

The largest churches, however, are in the South.[15] Congregations in the South are *more theologically conservative* (83 per cent), followed by congregations in the Midwest (57 per cent) and the western USA (54 per cent), and last – conservative congregations in the northeast (41 per cent). The northeast cluster of dioceses is also notable as being the area most likely to have theologically *very liberal* congregations (21 per cent), whereas the southern cluster is least likely (2 per cent).

Are the smaller churches more liberal then? Not necessarily. The answer depends more on where the church is located. Small churches in rural areas and small towns tend to be fairly conservative theologically. In the suburbs and cities, however, the smaller the congregation the more likely it is to be more liberal theologically, even in the South. It is the very large (over 600-member) urban and suburban congregations which are more conservative theologically on women's leadership.

These very liberal small congregations in more urban areas can be categorized as 'niche churches', serving a constituency typically not drawn to the larger nearby congregations of the denomination. Ammerman describes niche churches, particular those with liberal views on homosexuality, to be best able to flourish in a cosmopolitan culture setting, where more liberal people reside and where there is more acceptance and opportunity to shop for a congenial congregation.[16] At the same time, very liberal congregations, even in relatively cosmopolitan areas, may experience difficulty in growing, given the likelihood that the bulk of the population is either unchurched or attracted to more moderate congregations of the denomination.

Most current Episcopal parishioners are moderately liberal at best. *Very liberal* Episcopal congregations are likely to be relatively small and without the programme resources or potential members to grow substantially. Yet an increase in such niche congregations can increase the number of Episcopalians overall by providing a church home for those who are not drawn to the typical mainline parish.

Clergy leadership and theological match and mismatch in church growth
As might be expected, clergywomen are more theologically liberal on having women in church leadership than clergymen, laywomen or laymen. About two-thirds (69 per cent) of clergywomen are very liberal, and only 5 per cent rather conservative. About half the clergymen are very liberal and a quarter tend to be more conservative. Fewer laywomen (45 per cent) and even fewer laymen (34 per cent) are very liberal toward having women in church leadership positions.

Further, theologically liberal persons are more likely to be pastoring or members of congregations in the northeast and west USA, rather than in the Midwest and especially the South. Even clergywomen in the South are less likely to be liberal than clergywomen in other parts of the USA. To illustrate: while a strong majority (78 per cent) of the clergywomen in the Northeast are very liberal, this is true of somewhat lesser majority in the Midwest (69 per cent) and West (68 per cent), and true only of a tiny minority (14 per cent) of the clergywomen in the South.

In looking at the match in theological stances between priest congregation in the total sample, they were grouped as follows: (1) *liberal match* (the pastor is very liberal personally and most in his/her congregation are at least quite liberal); (2) *more conservative match* (the pastor and most of the congregation are somewhat to quite conservative); (3) *liberal-conservative mismatch* (the pastor is very liberal, while his/her congregation is more conservative). There were not enough cases where the pastor is conservative and the congregation liberal to use this as another or fourth category.

Not only are clergywomen more likely to be more liberal than clergymen generally, but they are more likely to be matched as pastors of liberal congregations. However, near equal proportions of both ordained women and men who espouse a liberal theological viewpoint find themselves to be somewhat to very 'mismatched' theologically with most in their congregations.

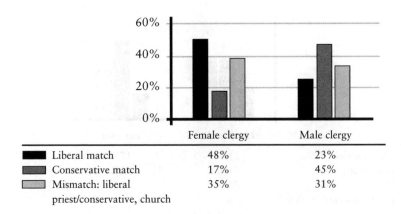

	Female clergy	Male clergy
■ Liberal match	48%	23%
■ Conservative match	17%	45%
☐ Mismatch: liberal priest/conservative, church	35%	31%

Figure 11.2: Clergy–church theological match

Regional location of clergy and congregations does make a difference, however. In the northeast, both male and female clergy are most likely to be in liberal matches. In contrast, in the South there are no instances of liberal matches (i.e., where strongly liberal clergy are pastoring fairly liberal parishes).

Does the presence or kind of theological match between pastor and congregation affect church growth directly? It does, but *only for clergywomen.* Clergywomen who are in a liberal match with their congregation are more likely to report congregation growth (67 per cent), than if they are in a more conservative match (59 per cent), or especially if they are in a mismatch (44 per cent), where they are liberal but most in the church conservative. Where this mismatch exists, the liberal clergywoman is probably eager to leave the conservative church.[17] This mismatch may contribute to conflict within such congregations, as the clergy try to change their members toward a more liberal, inclusive theological understanding. Consequently, in these clergy–congregation mismatches little is likely to be done by ordained or lay leaders to attract and retain more members.

Church growth and lay theological match

Those in the pews may also see themselves as matched or mismatched theologically with most other parishioners in their congregations. Individual members' sense of how well their theological views chime with those of their congregations has no direct relationship to whether they see their churches as growing, remaining the same or declining. However, laywomen who saw their value orientations on this matter as congruent with most others in their congregations, were somewhat more likely than those who felt mismatched to say that

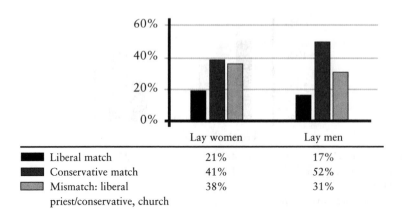

	Lay women	Lay men
Liberal match	21%	17%
Conservative match	41%	52%
Mismatch: liberal priest/conservative, church	38%	31%

Figure 11.3: Lay member–church theological match

they felt 'spiritually uplifted' and that their 'participation is appreciated' in their congregations. Laywomen matched theologically with most in their congregations are even more likely to believe that 'members are active in making this a vital parish', particularly if these women are in theologically liberal churches.[18] There is no significant relationship for laymen with theological match in these areas.

Several explanations for these findings seem plausible for laywomen. Theologically conservative women are probably not as active participants in Episcopal congregations as are theologically liberal women. Theologically liberal women actively involved in church programmes and mission activities might well find their efforts receiving greater appreciation in liberal rather than conservative churches. Laymen are another matter altogether. The relative rarity of men in the pews of all congregations helps ensure that for even their rarer presence, they are made to feel appreciated, especially if they are heterosexual, young or middle-aged men (Lummis 2004a).

Since women make up the active majority of members, it is important to note the positive effects of laywomen's theological match with most in their congregations on their feelings of being appreciated and for their perceiving that members in their congregations are active in contributing to church vitality. This result supports other research studies mentioned earlier, concluding that lay people who have a sense of 'belonging' to their congregations are more likely to be actively involved.

These findings on theological match hold whether or not laywomen have an ordained woman on the pastoral staff of their congregations. At the same time, liberal laywomen in liberal congregations who have a woman on the

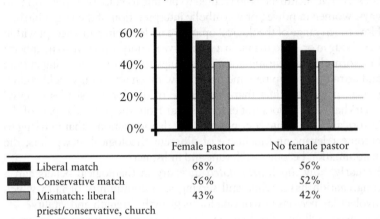

Figure 11.4: Laywomen theological match

pastoral staff are most likely to report that it is very much the case that 'members are active in making this a vital parish'. This suggests that female clergy are more able to encourage church growth when they have a cadre of liberal laywomen to work with them.

Summary and discussion

The research data and the results of other studies presented here seem to point to various hypotheses and questions for further examination:

- Clergy of very liberal churches are unlikely to be leading the majority of the growing congregations in their denominations. This is not because they are theologically liberal pastors in liberal congregations, but because there are other factors far more important that theology in predicting church growth.
- Liberal clergy may be particularly successful leaders in either starting or expanding theologically liberal 'niche' congregations attracting a special constituency.
- Niche congregations, however, are unlikely to exhibit shades of grey theologically, or to put it another way: if conservative churches are more black theologically, than niche would be more white theologically, even if there membership are all shades of the racial/ethnic rainbow. Niche congregations that are open and affirming of gay/lesbian lifestyles, as Ammerman found, also try to attract straights too (Ammerman 1997, pp. 196–7).

However, these niche congregations would not tolerate the presence of very conservative members, who wanted to be able to voice their objections to gays, women in power, or a symbolic interpretation of the virgin birth.

- How much range of theological opinion can denominations accept within their body in order to maintain a distinctive identity attractive to members? In reformulating denominational teachings to meet the changing culture and attract and keep new members, how much attention should church leaders pay to the fact that their range of theological 'shades of gray' (Markham 2003) does not extend so far from the particular part of the historical black–white continuum of the denomination – that in trying to become relevant and inclusive of different theological viewpoints, the denomination becomes irrelevant and indistinct?
- Similarly, how much *articulated* diversity in theological beliefs can a congregation have, while still serving as a community of faith which involves lay persons in working for its growth, strength and vitality?
- Is it easier to discuss theological values *across* faith traditions and denominations, rather than *within* a denomination, and particularly a congregation?

Communicating truth effectively when many voices are talking at once may need theological homogeneity provided by congregations with similar viewpoints, whether they fall to the black or white side of the grey continuum within a denomination. This being so, what congregational conditions or methods might be used to converse across the theological shades of liberalism–conservatism within a congregation?

Notes

1. Kevin Dougherty, in reviewing factors shown in studies to be causes or correlates of church growth, makes the point that there are a 'host of internal and external influences' that appear to be related to growth – and how these relate over time and in different denominations is likely to be different (Dougherty 2004, pp. 117–31).

2. Hadaway (2002, p. 39), using the *FACT* data reports that while 95 per cent of the denominations classified as conservative compared to 78 per cent of those classified as liberal: say the Bible is a foundational source of authority, even fewer (only 54 per cent) of the Episcopalians put this much weight on the Bible as a source of theological authority.

3. Ibid., p. 37. The *FACT* survey asked church leaders if their congregations had (1) definite expectations for members that are strictly enforced; (2) fairly clear expectations for members, but the enforcement of these expectations is not very strict; (3) only implicit expectations for members that are seldom, if ever, enforced. Few congregations in any denomination were in the very first category, and fully 70 per cent of the congregations even of the most conservative denominations were in the second category, compared to about 50 per cent of the congregations of the mainline denominations, including the Episcopal Church (46 per cent). At the same time, slightly over half of the 726 Episcopal congregations in the *FACT* study (52 per cent) were in the least strict third category.

4. Finke (2004, p. 20) argues that religious organizations to flourish have to achieve two seemingly opposing objectives: guarding core religious beliefs that are timeless; and generating

innovations for the local congregations adapting to a changing world. Successful denominations and congregations know what to change and what theological beliefs, teachings and rituals to retain.

5. Djupe and Gilbert (2003, p. 120) in illustration comment: 'The discussion of gay rights … has become very contentious in many denominations besides the ELCA and the Episcopal Church, with the very liberal stances of clergy and denomination clashing against general congregational discomfort of even hostility … but many congregations seem to wish the issues would disappear altogether.' Sachs and Holland (2003) also indicate that the divisions within the Episcopal Church around homosexuality are areas that their focus groups of lay persons in parishes around the country would not like to see divide their congregation, and hence would prefer not to discuss.

6. Mead (1993, pp. 12–13) gives definitions of these types of growth and devotes chapters to each.

7. Dougherty (2004) makes this empirical generalization in summarizing results of studies of church growth using resource mobilization theory. His review and own study lead him to conclude that a pivotal factor in congregational growth is whether members feel a 'sense of belonging', which in turn results in greater participation.

8. Hadaway (2002, p. 12); Dudley and Roozen (2001, p. 26). In a more recent study of Episcopal members and clergy nationally (2002), growing churches are substantially more likely to be the larger churches in the more populated areas. See the report by the Committee on the Status of Women (2003, pp. 46–7).

9. There is no linear relationship between theological liberalism/conservatism and church growth, as indicated in Hadaway (2002, p. 37). Hadaway reports that Episcopal congregations in the middle category of *strictness*, have 'fairly clear' expectations for members, rather than being very strict or very loose in their expectations. He argues that they are more likely to be seen as *vital/strong*; and even here this measure of vitality includes six measures, only one of which is growth in worship attendance. Bruce and Woolever (2004) also found no clear correlation between liberalism and growth. They reported that equal proportions of growing and non-growing churches are reported as being conservative theologically or politically.

10. Carroll (1991) discusses the importance of the pastoral leader listening carefully and responding to members' needs, in a way that gets them to work in conjunction with one another and the pastor in strengthening the church. Carroll (2000) goes further in describing the ideal pastor as also being the kind of innovator and prophetic leader who can develop a vision and who has the persuasive or charismatic abilities to get members to see the vision as theirs too, and work towards it.

11. Committee on the Status of Women (2003). The primary purpose of this survey was to investigate whether and how the status of women had changed since 1986–87, and to assess what obstacles still remain to the full participation of lay and ordained women in the Church. A total of 2,843 surveys were returned, 69 per cent women and 31 per cent men as designed, about a 45 per cent return rate over all. This is primarily a sample of lay persons, in that only 12 per cent of those who returned surveys are ordained. This research-based report, which includes action reports by the eighteen participating dioceses and recommendations to the whole Church, can be downloaded from http://www.episcopalchurch.org/women/ surveyreport.htm

12. On a 5-point answer-scale (1 very willing to 5 very unwilling) clergy and lay respondents were asked how willing they personally and most in their congregations would be to have a woman as: (a) senior warden in this parish; (b) assistant minister in this parish; (c) rector of this parish; and (c.1) if she had young children; (c.2) if she is lesbian with a partner; (d) diocesan bishop of this diocese; (e) suffragan or assistant bishop; (f) deputy to General Convention.

13. In illustration, in the total sample reporting on this question (2,271), in congregations of 150 members and under – 40 per cent said their church had grown in the last five years, in congregations of 150–359, 57 per cent reported growth; in congregations of 350–599, 63 per cent reported church growth, and in congregations of 600-plus members, fully 74 per cent said their congregations had grown.

14. In illustration, of the total sample who strongly agree that in their congregations 'members are active in making this a vital parish', 46 per cent are in churches under 150; 56

per cent in churches 150–349; 60 per cent in churches 350–599, and fully 72 per cent in churches of 600-plus members.

15. Of congregations over 600, 19 per cent of the respondents were from congregations in the South, 10 per cent from the west, 8 per cent from the northcentral cluster of dioceses, and 7 per cent from the northeast.

16. Ammerman (1997, pp. 130–33) defines niche congregations as fitting best in a cosmopolitan culture, particularly if these congregations are open and affirming of gay/lesbian lifestyles. Emmerson and Kim (2003) make a similar point about niche congregations which are trying to be multiracial.

17. Mueller and McDuff (2004, pp. 261–73) found that theologically liberal clergy in conservative denominations were most likely to want to leave these congregations.

18. For laywomen, the correlation between feeling spiritually uplifted and degree of perceived theological fit with most in the congregation is 0.12 (sig. 0.001) and with feeling appreciated for congregational participation is 0.14 (sig. 0.001); and believing that 'members are active in making this a vital parish' is 0.17 (sig. 0.000). In illustration, among laywomen who 'agree strongly' that their *participation is appreciated*, 76 per cent are in liberal matches, 66 per cent in conservative matches and 58 per cent mismatched with their congregations. In contrast, for lay men, the correlations are 0.002 and 0.04 respectively, which are not significant.

References

Ammerman, Nancy T., 1997 *Congregation and Community* (New Brunswick, NJ: Rutgers University Press).
———, 2005 *Pillars of Faith: American Congregations and their Partners* (Berkeley, CA: University of California Press).
Ammerman, Nancy T. and Lummis, Adair T., 1996 *Spiritually Vital Episcopal Congregations,* Final Report to the Trinity Church Grants Board, New York City.
Ault, James M. Jr, 2004 *Spirit and Flesh: Life in a Fundamentalist Baptist Church* (New York: Alfred A. Knopf).
Bennison, Charles. E. Jr, 1999 *In Praise of Congregations: Leadership in the Local Church Today* (Boston, MA: Cowley Publications).
Bruce, Deborah and Woolever, Cynthia, 2004 *Fastest Growing Presbyterian Churches* monograph (Louisville, KY: Research Services, Presbyterian Church USA).
Carroll, Jackson W., 1991 *As One with Authority: Reflective Leadership in Ministry* (Louisville, KY: Westminster John Knox).
———, 2000 *Mainline to the Future: Congregations for the 21st Century* (Louisville, KY; Westminister John Knox).
Committee on the Status of Women, Executive Council of the Episcopal Church, 2003 *Reaching toward Wholeness II: The 21st Century Survey* (New York: Episcopal Church Center).
Deckman, Melissa, Crawford, Sue E.S., Olson, Laura R., Green, John C., 2003 'Clergy and the politics of gender', *Journal of the Scientific Study of Religion* 43:621–31.
Djupe, Paul A. and Gilbert, Christopher P., 2003 *The Prophetic Pulpit: Clergy, Churches and Communities in American Politics* (Lanham, MD: Rowman and Littlefield).
Dougherty, Kevin D., 2004 'Institutional influences on growth in Southern Baptist congregations', *Review of Religious Research* 46:117–31.
———, 2003 'How monochromatic is church membership? Racial–Ethnic diversity in religious community', *Sociology of Religion* 64: 65–85.
Dudley, Carl S. and Roozen, David A., 2001 *Faith Communities Today* (Hartford: Hartford Seminary).
Emmerson, Michael O. and Chai Kim, Karen, 2003 'Multiracial congregations: an analysis of their development and a typology', *Journal for the Scientific Study of Religion* 42: 217–27.
Finke, Roger, 2004 'Innovative returns to tradition: using core teachings at the foundation for

innovative accommodation', *Journal for the Scientific Study of Religion*, :19–34.

Hadaway, C. Kirk, 2002 *A Report on Episcopal Churches in the United States* (Office of Congregational Development, The Episcopal Church).

Jenkins, Phillip, 2002 *The Next Christendom: The Coming of Global Christianity* (Oxford: Oxford University Press).

Lummis, Adair T., 2004a 'A research note: real men and church participation', *Review of Religious Research* 25:404–14.

————, 2004b '*The Interdenominational Executives Group*: As a National Denominational Leader Support Group and as a Research-Based Learning Community of Practice', Evaluation Report for the Lilly Endowment. Hartford Seminary.

————, 2003 *What Do Lay People Want in Pastors? Answers from Lay Search Committee Chairs and Regional Judicatory Leaders* (Durham, NC: Pulpit and Pew Research Reports; Duke Divinity School).

Markham, Ian S., 2003 *A Theology of Engagement* (Oxford: Blackwell).

Mead, Loren B., 1993 *More than Numbers. The Way Churches Grow* (Washington, DC: Alban Institute).

Mueller, Charles W. and McDuff, Elaine, 2004 'Clergy–congregation mismatches and clergy job satisfaction', *Journal for the Scientific Study of Religion* 43:261–73.

Nesbitt, Paula, 1997 *The Feminization of the Clergy in America: Occupational and Organizational Perspectives* (New York: Oxford University Press).

Percy, Martyn, 2001 *The Salt of the Earth: Religious Resistance in a Secular Age* (London: Sheffield Academic Press).

Sachs, William and Holland, Thomas, 2003 *Restoring the Ties that Bind: The Grassroots Transformation of the Episcopal Church* (New York: Church Publishing).

Woolever, Cynthia and Bruce, Deborah, 2004 *Beyond the Ordinary: Ten Strengths of US Congregations* (Louisville KY: Westminster John Knox Press).

Zikmund, Barbara Brown, Lummis, Adair T. and Chang, Patricia M.Y., 1998 *Clergy Women: An Uphill Calling* (Louisville, KY: Westminster John Knox Press).

Chapter 12

Two Conditions for a Growing Liberal Church: Right Theology and Right Clergy

Ian Markham

Progressive Christians are often bewildered. Why is it that conservative churches are so strong? A typical response tends to offer a semi-psychological analysis: the evangelicals, explains the liberal, are so insecure that they need the certainties provided by conservative religion. The assumption made in this analysis is that it is a problem with the evangelical not a problem with the liberal church. Others are blamed for the empty liberal church.

In this chapter, I want to challenge this liberal blame culture. The successful progressive churches are those who do not blame the empty church on the psychology of the Christian attending the large evangelical church two blocks away. Instead they recognize that there is no reason why a liberal church cannot be an interesting, demanding and stimulating church. In this chapter, we look at the two conditions that enable a liberal church to be an attractive church: the type of liberal theology and the nature of the liberal clergy-person. We start with the theology.

What sort of liberal theology?

Given the word 'liberal' means entirely different things to different people, it is helpful to clarify precisely what the word 'liberal' means when linked with growing churches. For much of the twentieth century 'liberal' was associated with the Anglo-American project of making the gospel relevant. Relevance in this context meant enabling the gospel to relate to our post-Enlightenment modern society. So the argument ran thus: Newtonian science made miracles impossible; Darwinian evolution made the historicity of Genesis 1 unlikely; and the relativism of Einstein's theory of relativity made the quest for absolutes impossible.[1] This scientific argument was coupled with the Enlightenment's sensitivity to history. Modern historians worked with the assumption that the world has always been much as it is. So the argument goes, it is political and social explanations that account for the change in the government of a country, not God. For historians examining the Bible, the claim that God was responsible for the triumph of the Babylonians over the Judaeans disappeared behind a political explanation that concentrates on the emergence of a fourth-century

BCE Babylonian empire. When it came to Jesus, a growing literature suggested a plausible narrative in the development of Christology. So the argument ran: Jesus was a Jew who thought in theocratic terms, which slowly evolved into the pre-existent Son of God in Paul, and then finally into the Incarnation of God in the Gospel of John.[2] Given the distance – historically – between John and the life of Jesus, the presumption was that Incarnational Christology is unlikely to be true.

Science and history, then, became the key challenges that shaped much liberal theology. Add to this mix the demands provoked by justice for a theology that does not support patriarchy, racism, exclusivism and colonialism, and a new theology emerged. This liberal theology was non-Incarnational, non-Trinitarian, sceptical of divine action, committed to a pluralist theology of other religions and to campaigning for theological reform on a whole host of justice issues. The major worry on this account was the much-talked-about 'gap' between pulpit and pew.[3] Clergy trained in this liberal theology that dominated the seminaries in the 1960s and 70s found themselves a decade or so later working in churches that didn't share this theology. 'How to move congregations along?' became a key issue of this period.

This approach to theology collapsed towards the end of the twentieth century. Although there are still elegant representatives[4] articulating this approach, there were four key difficulties with it. The first was that the world of science changed. The New Physics was much friendlier to religion. Tom Driver attempts to show otherwise, but many physicists became religion-friendly. Keith Ward describes the shift in his book of the BBC Radio series *Turn of the Tide*. Ward takes as his illustration the distinguished physicist John Polkinghorne. Ward writes:

> A physicist such as Polkinghorne, then, sees the world as having the character of intellectual beauty; as showing an amazingly delicate balance and order which arouses awe and wonder as we see it. This is not only consistent with the thought of a wise creator; it almost inevitably leads the mind to that hypothesis. Indeed, it might even be said, not that science leads to God, but that it was the idea of God which gives birth to science as we know it. The world as physics sees it is not just 'one damn thing after another'. It is a highly ordered and beautiful structure, and it is natural for anyone with a scientific mind to ask, 'Why is it the way it is?'[5]

The New Physics compounds the sense of awe and beauty. Indeed the holistic, interconnected universe made divine action seem much more plausible. Science was no longer an enemy but a friend. Naturally, evolution still had to be accommodated, but this was seen as less problematic and relatively easy to reconcile with the biblical narrative.

The second difficulty was that our postmodern sensitivity to history challenged the assumption that the world is experienced by all in the same way as it is experienced by the post-Enlightenment person. Perhaps we should not assume the universal nature of our worldview. William Abrahams in his *Divine Revelation and the Limits of Historical Criticism* challenged the assumptions underpinning many of the liberal readings of the Bible.[6]

The third difficulty was that some of the justice causes did not want to build on an impoverished faith. John Macquarrie, when describing the Christology of Jon Sobrino, writes:

> The Christology presented in this book, though it has radical political implications, remains theologically in the orthodox tradition. This is typical of liberation theologians in general. A few years ago I heard Dr Sobrino declare at a symposium in the United States, 'No liberation theologian known to me has ever denied the divinity of Christ'.[7]

The oppressed, then, are not interested in a demythologized Christ. Black theology believes in an active God and has retained a strong evangelical set of assumptions. The demands of justice did not want to be hijacked for increasing scepticism about God. However, it was the fourth difficulty that proved decisive.

The fourth (and final) difficulty was that certain strands of liberal theology did not know where to stop. Some of the key thinkers did not stop at a cosmic deism, but went further. The factors that propelled them to doubt the Incarnation and Trinity slowly led them to doubt the existence of God.[8] Don Cupitt is a good example. God, in Cupitt's theology, evolved into a symbol of goodness and love. The liberal theology of increasing doubt had reached its nadir.

Given all this, the temptation was to reject the word 'liberal' entirely. And much of the academy succumbed to the temptation. For all the differences between the post-liberal, radical orthodox and neo-Barthians, they shared a commitment to a conservative theology. Now engagement with non-Christian sources was problematic; the Enlightenment and secularism became the big enemy; and the Bible and Trinity were suddenly uncomplicated. Instead of a nuanced reaction to liberal theology, we found imaginative, often postmodern, ways of going backwards. 'Liberal' became the ultimate insult.

In fact what was needed, and is needed, was a more discriminating engagement with twentieth-century theology. 'Liberal', which for so long was defined as 'increasing scepticism', needed to become associated with a different set of concepts. Keith Ward at Oxford led the way.[9] Theology needed to be liberal in the sense of generous, engaged, committed to justice and willing to learn from others. Liberalism was now redefined as a *modus operandi*. In terms of belief, we cannot and should not go back in a crude fashion to a premodern theology, but should commit to shaping our theology in conversation with modern science, the social sciences and other religions. A mid-twentieth-century liberal theology is bound to struggle as a foundation for a congregation; but a twenty-first-century liberal theology which commends a theological method can be, and often is, a basis for a thriving congregation.

What sort of clergy?

Having argued that a liberal theology as a method can play a vital role in a congregation, the next stage is to reflect on the disposition of the clergy. The fact is that very few of us start life as liberal Christians. When Bishop David

Jenkins (the former Bishop of Durham) was asked where the new members of the liberal churches would come from, he replied: 'where they have always come from – the evangelicals'.

Now is this true? From a recent sample of Episcopal membership in the USA, we find some 15.5 per cent in the North are from Catholic or evangelical denominations, while in the South the figure is nearer 25.4 per cent.[10] In both cases approximately half were always Anglican. Given, however, that you can be a cradle evangelical Anglican who then perhaps grows up into a liberal Anglican, it is difficult to get data on this question. However, we do know that some liberals are formed in reaction to the tradition in which they grew up. So a significant number of members in a liberal church are either from the Roman Catholic or evangelical communities. And we have ample biographical evidence for how the change occurs. For Roman Catholics, one tends to be born into the church and then, perhaps at university, find oneself repelled by the Catholic position on, say, sexuality.[11] Evangelicals tend to be converted to a fundamentalist form of Christianity at university and then subsequently discover the tensions with modern science or religious diversity and move away from the evangelical worldview. Theological education can then further entrench the reasons for being alienated from the conservative theologies of one's youth or conversion experience.

What follows is speculative. It is a reflection on the many hundreds of conversations I have had with progressive clergy. I do appreciate it is highly impressionistic; however, I invite others to engage with the following in a critical way. I see the problem thus: in the same way that the person who has stopped smoking is the most vitriolic anti-smoker so the person who was a Catholic or an evangelical becomes equally repulsed by the practices of these groups. The problem in religion is that a whole host of practices essential for a vibrant faith life and leadership of a thriving congregation are also associated with the tradition that the person has rejected. So as an evangelical, one was accustomed to seizing the opportunity to share faith with those outside the community. Now a liberal, one is embarrassed to do so. As an evangelical, one knew the importance of daily quiet time; now a liberal, the practice has stopped. When an evangelical, one's zeal for the Lord was infectious and attractive; now a liberal, zeal disappears.

Dean Kelley in his *Why Conservative Churches are Growing?* is right to argue that an undemanding church is unlikely to attract adherents. His famous hypothesis was that 'social strength and leniency do not seem to go together'.[12] However, Kelley does not stress sufficiently the leadership of the congregation. I want to suggest that the problem with many small liberal churches often lies in their clergy. They are semi-embarrassed to be at the front. They move through the liturgy imparting doubt and scepticism. They have a virtual allergic reaction to any committed 'conservative' Christian who happens to be in the congregation already. The preaching is often dry, detached and theoretical. John Bowden captures this when he describes a wife's picture of a tormented clergy-person trying to prepare a sermon:

It is Saturday night and her husband is crying in her arms in despair because he has two sermons to preach the next day and nothing at all to say. His mind is bland – no thought, no words. The appointed lessons seem to say nothing to him, and worse than that, he is acutely aware of his own emptiness – as though he himself had no real being. The feeling comes to him often. At other times it can take the form of an utter lack of direction, as though he were wandering alone in some unsignposted wilderness with no indication of what he should do, where he should go or what he should become. And yet in spite of this the life of the parish has to go on. The sermons have to be preached, the church roof has to be propped up if it is falling down. People come to him for advice and expect him to know the answers; he has to try to mediate the love of God to them, however little he is aware of it himself. No wonder they are beginning to ask how good he is. He asks himself the same question and answers it as they do.[13]

The tormented clergy-person is so far from the story of the Christian drama that the Scriptures no longer connect. The words 'I love the Lord' will never pass their lips. They say the creeds with their fingers crossed, while insisting on their liberal interpretation of every statement. They hope the habit will keep people coming. And they find and feed on fellow disillusioned Christians, celebrating their doubt and scepticism. The result is inevitable: it is often boring. It is a struggle enough to get out of bed on a Sunday morning, but to arrive at a service where the clergy-person sends signals of being uncomfortable with it all is enough to lead to despair.

Granted this is extreme, and perhaps a bit of a caricature. But as I have already argued, a liberal theology that survives and thrives must be a committed liberal theology. And the phrase a 'committed liberal theology' is not an oxymoron. A liberal theology associated with increasing unbelief and scepticism is problematic; but a liberal theology associated with generosity, openness, celebration and hope can invoke commitment. A church that positions itself as a community that loves God, strives to be Christlike, and doesn't feel obliged to assume that all non-Christians are damned and gays are a symptom of depravity can be deeply attractive.

It is important, however, that the clergy need to come to terms with their religious past. A mature response would involve the following. First, the devotional life must continue. It is the space between a clergy-person and God. A key goal of a worshipping community is to help all the members cultivate this space. When the clergy-person has lost that dimension, it makes it very difficult to inspire others. Second, it is vital that the clergy-person radiate passion and commitment. It must all matter. Third, the liberal generosity and openness must extend to the conservatives. It is tempting for many liberals to insist that hell is empty except for conservative Christians. But a liberalism which doesn't extend to conservatives is deeply illiberal. The passion and devotion of the conservative Christian needs to meet an equally passionate and devotional liberal response.

What sort of congregation?

In this concluding section of this chapter we shall identify some of the key ingredients of a growing liberal church. There are, as I see it, five aspects.

First, it is a congregation that continues to be recognizably in the Christian tradition. It acknowledges a debt to the tradition; it is not so uncomfortable with that tradition that it is endlessly complaining about it. Second, it encourages a genuine pluralism in the congregation. The brave evangelical in the congregation should know that the tradition and Scripture are appropriately celebrated. The doubter or the recovering Catholic should also know that there is space for them. It recognizes that the faith journey for one is different for the other; people end up in different places. It leaves to God the ultimate task of sorting out an individual's theology. Third, it sends clear signals that a committed Christian theology need not insist that every Muslim, Jew, Buddhist, etc. will end up in hell. It recognizes that many of the biblical and natural law arguments against same-sex relationships cannot be binding on the mind of the Church today. However, it will also be Incarnational and Trinitarian. Properly understood, such doctrines do shape the Christian interpretation of the world. Fourth, this congregation will witness to the social and political demands of the gospel. It will be willing to think, press and struggle with the propensity of the Church to be endlessly on the wrong side of many civil rights struggles. There is a world outside the Christian tribe which this congregation recognizes and to which, as part of the gospel witness, it makes a significant contribution. Fifth, arising from the last point, this congregation is deeply interested in the conversation with philosophy, the social sciences and the natural sciences. It wants to be a community that carries on the work of the tradition in engaging with these vitally important conversations.

Thanks in large measure to the various studies of congregations (much of it documented elsewhere in this book) we now know what creates a growing church. And *contra* Kelley, it is interesting to note that 'conservative' theology is not on the list. Although it is true that many of the growing churches are conservative ones, there is ample evidence that this is a contingent connection not a logically necessary one. We all know that there are many thousands of small churches which are deeply conservative; we also know that there are some large liberal churches; and at least one growing liberal denomination – namely, the Unitarian–Universalists. Cynthia Woolever and Deborah Bruce have produced two books that explain in a very accessible way the key factors that shape growth. They explain that of the ten strengths of US congregations, 'Three congregational strengths are positive predictors of numerical growth: Caring for Children and Youth, Participating in the Congregation, and Welcoming New People.'[14] The key factors that shape growth are at this basic level of making sure one welcomes new people, providing good programmes for children and encouraging people to get involved. All of these things can be done by a liberal congregation.

The puzzle perhaps is why so few liberal congregations have made this discovery. The argument of this chapter is that there is a barrier that makes these basic growth activities difficult. And this barrier needs to be broken by these liberal congregations revisiting the theology and the leadership. I am suggesting this is where the problem lies. If we revisit our theology and resist the creeping blame culture amongst the liberal clergy, then at last we could transform the faith scene.

Ultimately Kelley's book is a depressing work. If strict religion is the only sort that works, then we might as well resign ourselves to the inevitable religious wars that will occur as one tribal faith encounters another. However, it is precisely because I believe in goodness and love at the heart of the universe enabling everything that is and sustaining everything that is that I challenge the hypothesis. It is, ultimately, a statement of faith that the God who is will not leave the world without a witness to a faith which is open, generous and hospitable.

Notes

1. Tom F. Driver, *Christ in a Changing World* (Crossroad, 1981) argues that we need to recognize that in a relativist universe all our absolutes must go.

2. For a classic statement see James Dunn, *Christology in the Making: A New Testament Inquiry into the Origins of the Doctrine of the Incarnation*, 2nd edn (Grand Rapids, MI: Eerdmans, 1996).

3. See, for example, John Bowden, *Voices in the Wilderness* (London: SCM Press, 1977).

4. Perhaps the best scholar who continues to argue for this vision is John Hick. See his Gifford Lectures for a masterful survey of his thought. These were published as *An Interpretation of Religion* (Basingstoke: Macmillan, 1989). Perhaps the best popularizer is John Shelby Spong. For a typical text see his *Why Christianity Must Change or Die* (London: HarperCollins, 1999).

5. Keith Ward, *The Turn of the Tide* (London: BBC Publications, 1978), p. 50.

6. See William J. Abraham, *Divine Revelation and the Limits of Historical Criticism* (Oxford: Oxford University Press, 1982).

7. John Macquarrie, *Twentieth-century Religious Thought,* new edn (Harrisburg, NJ: Trinity Press International, 2002).

8. For a brilliant and moving summary of an individual's increasing doubt see Michael Goulder in Michael Goulder and John Hick (eds), *Why Believe in God?* (London: SCM Press, 1983), Ch 1.

9. Those who represent this movement include William Schweiker and his Christian Humanism, Martyn Percy and his Implicit Theology, Keith Ward and his Comparative Theology and George Newlands and his Theology of Generosity.

10. I am grateful to Adair Lummis for the statistics here.

11. See, for example, Libby Purves, *Holy Smoke* (London: Hodder & Stougton, 1999). Libby Purves did remain a Roman Catholic, albeit a liberal one.

12. Dean M. Kelley, *Why Conservative Churches are Growing. A Study in Sociology of Religion* (New York: Harper & Row, 1972), p. 83.

13. John Bowden, *Voices in the Wilderness* (London: SCM Press, 1977), pp. 5–6.

14. Cynthia Woolever and Deborah Bruce, *Beyond the Ordinary. Ten Strengths of US Congregations* (Louisville, KY: Westminster John Knox Press, 2004), p. 113.

Chapter 13

A View from the Pew: Ministry and Organic Church Growth

Martyn Percy and Emma Percy

There is more than a fair degree of certainty and simplicity in Kelley's thesis, *Why Conservative Churches are Growing*.[1] Kelley asserts that in order for a church to grow numerically, there has to be some kind of clarity about its purpose. Religion, claims Kelley, is about providing ultimate meaning for people: making sense out of existence and also answering the question 'why do bad things happen?' So Kelley argues that in order for a strong sustainable community to develop, there needs to be a sense that the community itself is so important that it *demands* commitment, and that this same commitment needs to be at some cost to the members. Correspondingly, for a church to grow numerically, there needs to be a sense that it has something to offer in making sense of life; and that it demands a commitment by return. If it costs nothing to belong to such a community, it can hardly be worth joining

Kelley discusses the importance of strictness in upholding the values and boundaries of such a community, and reflects on Kierkegaard's call for 'serious religion'. Here Kelley asserts that liberal and mainstream churches have lost the sense of 'defined boundaries', with the principle of religious tolerance and individual freedom being embraced to such an extent that the churches no longer espouse a faith that people deeply and sacrificially commit to. Such churches are 'lukewarm', and though they may be engaged in much good work, they do not have clarity in their religious expression. Correspondingly, energy is expended into espousing a good cause or practical service, which though implicitly connected to the understanding of faith, is not about the Church's main purpose of drawing people in to a community of salvation. Kelley therefore argues that the more conservative churches have a better record in turning round the lives of the socially excluded, by converting them to a new meaning in life which demands a changed lifestyle.

To be sure, Kelley's ideas constitute a simple, compacted and logically coherent thesis. But the question contemporary ecclesiologists, missiologists, practical theologians and sociologists of religion might ask is also simple: does it make sense? The answer here must at least be in some doubt, for we know that even in measuring numerical strength, there are multiple ambiguities. How does one account for the large rise in numbers attending cathedral services in the Church of England where there is patently no relationship between strictness and strength? Equally, how would one explain the burgeoning number of metropolitan churches that attract niche neoliberal groups? Even a preliminary survey of churchgoing habits in the twenty-first century suggests that there are more exceptions to Kelley's 'rules' for growth, which therefore renders his thesis somewhat unsafe.

That said, there can be no denying of the importance of meaning in churches. But defining the purpose of a church need not be strict or exclusive; it can also be inclusive and open (and no less attractive for this). The complex struggle for mainstream and liberal churches remains stubbornly centred on how to continue to encourage commitment, and how to communicate the seriousness of the gospel and teach people about the cost of discipleship. Or put another way, the task might be to discover ways of being unapologetic about faith, which do not inhibit those same churches from being tolerant. Is it possible to be religiously tolerant and yet truly communicate a faith that is life-changing?   Can liberal and mainstream churches teach about lifestyle, but without interfering with individual liberty?

It might be said (and perhaps this is something of a caricature), that mainstream churches do not expect too much from their members. They tend not to worry about members who miss three of four Sundays. Anxious to avoid inducing guilt, and equally concerned to under-communicate a sense of urgency, mainstream churches typically adopt a mellow attitude to belonging, and tend to tolerate a variety of inchoate expressions of belief. In one sense, mainstream churches are reconciled to understanding their congregational composition: a mixture of loyalists and consumers. Yet this attitude should be contrasted with more evangelical churches, where the 'non-attendance' of a member is interpreted rather than tolerated. Perhaps the person is 'backsliding'? Maybe they are struggling with their faith and need support? Where Kelley is correct is in understanding that evangelical and conservative churches grow first and foremost by engaging their members in deep bonds of commitment; and then again through evangelism. Such churches readily accept that people want to make seriously informed choices about church attendance.

Yet church growth has never been such a simple matter. There are many institutional and contextual factors that may account for the numerical growth of a church. In England, a popular Church of England primary school can lead to extensive community involvement in the church. Other demographic factors may also have a bearing, such as class, ethnicity and wealth. If action flows from identity, then a community with a close-knit sense of itself may find its religious expression more 'productive' than a more disparate community. In general, effective evangelism flows out of a sense of purpose, excitement and mission. Correspondingly, strictness and strength may not be, as Kelley suggests, such decisive factors.

That said, the most fundamental problem for the ebbing mainstream churches is often the lack of compelling reasons for people to participate. Mainstream churches can be embarrassed about talking about God, and their fear of intolerance can then lead to a chronic lack of religious conversations and overt religious output in the local community. All too frequently, mainstream and liberal churches can lose their core public identity in asserting their breadth and diversity (i.e., tolerance), rather than communicating that they do, in fact, believe in God.

How do churches grow?

One of the more interesting questions any vicar of a parish might have to ponder is, 'why do people come to this church?' Granted, the answers that one is likely to get will reflect, to a certain extent, what the laity thinks it should say. Posing this question in a small group recently, we were offered two very different answers. The first person replied that he came to church 'to worship Jesus Christ as his Lord and saviour'. The second stated that 'she came out of habit'. Yet in encouraging people to come to church there is a sense in which both these answers become important. People need to know what it means to be a Christian, and that this involves worshipping the God who is known and encountered through Jesus Christ. They also need to develop a lifestyle in which church attendance becomes habitual (as well as desirable), and a normal part of their daily existence. More conservative churches tend to work hard on both, communicating a neat definition of faith (with a strong sense of obligation in personal lifestyle), which will in turn include regular attendance. This combination – of strong message and demanding commitment – is given as one of the reasons for the growth of conservative churches.

In agreement with Kelley, we would also wish to affirm that a healthy church is likely to be a numerically growing church (or at least 'self-replenishing'). Central to the Christian faith is the belief that Christ's message is for all, and that people can find their lives enriched and blessed if they turn to him. Therefore, all churches, whatever their theological position, should rejoice when new members join them, and indeed anticipate this. Yet numbers are very far from being the main rationale for being a church. Some of the most powerful forms of witness come from the smallest Christian communities, whose numbers do not obviously grow, but whose impact is extensive far beyond their slight membership. Equally, some (apparently) successful and large churches can turn out to have only slight and marginal impact upon a wider community. As the old adage goes, it is quality that counts, not quantity.

That said, we agree that a declining attendance will have a debilitating effect on a congregation at a number of levels. In practical terms, falling numbers impact on volunteers and on finance, and they also alter the feel of worship. A church which sees new members is, invariably, stimulated and encouraged. It usually benefits from new gifts and skills as well as better finances. Some traditions in the church are strongly driven by a missionary zeal to make disciples for Christ. This zeal is usually underpinned by a belief that those who do not profess faith in Jesus Christ will not attain the (eternal) rewards of belonging to God. Sharing one's faith is an obligation, and the concern for the eternal destiny of others can provide a clear motivation. Then again, if the theology of the church takes a more liberal view of salvation, then clearly the task of recruiting can become less urgent, as less depends on belonging and believing. If this is also coupled with a sense that the tradition is hesitant about articulating ultimate truths, and must also allow for individual freedom, then the missionary task becomes more complex. Yet we would also wish to argue that churches which hold a liberal position can do so with passion and commitment, and can still believe that the message of the gospel is life-enhancing and well worth sharing. How do they put this message across, and how do they draw others from interest into commitment?

Our own experience is in working within this theological tradition, and while we cannot claim rapid numerical growth, we have observed that the liberal or mainstream Anglican tradition of which we are part consistently and regularly welcomes new members. Reflecting on Kelley's assertion – that religion needs to give people a means of making sense of life – it is clear that people join churches across the traditions because of specific life experiences that they need to make sense of. What is perhaps especially interesting has been to observe that people have been attracted to ordinary, broad and mainstream churches precisely because they do *not* provide simplistic explanations of theology or life.

To earth this contextually, we note that over the seven-year period when Emma was vicar of Holy Trinity Millhouses (a parish of some 4,000 in a northern English city, with an electoral roll of about 160 and a weekly attendance of about a hundred), new members included a mother whose first child was born severely handicapped and died, a couple whose 30-year-old son died of a heart attack, two couples with mentally-ill sons, two mothers of adopted children and many others who have had to cope with complex bereavements. In different ways, each of these people were looking for a place which could give meaning to their life – but without trying to explain away their suffering. A theology that provides hope, knit together with the sustaining love of God, and at the same time without tidying up loose ends, seemed to provide for these people something they could not find either in the world or in a more conservative church. Some of the new members had in fact moved from more conservative churches, while others became involved for the first time or after a long break.

Another group who joined the church were mothers of children, and occasionally their fathers as well. The experience of becoming a mother leads some to want to return to church, having been taken as children themselves. They are often all too aware of the complexity and fragility of life, and sense a need for God to be watching over their child or children. They also find that children ask big questions about life and death, purpose and meaning. Interestingly, we encountered a number of parents brought to church by children who had expressed a strong desire to be part of our church without necessarily being drawn in by friends. They were attracted to a church that was not overprescriptive and that valued children, encouraging their involvement in its life.

Others who joined are much harder to categorize: individuals who have encountered the church through occasional offices or friends, and who have been drawn in because it provides a sacred space, an experience of worship and an encounter with others that is somehow deeply transcendent and satisfying. The church has also grown through simple transfer, as people who were already regular church worshippers moved into the area and came looking to be involved in the community, for which the church continued to provide a focus.

These simple observations lead us to reflect on the fact that one of the primary ways in which churches grow numerically is through ordinary pastoral, maternal and paternal ministry. In her recent *What Mothers Do: Especially when it Looks Like Nothing*,[2] Naomi Stadlen argues for a focus on 'being' rather than 'task-orientation' in motherhood, and we think that her observations translate well into the field of contemporary missiology and ecclesiology, by setting a fresh agenda for growth and development.

What Mothers Do offers a beautifully simple argument. Stadlen says that contemporary culture is gripped, almost mesmerizingly, by formulas and recipes that seldom correspond to reality. So-called 'Mother and Baby' books are a good example: they offer step-by-step advice, which appears to be simple and effective. But, argues Stadlen, most of these kinds of books actually tend to infantilize the mother. What happens if I have a baby that doesn't do what the book says? Guilt, frustration and anger can quickly set in. I can try another book, but then what happens if that also fails to mould the child in the image of the author? The 'how to' books, says Stadlen, reduce motherhood to a series of tasks, instead of concentrating on the *relationship* between mother and child. She argues that mothers rarely need to be told how to care; it is learned and developed in relationships, not through advice-lines and programmatic books.

The heart of the book suggests that mothers are always doing something with their offspring, and most especially when it looks like *nothing*. They are *engaged* with their child. They are relating. They are being with and being for the child. So the question 'what have you done today' – often asked of a young mother – needs no obvious reply, even though it often prompts guilt and embarrassment. Simply to have been with the child is enough; to have discovered a song or a sound that comforts him; or something visual that simply amuses and stimulates her. This is enough.

We have opened up the argument in this way, because it seems to us that one of the most pressing problems that besets the church today is that it too is gripped by a culture of formulae. Many ecclesial recipe books have appeared in recent times: *How to Grow your Church*; *How to Manage your Congregation* (surely a work of satire?); *Ten Steps to Growth*; *Mission-Shaped Church*; *The Purpose-Driven Church*; or Alpha courses; and who can forget 'the decade of evangelism' (RIP)? Each of these initiatives is well meaning but deeply formulaic: a kind of panacea for panickers. And clergy (and sometimes congregations) are easily seduced by such things. Many wince at Christmas when someone sidles up to them at a drinks party and says: 'So

Vicar, your busy time then.' Because the flip-side of the question often asked of clergy is also implied by this remark: 'What exactly do you do all day, Vicar?'

Clergy are often stumped for an answer. Communion in a residential or nursing home for five senior citizens, a couple of visits, some paperwork, morning and evening prayer, one meeting and some thinking doesn't sound like a very productive day. But here clergy are at one with mothers. They have been doing a lot; it just seems like nothing. They have formed, deepened and kindled relationships. They have related to lots of people for whom dependency is a fact of life, and concentrated deeply on being, not just doing. They have made somebody's day, simply by dropping in, or just by smiling and talking to them.

Formulas, like recipes, anticipate success: and churches are usually too tempted to worship both the rubric and the outcome. But unlike recipe books, those courses and books that address the apparent malaise of the Church forget that just as every child is different, so is every congregation: a uniquely constituted set of ingredients. What works in one place may not work in another. So, the moral of this analogy is simple: don't impose formulas for growth on children or churches, and don't try to conjure up congregations in the same way that you might try to conjure up a meal. Respect what has come naturally and work with that. Even if it simply means just being, and apparently doing nothing.

We are struck by how many of the metaphors that Jesus uses to describe the numerical increase of the kingdom are organic, suggesting a slow patience in husbanding growth. The parable of the sower, for one, hardly anticipates a packed schedule for the sower. After his work is finished for the day, what does he do? He will need to wait, water and wait. Similarly, the parable of the mustard seed reminds us that although there is an extensive outcome to be enjoyed, the process of moving from seed to tree is 'natural' rather than 'driven'. We do not, of course, think that the organic parables on kingdom growth that Jesus tells give licence to clergy sit back and do nothing. But we do think that they suggest that the true growth worth striving for is more likely to be crafted through patient tending, working empathetically with natural ingredients, rather than with 'instant' formulas that produce growth for its own sake. We have consistently levelled a criticism at Donald McGravran's work on church growth in this respect, namely that his relentless push for growth was not unlike introducing steroids into the body of Christ. The results were fast and looked spectacular (judged from one perspective), but the long-term health implications were less than convincing. Building up the mass of the body can be a form of idolatry. There is no real substitute for healthy, natural and sustained growth.

Ministry and growth

The question naturally arises: what would ministry to a developing congregation look like? From our perspective as Anglican priests, we suggest that there are several ways of being in a congregation that shape the task of ministry, but are fundamentally centred on role rather than any particular outcomes. We recognize, to begin with, that the Church as the body of Christ – as a metaphor – is imperfect, since the Church is never complete and cannot complete or delimit itself. In one sense, the Church has an open definition because its boundaries and identity are, at a fundamental level, contested and open. Who belongs, who attends occasionally but not frequently, who believes this or that, will be a feature of even the most conservative congregation. Tight definitions of a church will seldom correspond to its grounded context; there is always a gap between ideology and reality.

What then, is the minister or priest to be or do in such an ambiguous situation? Clearly, it is tempting to be seduced by recipes and formulas that deliver clarity. But we would suggest that a focus on the role and identity of the minister (and minister) is a more fruitful path towards encouraging sustained, natural, organic church growth. We offer four hallmarks of priesthood and a priestly church by way of conclusion.

First, ministry is sacramental–transformative. To be a priest or a priestly church is to have an understanding that ordinary material (such as bread, wine, water, etc.) can be transformed by prayer and worship into something through which God speaks to us and spiritually nourishes us. But we do not confine this axis to the standard tokens of the sacramental life of the church. We observe that congregations and ministers find that casual conversations, pastoral encounters, acts of service and other activities are also sacramental and transformative; they become 'places' where the life of God meets the life of the world. The more alert a congregation is to how God feeds and sustains his people, the more likely it is that this food will be shared, and more people transformed.

Second, ministry is reciprocal–representative: that is to say, that while the minister or priest may undoubtedly represent Christ to the people, the congregation continually looks for the ways in which Christ is present within them and outside itself. This is an important dimension in mission, for it affirms the activity of the Holy Spirit beyond the borders of the church, and reminds congregations that Christ can be encountered in new and alien ways, to which the congregation needs to be receptive. At a contextual level, congregations that grow organically will tend to have deep partnerships with a variety of secular agencies that complement its work and mission, so that the 'common good' and the blessing of social capital becomes an enlarged and shared task.

Third, ministry has a sacrificial–receptive dynamic. Obviously, priesthood, as with other forms of ministry, is costly. But the cost is often found not in the output, but in the receptivity to the input. As priests, we observe that individuals will confess and confide all kinds of things that go no further. Here, the priest has a role as absorber of pain; of receiving knowledge that cannot be shared; of taking upon herself burdens that are being finally deposited, once and for all. There is some salvific and cathartic here, to be sure. But we also note how, when individuals finally feel 'they can tell you anything' (and not be judged, but simply loved), they finally feel free to belong to the body of Christ. The costly ministry of sacrificially receiving people's lives and stories allows them to be grafted into the church.

Fourth, ministry is a also a delicate combination of the pastoral–prophetic. The old English adage expresses it well: clergy are there to comfort the afflicted and afflict the comfortable. The imperative to offer love, nurture and tenderness has to be balanced with the responsibility to speak out, which can be costly. We are mindful that, sometimes, growth and popularity must be sacrificed to truth and justice. Natural, organic church growth sometimes requires heavy pruning and an interventionist cultivation. In all of this, we remember that it is God alone who gives the growth. We know that it can be engineered, and we know that such engineering can be effective in terms of numerical growth. However, we remain convinced that the only true growth is the natural and deep kind that God invariably bestows upon a faithful, hopeful and joyful people.

Notes

1.   Dean M. Kelley, *Why Conservative Churches are Growing. A Study in Sociology of Religion* (New York: Harper & Row, 1972), p. 83.

2.   Naomi Stadlen, *What Mothers Do: Especially when it looks like nothing* (London: Piatkus Books, 2004).

INDEX